Jane Austen and Comedy

TRANSITS:
LITERATURE, THOUGHT & CULTURE 1650–1850

Series Editors
Greg Clingham, Bucknell University
Kathryn Parker, University of Wisconsin—La Crosse
Miriam Wallace, New College of Florida

Transits is a series of scholarly monographs and edited volumes publishing beautiful and surprising work. Without ideological bias the series seeks transformative readings of the literary, artistic, cultural, and historical interconnections between Britain, Europe, the Far East, Oceania, and the Americas during the years 1650 and 1850, and as their implications extend down to the present time. In addition to literature, art and history, such "global" perspectives might entail considerations of time, space, nature, economics, politics, environment, gender, sex, race, bodies, and material culture, and might necessitate the development of new modes of critical imagination. At the same time, the series welcomes considerations of the local and the national, for original new work on particular writers and readers in particular places in time continues to be foundational to the discipline.

Since 2011, sixty-five *Transits* titles have been published or are in production.

Recent Titles in the Series

Fire on the Water: Sailors, Slaves, and Insurrection in Early American Literature, 1789–1886
Lenora Warren

Community and Solitude: New Essays on Johnson's Circle
Anthony W. Lee, ed.

The Global Wordsworth: Romanticism Out of Place
Katherine Bergren

Cultivating Peace: The Virgilian Georgic in English, 1650–1750
Melissa Schoenberger

Intelligent Souls? Feminist Orientalism in Eighteenth-Century English Literature
Samara Anne Cahill

The Printed Reader: Gender, Quixotism, and Textual Bodies in Eighteenth-Century Britain
Amelia Dale

For a full list of *Transits* titles go to https://www.bucknell.edu/script/upress/series.asp?id=33

Jane Austen and Comedy

Edited by

ERIN M. GOSS

Bucknell | BUCKNELL
UNIVERSITY | UNIVERSITY
| PRESS

LEWISBURG, PENNSYLVANIA

Library of Congress Cataloging-in-Publication Data

Names: Goss, Erin M., 1976- editor.
Title: Jane Austen and comedy / edited by Erin M. Goss.
Description: Lewisburg : Bucknell University Press, [2019] | Series:
    Transits : literature, thought & culture 1650-1850 | Includes
    bibliographical references and index.
Identifiers: LCCN 2018036388 | ISBN 9781684480784 (cloth : alk.
    paper) | ISBN 9781684480777 (paperback : alk. paper)
Subjects: LCSH: Austen, Jane, 1775-1817—Humor. | Comic,
    The, in literature.
Classification: LCC PR4037 .J314 2019 | DDC 823/.7—dc23
LC record available at https://lccn.loc.gov/2018036388

A British Cataloging-in-Publication record for this book is available
from the British Library.

♾ The paper used in this publication meets the requirements of the
American National Standard for Information Sciences—
Permanence of Paper for Printed Library Materials, ANSI
Z39.48-1992.

www.bucknell.edu/UniversityPress
Distributed worldwide by Rutgers University Press

Manufactured in the United States of America

For laughers

E   *Emma*, ed. Richard Cronin and Dorothy McMillan in *The Cambridge Edition of the Works of Jane Austen* (Cambridge: Cambridge: University Press, 2005).

J   *Juvenilia*, ed. Peter Sabor, in *The Cambridge Edition of the Works of Jane Austen* (Cambridge: Cambridge University Press, 2006).

L   *Jane Austen's Letters*, ed. Deirdre Le Faye, 3rd ed. (Oxford: Oxford University Press, 1995).

LM   *Later Manuscripts*, ed. Janet Todd and Linda Bree, in *The Cambridge Edition of the Works of Jane Austen* (Cambridge: Cambridge: University Press, 2008).

MP   *Mansfield Park*, ed. John Wiltshire, in *The Cambridge Edition of the Works of Jane Austen* (Cambridge: Cambridge: University Press, 2005).

NA   *Northanger Abbey*, ed. Barbara M. Benedict and Deirdre Le Faye, in *The Cambridge Edition of the Works of Jane Austen* (Cambridge: Cambridge: University Press, 2006).

P   *Persuasion*, ed. Janet Todd and Antje Blank, in *The Cambridge Edition of the Works of Jane Austen* (Cambridge: Cambridge: University Press, 2006).

P&P   *Pride and Prejudice*, ed. Pat Rogers, in *The Cambridge Edition of the Works of Jane Austen* (Cambridge: Cambridge: University Press, 2006).

S&S   *Sense and Sensibility*, ed. Edward Copeland, in *The Cambridge Edition of the Works of Jane Austen* (Cambridge: Cambridge: University Press, 2006).

Jane Austen
and Comedy

Jane Austen and Comedy

Erin M. Goss

Y OU WILL HAVE TO EXCUSE ME," a review article in the *Baltimore Sun* of July 12, 1981, begins, "I've been away. Not out of Washington, in person, but in spirit. I can't tell you anything about the shake-up in the Polish Communist Party, the tax cut or the revisionist Marxist theory about Mao-Tse-tung, if that's how you spell his name."[1] Excusing the absenteeism that has made this writer apparently rather blithely unaware of current political events on both the national and international stage appears one simple explanation: "I was, in short, out to lunch with Jane Austen."

There seems to be something about the reading of Jane Austen that invites just this sort of joke from a reader who proudly rejects an outside world and celebrates a delighted distance from the "shake-ups" and "theories" that may indeed affect many—but evidently not all—co-inhabitants in this life of ours. Such a gesture enlists Austen in a joke that is also made at her expense, as she provides the excuse for a turn away from the world rather than offering a way into it. That is, of course, only half of the joke. The other half comes in the identification of what the speaker has been doing with Jane Austen. Out to lunch, she and Jane Austen have apparently indulged together in their refusal to participate in the outside world. Instead of learning about tax codes, the two have shared the expansive time of a Ladies' Lunch in which laughter replaces political anxiety and gossip replaces theorizing.[2]

While an escape hatch from our current political moment may always sound welcome enough, in bringing together Austen and Comedy—these two potential superfluities so easily designated apolitical—this collection asks its reader to focus on two things always at risk of being dismissed as distractions. These essays consider the social value of the comedic and the funny as they assert that Austen is both. Showing how Austen may be read through the lens of the comedic—and its various associations in humor, laughter, farce, and so on—the collection ultimately invites a taking seriously of things not always taken seriously.[3] Instead of using Austen's comedy as an excuse for not thinking about the world, this collection invites its reader to do precisely the opposite.

Invoking an often-held assumption that comedy is that stuff we do when we should be doing something more serious, the 1981 Baltimore critic crystallizes a long-held belief in Austen's pointed irrelevance to—and thus, value as a distraction from—a world of political reality. Insistence on Austenian irrelevance was marked as a selling point by her early biographer and nephew, James Edward Austen-Leigh, who listed among her accomplishments his declaration that "the politics of the day occupied very little of her attention."[4] Such an assertion, as Jocelyn Harris points out, is belied by Austen's references throughout her work and letters to any number of contemporary events; these references, Harris asserts, "reveal her to be fully engaged with the politics of the day."[5] Nevertheless, imagined liberation from lived consequence has constituted the grounds for Austen's appeal to a certain class of reader at least since Janeites like Rudyard Kipling established the love of Jane as one of those things men did in secret as a way to evade their more pressing responsibilities.[6] As the franchise for such amorous reading opened to women, it became both less secret and less suggestive of an evasion of responsibility; rather, the adoration of Austen came to seem the purview of those who, whether on account of sex, class, or intellectual proclivity, had no responsibility in the first place. Her attractiveness as an escape from reality has by turn become a sign that neither she nor her work bears much connection to it. Jane Austen has come to serve as what Mary Ann O'Farrell calls a "figure of Western ignorance"[7] held up as a lady writer offering safe haven to tired white people who cannot cope fully with the call to respond to a world that they do not find easy. As the author who in 1975 completed Austen's fragmentary *Sanditon* (under the title of a "Collaborator," no less) pronounced, "we turn to her for relaxation on plane journeys, in family crises and after the sheer exhaustion of our servantless world."[8] There is little question about who constitutes this "we" whose experience is included in a world only recently marked as "servantless," and the Collaborator insists that in turning to such a version of Austen this *we* remains "unrepentant" about *our* choice. Love of Austen has offered an insistence upon unapologetic classism and a flight from the burdens of modernity for those on whom such burdens may fall most lightly. At the same time, of course, that Austen has been mobilized on behalf of an insistent cultural ignorance for the privileged, she also has provided an avenue to what O'Farrell calls a "disavowal" of that ignorance under the auspices of cultural literacy. As implied by any number of online quizzes [ABC, OUPBlog, the *Guardian*, etc.], in the year 2017 alone, knowledge of Austen is both attainable and necessary to consider oneself properly cultured, though it is, also, of course, possible to get it wrong, as Helena Kelly's May 2017 *LitHub* piece reminds.[9] To know Jane Austen is to have arrived, culturally and intellectually, and to offer as an excuse for one's retreat from the world a privileged knowledge that used to be called cultural capital. Such a knowledge may indeed require leaving behind—whether temporarily or permanently—the extant world and eschewing the expanse of globalized politics for the much more manageable topography of the country estate. Austen's world has always offered a look backward, and these days perhaps the insular nostalgia her novels produce for an England That Was may seem a remarkably better option than many views available to English-speaking readers looking around them. Whether the year is 1981 or 2017, the relative innocuousness and genteel stability of Austen's Regency drawing room may certainly offer respite, for some.

The recent explosion of scholarship and popular writing (and fan fiction, comic books, video blogs, ten-pound notes, and so much more) accompanying the bicentenary of Austen's death has of course belied any claims to Austen's purely insular appeal. She has been claimed by everyone, it seems, popping up in the speeches of alt-right misogynist provocateurs,[10] and in the high teas of Pakistan's upper echelon.[11] Indeed, 2017 provided a Jane Austen so ubiquitous that imagining her as a provider of refuge or escape seems an absurdity, especially if, as the *Atlantic* would tell us, "Jane Austen is Everything."[12] These days one perhaps wishes one could get away from Jane Austen.

As Devoney Looser has shown, at least to some extent 'twas ever thus. Austen has long been bandied about on one side of an issue or another, whether she is conscripted, in one of Looser's most compelling studies, on the side of or in adamant opposition to women's suffrage; or recruited not only on the side of a reactionary conservatism but also on the side of the radicals, whoever they might be.[13] Austen has only become *Austen* relatively recently, and yet the process of her creation as the most legitimate female author the English language has managed to produce has been, as Looser demonstrates, more contentious along the way than we may usually acknowledge. Does Jane Austen belong most properly to the right, to the alt-right, or to the left? Does she provide a global vision or merely offer an insidiously exportable and perpetually colonizing Englishness the tendrils of which continue to find their ways across the globe long after the global power that secured them has faded and waned? And what, and whose, will her work have become after this year of bicentenary reckoning?

The very fact that these questions remain askable may signal the aspect of Jane Austen's work that has remained most consistent across the decades and years of thinking about her. Austen can be many things to many people because her work remains so properly its own and so precisely positioned in its own space and place. Austen's work sings its self-sufficiency and remains best caricatured by Austen herself as those fine brushstrokes on two inches of, among all things, ivory. There is a whole world that must be excluded for such brush-strokes to take shape, and it is a world of commerce, and sea travel, and violent animal death. Once all that is set aside, however, those brushstrokes can present a scene so complete that a person loses him- or herself within it. There is perhaps no better image for Austen's work, however overquoted it may be. As they say, clichés become that way for a reason, and universal truths don't pop up without precedent.

To be "out to lunch with Jane Austen," as the *Baltimore Sun* columnist claimed to be, or to "escape" into her, as Katherine Reay's 2017 novel promised one could do,[14] is to take her as the blissfully blank slate that is a version of the world unconnected to this one. To imagine oneself into such a world, of course, may depend upon one's ability to fit one's desire into the white bourgeois English society that is Austen's bailiwick, but there are certainly many who claim the power of such an act. Indeed, according to Ayesha Mattu and Nura Maznavi, it may well be those who insist on Austen's narrowness that become her worst readers;[15] despite apparent differences, the drive for Austenian identification runs both deep and wide. Even if, as one 2017 *New York Times* article would have it, she is "not your bestie,"[16] Austen has been designated a passport out of a nasty, too-real world that persistently denies one's desires. Hers is a world of wish fulfillment, of upheaval rectified and complications satisfactorily resolved. Hers is a world of comedy, both most generally and most precisely understood.

If Austen has been designated a passport out of a nasty, too-real world, so too has comedy, which, as Lauren Berlant and Sianne Ngai's recent special issue reminds, produces its pleasure "from its ability to dispel anxiety."[17] The light and frivolous stuff of pastime, comedy often appears at best culturally superfluous, and at worst ideologically moribund. A form that makes light of social concerns warranting more weighty attention, that promises easy answers in its neatly tied-up resolutions, and that insists everyone pair off into perfectly matched and generally heteronormative marriages, comedy—like Austen—invites suspicion on ideological grounds from lovers of justice and things that matter.

Escapist fantasies surrounding Austen's work have indeed often resided in its purported comedy. A 1978 review in the *Listener*, for example, distinguishes Austen from egoist academics (and George Eliot) through a turn to her good humor: "Jane Austen is really more like a way of life, and of feeling and thinking and finding things funny. She is the essence of a particular sort of domestic civilisation."[18] Such humor, set apart from the threat of the satirist, offers instead a gentle ease. "Her genius was for comedy," offers up the *Times* in 1978, "for humorous observation of social and domestic life: 'Two or three families in a country village,' she said, 'is the very thing to work on.'"[19] And as Anthony Burgess wrote in the same year, "she knew that the gentle pillorying of folly could be construed as lack of charity. No one more charitable, more chaste, more vital, more civilised ever existed. As Kipling recognised, there has to be a heaven to accommodate her."[20] To travel back in critical time a bit, we find the *Cornhill Magazine* in 1871 establishing the understanding of Austenian humor that would persist for a century and beyond: "There is no malice in Jane Austen. Hers is the charity of all clear minds, it is only the muddled who are intolerant."[21]

Even if her world is a comedic one, Austen's comedy is to be understood as her own particular version of the form she inherits, just as her humor must be understood as hers alone. Rather famously, the popular notion of Austen as a genteel humorist laughing delicately and utterly without malice was exploded, in academic circles at least, by D. W. Harding's 1940 reinvention of Austen as the masterful wielder of what he called "regulated hatred," which he offered up as the foil to the "urbanity" and "gentler virtues" extolled by so many of her adoring readers; Harding proposed that "her books are, as she meant them to be, read and enjoyed by precisely the sort of people whom she disliked."[22] For Wendy Anne Lee, who claims that it "would be hard to overestimate the influence of Harding's ideas" on the field of Austen studies, Harding opened the door to a political Austen, not only an author whose representations might have some resemblance to events of the outside world but more crucially a strategist who could help navigate the difficulties of being among others.[23] Harding's Austen was a thinker who imagined politics through the lens of comedy, rather than an entertainer who provided a retreat from politics through comedic distraction. This sense of Austen and even of Harding, Lee writes, "was soon lost," replaced by the "hater" that Harding provided to Austen's readers.[24] The naming of Austen's "hatred" opened the door easily to accusations of a misanthropy that had been held at bay through repeated insistences on her gentle and even demure humor. A key example and progenitor of this latter position appears in Marvin Mudrick's assertion that Austen's "inhumanly cold and penetrating" irony was the result of her own personal defensiveness and ultimately of her awareness of her own sexual inadequacy.[25] The Janeites' gentle humorist is replaced by Harding's political comedian, who is then replaced by a strident and perhaps markedly unfunny pathological spinster, readily recognized by the likes of D. H. Lawrence, who in *Sex, Literature, and Censorship* (1959) called her a "mean" "old maid" who was, among other things, "thoroughly unpleasant."[26] It is difficult, evidently, to know how to respond to a woman who laughs.

In response to accusations of triviality and insistent escapism has arisen a different strategy for reading Jane Austen, one that often asserts her relevance, sometimes insists upon her universality, and nearly always begins with an assumption of her unquestionable and current topicality. Exploiting what O'Farrell calls in a slightly different context the "impulse toward the conjugal," critics and scholars have found ways to align Austen's name with other historical and philosophical concerns through the, at times, largely performative act of inserting an *and* between them.[27] Beginning with Marilyn Butler's *Jane Austen and the War of Ideas* (1975) and Warren Roberts's *Jane Austen and the French Revolution* (1979), and carrying through Peter Knox-Shaw's *Jane Austen and the Enlightenment* (2004) and William Deresiewicz's *Jane Austen and the Romantic Poets* (2004), Austen has also been linked, married as O'Farrell would have it, to religion by Michael Giffon (2002), to the theater by Penny Gay (2002), and to animals by Barbara K. Seeber (2013). Outside the realm of books, the broader culture has married her off even more expediently and at times outlandishly: to zombies and sea monsters, to William Shakespeare in the Folger Library's "Will & Jane" exhibition, to feminism, to game theory, to whatever might seem useful either to provide a culturally legitimized way in to the second term or to assert the continued relevance and cultural viability of the first. None of this is, of course, to be too critical about the impulse, since this collection of essays rather clearly partakes in it.

In pairing Austen with comedy, this collection performs a doubly conjugal act, or perhaps a meta-conjugal act. One way to understand the various pairings-off in which Austen is imbricated, after all, is through the form of comedy itself. Such pairings are, first, often intended to be funny, as we imagine Austen all cozied up with Charles Darwin[28] or, as O'Farrell discusses, Osama bin Laden. They also, however, engage more formally with comedy in their suggestion, however oblique, that Jane Austen might finally after all these years have met her match and be ready to settle down—with Romantic poets, or religion, or animals. They suggest, that is, the finale of a comedy understood through the lens of genre; such a comedy must end in a triumphant marriage that ties up loose ends (like unmarried women) and offers an audience the promise of a future governed by a restoration of reason and order. Each of Austen's bibliographic pairings suggests that it will be the last, as Austen will finally be happily settled, and the intellectual quest to sort her out—a kind of courtship, perhaps—will be complete. If other critics and scholars have been aiming to enlist Austen in such a comedy, this collection aims, among other things, to consider what she and her work might have to say about it.

That there has been no previous collection of essays taking up the confluence of Austen studies with either the formal and generic consideration of comedy or the broader field of humor studies seems surprising; and yet, it may simply be the case that both humor and comedy are so pervasive in Austen's work that the combination has not seemed to warrant special attention. Perhaps there has seemed little reason to conjoin Austen to that with which her work is so ubiquitously permeated. Or, perhaps, uniting Austen with comedy has not been seen to do the sort of work that such a union so often seems aimed to do. If both Jane Austen and comedy can be seen to be insignificant and escapist fluff, the kind of cultural frippery that in keeping their audiences happy distract them from the world, then putting them together affords neither greater weight. This volume will not precisely insist on the contrary to that position, largely because insisting on the contrary comes too close to conceding the original point. In considering Jane Austen *and* comedy, rather than describing the comedy *of* Jane Austen, this collection seeks to turn a new critical eye on both, asking what and how comedy thinks, and how Austen's engagement with comedy—in terms of both content and form—may provide another way to read her as a thinker as well as an entertainer.

The essays in the book that follows take for granted two not unrelated notions. First, Jane Austen's books are funny; they induce laughter, and that laughter is worth attending to for a variety of reasons that the contributors will delineate. Whether our laughter comes from the raillery of Mrs. Jennings, the carefully contrived confusion of *Northanger Abbey*'s "something very shocking indeed," or from Elizabeth Bennet's proud laughing "whenever she can" at "follies and nonsense, whims and inconsistencies," Austen's novels produce as one of their primary effects at least a periodic gentle chuckle.[29] Second, Jane Austen's books are comedies—understandable on the one hand through a generic form that rewards its reader with a connubial triumph following the potential hilarity of romantic adversity, and on the other through the more general promise of wish fulfillment. After all, as Pam Perkins succinctly writes in her assertion of the generic coherence of *Mansfield Park*, comedy, "in its broadest sense," "describes any movement from despair to happiness."[30] In approaching comedy theoretically, historically, and generically, the book's contributors think of comedy and of humor not only as effects but also as part of a mode of thinking that recognizes comedy as having its own particular intellectual and social value. In acknowledging that Austen's work is both funny and comedic, the contributors to this book seek a way to think about the kind of work that Austen's comedy is doing.

There are as many ways to think about comedy as there are ways to laugh, and the essays that follow will not be entirely exhaustive about either. However, through the specific approaches that each essay brings to bear on the concepts of humor, laughter, and comedy, the book in aggregate offers ways of thinking about Austen's work not only as it invokes a Hobbesian notion of laughter as ridicule but also in relation to psychoanalytic notions of laughter as relief mechanism, to Bakhtinian notions of comedy as an invitation to the carnivalesque, to Kantian notions of laughter's dependence on incongruity, and even to the distinctly Bergsonian idea of laughter as apotropaic warding off of the human made mechanical. For some, comedy invites reflection on social justice; for others, it makes possible a form of thinking available in no other way; and for others, recognition of the historical and contextual frame for Austen's comedy invites readers to see anew both that frame and Austen's texts themselves. For all of the contributors, reading Jane Austen with a specific focus on comedy brings to light a vision of her work in its specific representation of a social world defined by the interactions of individuals jockeying for position and power. While this latter is not the only definition of politics, it is among the more immediately felt, and I suggest that a greater attention to Harding's insistence that Austen's laughter provided a tactical philosophy might be an idea whose time has come again.

One way to understand both the politics of comedy and the political ramifications of laughter is to see laughter as a form of resistance, especially for those who are adjured not to engage in it. And it has become something of a commonplace, even if one knows better than to call it a truth universally acknowledged, that the moment into which Jane Austen wrote was one that sought to foreclose the possibility of women's laughter. Audrey Bilger describes the ways that the idealized femininity imagined over the course of the eighteenth century operated in opposition to the possibility that women might be funny, as "numerous conduct books of the period defined proper feminine behavior for middle-class women largely in terms antithetical to the critical spirit of comedy."[31] While Bilger cites James Fordyce—always appropriate in the context of Austen—any number of others can be found to make the case against women's laughter, and Soha Chung's essay in this collection includes several of the voices raised against laughter's excess. Listed by Thomas Gisborne as one of the weaknesses to which women are particularly prone, "an unreasonable regard for wit" can only get women into trouble, leading as it does to the "thirst for admiration and applause; to vanity and affectation."[32] Erasmus Darwin's *Plan for the Conduct of Female Education in Boarding Schools* (1797) similarly bemoans the horrors of the "laughing vehemently aloud, or tittering with short shrieks, in which some young ladies, who have left school, indulge themselves at cards or other amusements . . . as their dignity of character must suffer by appearing too violently agitated at trivial circumstances."[33] Similarly, "A letter from a father to his daughter at a boarding-school" (1774) warns its addressee to "beware of wit and wanton humour, which are dangerous things, and may bring you into trouble."[34] The particular trouble into which the "dangerous things" of humor and wit may bring a young lady is outlined by Fordyce, who warns his readers with all perspicacity against displaying the wit that might make it impossible that they would ever marry, since, as he explains, "men of the best sense have been usually averse to the thought of marrying a witty female."[35] Such men are opposed to the thought because, Fordyce insists, including himself among their number, "we cannot be easy, where we are not safe. We are never safe in the company of a critic; and almost every wit is a critic by profession."[36] As a more contemporary novelist has suggested, men may fear nothing more than they fear that women might find it possible to laugh at them.[37]

Even if, as Simon Dickie has recently suggested, eighteenth-century "cautions about delicacy, benevolence, sexual modesty, and the proper use of time would hardly be necessary if women were already following them," the imagined foreclosure upon women's humor has made the acknowledgment of Jane Austen's comedy, and indeed of women's comedy more generally, something of a recovery project.[38] For Regina Barreca, for example, women's humor becomes necessarily countercultural and rebellious, as she insists that the fundamental difference "between men's humor and women's humor, is the difference between revolt and revolution."[39] For Barreca, who suggests that "women's comedies have often been misread since they often do not adhere to these essentially conservative conventions of comedy," the key to Austen's comedy in particular is what she calls a "meta-narrative of refusal," a structure that reveals "the absurdities of a world which can only be effectively presented in a comic frame."[40] Eileen Gillooly similarly summarizes Austen's humor under the rubric of "maternal aggression," a vehement refusal to submit to the cultural rules that "strenuously [restrict] a daughter's identity and destiny."[41] For Barreca, for Gillooly, and for Bilger, women's comedy in general and Austen's comedy in particular enact rebellion through the simple act of laughing amid a culture that suggests that such an act undermines their proper demeanor and dignity. Doubling down on this assertion of humor's rebellious nature, perhaps especially within the at times rarefied air of Austen studies, Jillian Heydt-Stevenson's *Austen's Unbecoming Conjunctions* provides a compendium of "Austen's comic irreverence" and finds within its catalog of comedic expression a version of Austen who "expands the space normally allowed to a woman during this period" and who "finesses" and ultimately explodes "the restrictions regarding women's sexuality."[42] Not only in Austen's letters, where Heydt-Stevenson finds "a freedom and an agency for women that some historians have not allowed," but also throughout the novels, *Unbecoming Conjunctions* uncovers a Jane Austen who laughs freely, who laughs openly, and who laughs most predictably at the kind of joke that is often deemed to fall well outside the purview of women's interest and capacity.[43] Heydt-Stevenson seeks to reveal a bawdy Austen, and in doing so to overturn the set of assumptions that has governed the discussion of Austen's propriety, morality, and adherence to convention.

Despite such assertions about women's comedy's necessarily radical status, Austen's comedy in particular (and perhaps all comedy, women's and otherwise) can be roped back into a party line without too much difficulty. Angus Fletcher has recently reminded that "comedy's very form—nakedly shaped as it is by an obsequious desire to please," is as often enlisted on the side of the conservation of things as they are as it is on the side of resistance to them.[44] Comedy, that is, can be the tool of demagoguery as easily as the hope of democracy. Such a dual possibility certainly lurks within Austen's comedy, even as it pertains to women and women's laughter. As Heydt-Stevenson points out, "Austen laughs both at and with women who break rules governing gender and sexual behavior."[45] Hers is not an ideological laughter. Neither, though, is it one that can be deemed simply rebellious. Rachel Brownstein writes of a desire to claim Jane Austen for the cause of feminism and to use her humor to enlist her, remarking, "in the struggle for power between politically radical and conservative critics, she has for years been claimed by both parties."[46] For Brownstein, it is irony—that hallmark of wit and sometime grumpy sister of humor—that allows Austen both to assert the power that a too-simple version of feminist scholarship needs her to have and to undermine the very desire for that power: "through irony, by pointing to the limits of definitive and assertive language, Jane Austen suggests a powerful and pleasurable relation women in patriarchy may have to discursive authority."[47] What Austen's comedy, or humor, or irony might thus show, according to a reader like Brownstein, is not only the capacity of a woman writer's resistance but also her acknowledgment of the pleasure afforded by a mere performance of resistance that nevertheless reinforces the oppression it pretends to undermine.

Comedy is a tricky thing, it turns out.

Whether focusing on work Austen never published, the work we all know well, or work she never wrote, the essays collected here seek to find in their attention to Austen's comedy a way to describe the kind of thinking her writing makes possible. There is resonance and common ground to be found across all eight essays as each locates in Austen a way to think about what it means to laugh and to find pleasure in humor. The three parts focus on three main approaches to the study of comedy. First, in Part One. Comic Energy and Explosive Humor, appear three essays considering Austen's work as productive of, and participating in, humor, or in that which is amusing or productive of laughter. These three essays offer ways to theorize humor both as experience and as effect, and each also provides ways to consider the function of humor. Concerned more precisely with the comic than the comedic, these essays invite us to consider the relationship of humor to a social world.

The first essay, Eric Lindstrom's "Austen, Philosophy, and Comic Stylistics" opens Part One by drawing attention not only to the value of Austen's writing to philosophy but also to its status as philosophical. Contending that "Jane Austen remains underappreciated as a philosophical writer to just the extent, and also in the same way, that comedy is undervalued as a mode of philosophical discourse," Lindstrom's essay locates in Austen's juvenilia access to what he calls a "comic energy" that has been occluded by critical insistence on the stylistic perfection of the published novels. In Austen's writing, Lindstrom demonstrates, emerges a stylistic and comedic approach to a philosophy of action that depends on comedy's striking insistence that one must think more than one thing at once. In Austen's humor Lindstrom finds a particular mode of thinking that is available most specifically through the laughter her writing produces.

Moving from the Ordinary Language Philosophy with which Lindstrom aligns Austen to the field of psychoanalysis and poststructuralist thought, David Sigler's "Jane Austen: Comedy against Happiness" reflects on Austen's humor in relation to the possibility of community. Describing the ways that comedy registers a split subject, at once striving for a happiness that social normativity holds up as ideal and resisting the coercive subjugation of the unconscious that such happiness requires, Sigler shows the ways that Austen's humor undermines the very drive for happiness that her novels seem to assert as primary. Ultimately, Sigler offers Austen's jokes as reflections on the formal insistence on happiness on which comedy relies, and his essay shows the ways that Austen's jokes throw into relief the structural paradigms of continuity that make them possible in the first place. Austen's jokes explode communal assurances that make them possible, and that explosion produces their humor.

For Sean Dempsey's "'Open-Hearted': *Persuasion* and the Cultivation of Good Humor," the energetic explosions of the first two essays become a way to think about comedy's particular relationship to the body, and the way that the experience of the comic is not only psychological or intellectual but also physiological. Considering the relation of "good humour" to the historically grounded concept of the "humors," Dempsey explores Austen's representation of a self whose openness to experience and the world manifests as what she calls "humor." Considering what is to be gained through a return of humoral theory to a consideration of humor, Dempsey's essay sees in Austen's focus on humor a way to include the energy of the body in a consideration of the self.

All three of the essays in the collection's first part suggest comedy's relation to the lived world through their emphasis on comic effects. In the collection's Part Two, (*Emma's*) Laughter with a Purpose, appear two essays emphasizing the function of laughter in the development of an individual consciousness. For the two essays in this part, Austen's comedy emerges in its capacity both to represent and generate laughter. In their suggestion that Austen's represented laughter produces her characters' emotional and psychological growth, these essays also suggest that the laughter Austen's texts generate in their readers may produce such growth in them as well. Perhaps unsurprisingly, both of the essays taking up this topic do so through attention to *Emma*.

First, Soha Chung's "After the Laughter: Seeking Perfect Happiness in *Emma*" considers Austen's representation of laughter as it echoes and also opposes the representation and proscription of laughter found in Austen's contemporary conduct literature. Seeing an analysis of Emma's laughter as a way to think about the laughter of Jane Austen herself, Chung focuses on the moral assumptions that Austen invites her reader to make about Emma's laughter, as well as the assumptions that such laughter seems to produce in her fellow characters. Ultimately, Chung shows how laughter can be read as an index of an individual's ability to reconcile personal with communal happiness. For Chung, Austen's text comes to offer a sort of case study in a variety of types of laughter signifying a differential relation between the individual in pursuit of pleasure and the community in pursuit of equanimity.

Also taking up the question of laughter in *Emma*, Timothy Erwin's "The Comic Visions of Emma Woodhouse" focuses on how the interplay of the visual and the verbal throughout *Emma* generates much of the novel's humor, as well as mapping the trajectory of Emma's own growth. Calling attention to the ways that film adaptations of *Emma* have translated Austen's verbal comedy into a simpler form of visual joke and attending to what he calls the visual-verbal humor of Austen's narrative, Erwin focuses attention on Emma's education, which allows her to move from an "outdated visual regime" to a more vibrant and open vision marked by her capacity for improvement and sympathy. Ultimately, Erwin suggests, the fact that film adaptations miss Austen's joke allows her reader to get it more clearly.

Part Three of the collection, Comedic Form, Comedic Effect, turns to the social effects of comedy taken as a form and genre and examines the relationship of Austen's comedy as genre to the world it represents (or refuses to do). While the essays in both earlier parts have strong interests in social questions and the larger world, these final three essays seek to think more specifically about the political and social ramifications of Austen's comedic form.

First, my own essay, "On Austen, Comedy, and Future Possibility," considers the tension between the potential conservatism of the form of traditional comedy and the disruptive quality of laughter. Examining the endings of Austen's novels and acknowledging both comedy's tendency to reify social norms (heterosexuality, marriage, the primacy of property) and the risk of laughter's aggressive and even violent tendencies, this essay finds an inherent hopefulness in Austen's employment of both. For laughter, as the essay describes, can be understood in many ways other than as a Hobbesian act of aggression, and comedy as much as it may risk reification of present problems and injustices nevertheless promises a future in which women's identity exceeds the marriage plot on which Austen's comedy depends.

A less hopeful approach to Austen's comedy appears in Michael Kramp's "Lost in the Comedy: Austen's Paternalistic Men and the Problem of Accountability." While my own essay finds a certain hope in the machinic nature of Austen's comedic plots, Kramp's examination of farce connects such machination to the normalizing or naturalizing function of comedy that conceals the potential horrors it represents. Reading Austen's depictions of General Tilney's anachronistic chivalry and Mr. Bennet's paternalistic benevolence, Kramp shows that Austen's text depicts the consequences of her male characters' paternalism but also all too often protects them from judgment by allowing them to remain cloaked in comedy. Austen's use of comedy to conceal the harm propagated by characters like Tilney and Bennet provides for Kramp an avenue toward a larger exploration of comedy's complicity in patriarchal systems of hierarchy and control. Ultimately, Kramp demonstrates, comedy may allow us to laugh at patriarchal hegemony, but it may also prohibit us from knowing or seeing the very thing at which we laugh.

The last essay in Part Three, Misty Krueger's "Sense, Sensibility, Sea Monsters, and Carnivalesque Caricature," concludes the collection by asking not what Austen has made of comedy but what comedy has been made with Austen. Focusing on the twenty-first-century proliferation of pastiche exemplified in Ben Winters's (and Jane Austen's) *Sense and Sensibility and Sea Monsters*, Krueger considers how the form of the mash up "literalizes conceptual problems embedded" in Austen's text, especially the imbrication of the bodily and the nonbodily as it appears in the fraught relationship between sensibility and eroticism. A liminal category even in Austen's text, the sensibility of the Austen and Winters mash up is one that exceeds any subtle suggestion of nerves and emerges to be fully represented in a monstrous Colonel Brandon whose face includes often uncontrolled tentacles, the reactivity of which bear witness to his otherwise invisible feelings. For Krueger, the mash up exposes a humor that was always present in Austen's text, and offers a means of analysis and reflection on the ideas that it seems to mock.

In a moment that seems urgently to require something other than genteel escapism, and maybe even something other than laughter, this collection of essays aims to direct attention to the ways we laugh, the ways that Austen may make us do so, and to the ways that our laughter is conditioned by the form in which Austen writes: the form of comedy. Efforts to join Austen to some other topic—however germane and significant it may be—engage in a sort of dance with comedy, as efforts to rescue her from charges of escapism and irrelevance lead us to marry her off again and again, writing one after another comedy in which she and her work play a starring role—though they may be, like so many heroines, subsumed into the marriage that concludes the trajectory of their plot. In drawing attention to the comedy that is so integral to Austen's work, this collection invites reflection not only on her inclusion of laughter and humor, and the comic, and the comedic, and jokes, and wit, and all the other topics that can so readily be grouped under the broad umbrella that is comedy but also on the idea or form of comedy itself, and on the way that this form may govern our thinking about so many things outside the realm of Austen's work.

In a remarkable and recently rereleased book called *Hope in the Dark*, Rebecca Solnit describes a history of leftist political activism not as the tragedy that it might at times appear to be, but as comedy. She reminds her reader that even though tragedy is "seductive" and may even make "the greatest art," it is comedy that allows for survival and that makes future action possible. While tragedy may be beautiful, sublime even, "Survival is funny," Solnit writes.[48] Whether we are ready to sign on to that assertion, we can at least acknowledge that comedy offers more promise for survival than does tragedy.[49] Comedy, after all, asserts a future while tragedy forecloses its possibility. Even as tragedy may get the best lines and demand the most obvious assertions of cultural relevance, comedy insists that life will continue and that the future has room for us to enter it. Comedy is insistently hopeful, and in this moment as in all moments, hope may be a thing worth embracing. Such a vision of the comic lies behind my own interest in comedy and in laughter, and my interest in laughter governs my approach to Austen. Suspect as he is, I believe that Mr. Bennet is not wrong to wonder for what we might live if not "to make sport for our neighbours, and laugh at them in our turn" (P&P, 403). Despite Patricia Meyer Spacks's insistence that to laugh with Mr. Bennet is to expose our own "moral insufficiency," I and the contributors to this collection suggest that what it means to laugh and even to be laughed at is a matter open to much more discussion than either Mr. Bennet or his many readers may believe.[50] Indeed, part of the point of this collection is to open the question of what Mr. Bennet's utterance might mean—not to Mr. Bennet (he takes his pleasure in a rather straightforwardly Hobbesian laughter of ridicule) but to us. What kinds of laughter and what understandings of comedy are available to us as readers of Austen? We hope this collection goes some way toward giving its readers a chance to think through these questions with us.

NOTES

1. Mary McGrory, "Snobs, Frauds and Social Climbers," *Baltimore Sun*, Sunday July 12, 1981.
2. For a consideration of gossip as a consequence rather than a cause of a circumscribed world, see Erin M. Goss, "Homespun Gossip: Jane West, Jane Austen, and the Task of Literary Criticism," *Eighteenth Century: Theory and Interpretation* 56, no. 2 (2015): 165–77.
3. It should be noted that the extraordinary recent special issue of *Critical Inquiry* 43, no. 2 (Winter 2017), edited by Lauren Berlant and Sianne Ngai, does take comedy rather seriously, though the issue's introduction is more invested in a consideration of humor and the funny than in a specific form that might be called comedy ("Comedy Has Issues," Introduction to Special Issue, 233–49).
4. James Edward Austen-Leigh, A *Memoir of Jane Austen: And Other Family Recollections*, ed. Kathryn Sutherland (Oxford: Oxford University Press, 2008), 71.
5. Jocelyn Harris, *Satire, Celebrity, and Politics in Jane Austen* (Lewisburg: Bucknell University Press, 2017), xviii.
6. Rudyard Kipling, "The Janeites," in *Debits and Credits* (London: Macmillan, 1926), 147–74. Also see William Galperin, "Austen's Earliest Readers and the Rise of the Janeites," in *Janeites: Austen's Disciplines and Devotees*, ed. Deidre Lynch (Princeton: Princeton University Press, 2000), 87–114.
7. Mary Ann O'Farrell, "'Bin Laden a Huge Jane Austen Fan': Jane Austen in Contemporary Political Discourse," in *The Uses of Austen: Jane's Afterlives*, ed. Gillian Dow and Clare Hanson (New York: St. Martin's Press, 2012), 198.
8. Quoted in Martin Amis, "Tinkering with Jane," *Observer*, July 20, 1975.
9. Helena Kelly, "The Many Ways in Which We Are Wrong About Jane Austen: Lies, Damn Lies, and Literary Scholarship," *LitHub*, May 3, 2017, http://lithub.com/the-many-ways-in-which-we-are-wrong-about-jane-austen/ (accessed May 19, 2018).
10. See Nicole M. Wright, "Alt-Right Jane Austen," *Chronicle of Higher Education* 53, no. 28 (March 12, 2017).
11. See Moni Mohsin, "Austenistan," *Economist 1843* (October/November 2017): 90–95.
12. Nicholas Dames, "Jane Austen is Everything," *Atlantic* 320, no. 2 (September 2017): 92–103.
13. Devoney Looser, *The Making of Jane Austen* (Baltimore: Johns Hopkins University Press, 2017), 141–44; Helena Kelly, *Jane Austen, The Secret Radical* (London: Icon Books, 2016).
14. Katherine Reay, *The Austen Escape* (Nashville, TN: Thomas Nelson Press, 2017).
15. Ayesha Mattu and Nura Maznavi, "Jane Austen and the Persistent Failure of the White Imagination," *Establishment*, May 15, 2017, https://theestablishment.co/jane-austen-and-the-persistent-failure-of-the-white-imagination-9a3c75c4bb5d (accessed May 18, 2018).
16. Howard Jacobson, "No, Jane Austen Is Not Your Bestie," *New York Times*, July 19, 2017, https://www.nytimes.com/2017/07/19/opinion/jane-austen-sexism.html (accessed May 18, 2018).
17. Berlant and Ngai, "Comedy Has Issues," 233.
18. John Bayley, "Calling on Jane Austen," *Listener*, August 26, 1978.
19. Derek Hudson, "Review of David Cecil's *A Portrait of Jane Austen*," *Times*, October 23, 1978.
20. Anthony Burgess, "Formidable Jane," *Observer*, Oct 29, 1978.
21. Ritchie, Anne Isabella Thackeray, "Jane Austen," *Cornhill Magazine* Volume 24, July-December, 1871: 171.
22. D. W. Harding, "Regulated Hatred: An Aspect of the Work of Jane Austen," *Scrutiny* 8 (1940): 347.
23. Wendy Anne Lee, "Resituating 'Regulated Hatred': D. W. Harding's Jane Austen, *ELH* 77, no. 4 (2010): 995.

24. Lee, "Resituating 'Regulated Hatred,'" 996.
25. Marvin Mudrick, *Jane Austen: Irony as Defense and Discovery* (Berkeley: University of California Press, 1974), 1.
26. D. H. Lawrence, *Sex, Literature, and Censorship* (1959), rprt. in *Erotic Works of D. H. Lawrence* (New York: Avenel Books, 1989), 436.
27. O'Farrell, "Bin Laden a Huge Jane Austen Fan," 193.
28. Peter Graham, *Jane Austen & Charles Darwin: Naturalists and Novelists.* Aldershot, UK: Ashgate, 2008.
29. Jane Austen, *Northanger Abbey*, ed. Barbara M. Benedict and Deirdre Le Faye. in *The Cambridge Edition of the Works of Jane Austen* (Cambridge: Cambridge: University Press, 2006), 113 (hereafter cited as NA); and *Pride and Prejudice*, ed. Pat Rogers, in *The Cambridge Edition of the Works of Jane Austen* (Cambridge: Cambridge: University Press, 2006), 62 (hereafter cited as P&P).
30. Pam Perkins, "A Subdued Gaiety: The Comedy of Mansfield Park," *Nineteenth-Century Literature* 48, no. 1 (1993): 2; see also Jane Austen, *Mansfield Park*, ed. John Wiltshire, in *The Cambridge Edition of the Works of Jane Austen* (Cambridge: Cambridge: University Press, 2005) (hereafter cited as MP).
31. Audrey Bilger, *Laughing Feminism: Subversive Comedy in Frances Burney, Maria Edgeworth, and Jane Austen* (Detroit: Wayne State University Press, 1998), 24.
32. Thomas Gisborne, *An Enquiry into the Duties of the Female Sex*, 3rd ed. (London, printed for T. Cadell, 1798), 34.
33. Erasmus Darwin, *A Plan for the Conduct of Female Education in Boarding Schools* (London: J. Drewry for J. Johnson, 1797), 66.
34. *A Letter from a Father to His Daughter at a Boarding-School* (London. Printed for G. Robinson, in Pater-noster-Rowe, 1774), 25.
35. James Fordyce, *Sermons to Young Women, in Two Volumes* (London: A. Millar and T. Cadell, 1766), vol. 1, 192.
36. Fordyce, *Sermons* (1766), vol. 1, 194.
37. Here I refer to Margaret Atwood's rather famous statement usually truncated to assert that while men fear that women might laugh at them, women fear that men might kill them. Atwood makes the statement in a more roundabout way than is usually quoted in "Writing the Male Character," delivered as the Hagey Lecture at the University of Waterloo in 1982. In that lecture, she offers the dichotomy as a response given to two questions asked of others. Upon asking, "Why do men feel threatened by women?" Atwood reports being told by a man, "They're afraid women will laugh at them." Having asked her female students, "Why do women feel threatened by men?" she reports having been told, "They're afraid of being killed." *Second Words: Selected Critical Prose 1960–1982* (Toronto: Anansi, 1982), 413.
38. Simon Dickie, *Cruelty & Laughter: Forgotten Comic Literature and the Unsentimental Eighteenth Century* (Chicago: University of Chicago Press, 2011), 6.
39. Regina Barreca, *Untamed and Unabashed: Essays on Women and Humor in British Literature* (Detroit: Wayne State University Press, 1994), 16.
40. Barreca, *Untamed and Unabashed*, 18, 43, 44.
41. Eileen Gillooly, *Smile of Discontent: Humor, Gender, and Nineteenth-Century British Fiction* (Chicago: University of Chicago Press, 1999), 81.
42. Jillian Heydt-Stevenson, *Austen's Unbecoming Conjunctions: Subversive Laughter, Embodied History* (New York: Palgrave Macmillan, 2005), 5, 16.
43. Heydt-Stevenson, *Austen's Unbecoming Conjunctions*, 16.
44. Angus Fletcher, *Comic Democracies* (Baltimore: Johns Hopkins University Press, 2016), 2.
45. Heydt-Stevenson, *Austen's Unbecoming Conjunctions*, 101.

46. Rachel Brownstein, "Jane Austen: Irony and Authority," *Women's Studies* 15 (1988): 57.

47. Brownstein, "Jane Austen," 58.

48. Rebecca Solnit, *Hope in the Dark: Untold Histories, Wild Possibilities*, 3rd ed. (Chicago: Haymarket Books, 2016), 70.

49. Berlant and Ngai wonder if tragedy still offers the most operative opposition to comedy; I agree with their suggestion that, to the extent that comedy marks that which is funny (the comic, the humorous), tragedy may no longer provide the best "foil." However, to the extent that comedy still holds within itself the formal promise of a happy ending, the specific opposition continues to be crucial ("Comedy Has Issues," 233–49).

50. Patricia Meyer Spacks, "Austen's Laughter," *Women's Studies* 15, nos. 1–3 (1988): 71.

Part One

COMIC ENERGY AND EXPLOSIVE HUMOR

AUSTEN, PHILOSOPHY, AND COMIC STYLISTICS

Eric Lindstrom

> When I am doing something intelligently, i.e., thinking what I am doing,
> I am doing one thing and not two. . . . The clown's trippings and
> tumblings are the workings of his mind, for they are his jokes; but the
> visibly similar trippings and tumblings of a clumsy man are not the
> workings of that man's mind. For he does not trip on purpose. Tripping on
> purpose is both a bodily and a mental process.
> —Gilbert Ryle, *The Concept of Mind* (1949)[1]

1

Side by side in Jane Austen's youthful manuscript writings ("Volume the Second"[2]) appear two short texts entitled "The female philosopher—a Letter" and "The first Act of a Comedy."[3] Each of these texts indicates a writerly identity toward which Austen was energetically drawn but from the practice of which she felt herself excluded. I reach this conclusion not mainly on account of the fragmentary nature of these pieces (they are, in fact, complete at an intentionally small scale), but from the downright zany perspective of their foreshortening. These productions are not little bits of ivory, two inches wide, labored over with great effort, but clowning skits likely dashed off in a sequence of moments. Their "trippings and tumblings" count among the rehearsals for Austen's later more complex comedy. Highly valued objects to be sure, nonetheless these texts and others in the *Juvenilia* volumes do not focus the reader's attention on the polished finish of the writing, but on the dynamic intelligence and humor of the writing act. In testifying against the sometimes clung-to image of the later novels as pictures of perfection, such rough and ebullient early pieces can help us do needed work on the comic energies of Austen's prose, early and late.

The philosophical stylistics of Austen's practice as a writer of comic prose is my subject in this chapter.[4] My argument will draw from twentieth-century Ordinary Language philosophy (including J. L. Austin, Gilbert Ryle, and Stanley

Cavell) in discussing the exemplary attention that such an unofficial grouping of thinkers awards to Jane Austen. Starting with the anecdote told about Ryle that, when asked if he read novels, he replied, "Yes, all six, every year"[5] (the honoring of Austen, via a joke, both a stand-in for all novels and their stand-out example), the Ordinary Language philosophers repeatedly use Austen's fiction as a touchstone in arguments about affective responsiveness and emotive intelligence. While admittedly using Austen as the currency of honor for a male homosocial gesture of bonding, they also indicate the grounds and leave suggestions for how to explore a performative philosophical conduct pioneered long before them in Austen's own writing.

Austin takes the Austenian title *Sense and Sensibilia* for his 1947–1948 lecture series on modern sense-perception philosophy. In these lectures Austin critiques the dummy usage of philosophical notions of sense-data and material things. Austin satirizes the relation through which these forms of thought "live by taking in each other's washing."[6] He contends that the attention shown by positivist philosophers to examples from everyday life has the sole purpose of referring the world of material things to the underlying reality of *sensa*—and from the start gives such "things" no other role to play. In his 2005 book *Philosophy the Day After Tomorrow*, Cavell in turn relates the "passionate exchanges" and rational play found in Jane Austen's novels in an aim to honor his teacher in the field of Ordinary Language philosophy:

> Because it is not to my hand here, or perhaps ever, to lay out a fuller geography of the courses that 'endless' passionate exchanges can take in satisfying the conditions of perlocutionary utterance, and because I think of myself here as wishing to honor Austin's work, I cite one brilliant source of such passionate exchanges that I imagine Austin would feel quite happy to be associated with, indicated in his announcing one of his once famous courses of lectures at Oxford, the one on the foundations of empirical knowledge, in roughly the following form: SENSE and SENSIBILIA. J. AUSTIN.[7]

Finally—from a philosophical theorist known widely for his jokes if not as a practitioner of ordinary language—Slavoj Zizek maintains in a section titled "Hegel with Austen" from *The Sublime Object of Ideology* (his first book published in English): "Aust*e*n, not Aust*i*n: it is Jane Austen who is perhaps the only counterpart to Hegel in literature: *Pride and Prejudice* is the literary *Phenomenology of Spirit*; *Mansfield Park* the *Science of Logic* and *Emma* the *Encyclopedia.* . . . No wonder, then, that we find in *Pride and Prejudice* the perfect case of this dialectic of truth arising from misrecognition."[8]

Misrecognition surely is in the very genetic stuff of comedy. I want to take a step aside, though, in what is perhaps a more idiosyncratic direction, philosophically speaking, and argue that at the level of prose style we may discover (or recover) something of the philosophical standing of Jane Austen the writer. As intellectual drive, Austen's main theme of love lies at the root of philosophy. Just as there can be no aspiration toward philosophy without the aspiration to love, there is no motive or method for thinking about the relation of philosophy to literature without considering the dimension of style. Attention to style may reintegrate what reason in academic philosophy has put asunder.[9] Not for nothing does the 1818 "Biographical Notice" appended to *Persuasion* and *Northanger Abbey* commend the author as "sensible to the charms of style, and enthusiastic in the cultivation of her own language."[10] With its implied syllepsis (a figure where one clause bears two divergent references divided in type, a joke springing forth from a category mistake), or zeugma, Austin's *Sense and Sensibilia* points my way in this approach.[11]

Syllepsis and zeugma figure prominently in the response of Ordinary Language philosophy to what Ryle calls the impact of "Descartes' Myth" on the theory of mind. Ryle summarizes in *The Concept of Mind*:

> If my argument is successful, there will follow some interesting consequences. First, the hallowed contrast between Mind and Matter will be dissipated, but dissipated not by either of the equally hallowed absorptions of Mind by Matter or of Matter by Mind, but in quite a different way. For the seeming contrast of the two will be shown to be as illegitimate as would be the contrast of 'she came home in a flood of tears' and 'she came home in a sedan-chair'. The belief that there is a polar opposition between Mind and Matter is the belief that they are terms of the same logical type.[12]

Perhaps the most famous literary example of syllepsis comes from Alexander Pope's verse in *The Rape of the Lock*. The line, "Or stain her Honour, or her new Brocade," relates a dualistic moral tenor of serious and nonserious concerns—and underlines it through a contrast of the figurative (and spiritual) with the literal (and material). Yet Pope's wit, in making the line, arguably undoes its controlling symbolic perspective as suggestive of legitimate contrast. In his allusion to Dickens's *Pickwick Papers*, Ryle uses the figure of syllepsis in order to "dissipate" the "hallowed contrast" of mind to matter as briskly as possible.[13] Similarly, both the title and the full argument of Austin's *Sense and Sensibilia* lectures aim to identify and dismiss the grounds of what he views as a powerful and long-standing philosophical myth. (Incidentally, Austen exemplifies the use of syllepsis or zeugma to perform the gesture of dismissal in *Sense and Sensibility* when, "Thomas and the table-cloth, now alike needless, were soon afterwards dismissed.")[14]

Henry Austen's account of Jane Austen's cultivation of style misses its largest potential insight by maintaining that her comic practice is anodyne. Playing upon more than the social, sentimental, and gendered script of Pope's Belinda, or the comic grotesquerie of Dickens in "She came home in a flood of tears and in a sedan-chair," the zeugmatic style renders a way of thinking critically and comically about category mistakes. The kind of positivist philosophy that would exclude style here stands accused by style (through the figure of zeugma, syllepsis) of making an error of logical type. The Dashwoods's servant, Thomas, is not fired, but is served his ordinary dismissal stylistically along with the cloth he has spread on the table (that "material thing" par excellence). How "ordinary" and unburdened can such a moment be, and bear any philosophical weight?

Historically, Jane Austen has seldom been claimed as a "philosophical" writer on her own terms—that is, without externally grounding her claim to philosophical thought through comparison of her self-described fine brush to, say, the big bow wow of an Aristotle, Adam Smith, or David Hume. This chapter argues that Austen is underappreciated at large as a philosophical novelist even as she is acknowledged by Ryle and others as an underappreciated resource to philosophy.[15]

2

One reason that Austen is seldom understood as a philosophical novelist reflects the legacy of a constraining historical discourse. The passage in volume 2 of *Sense and Sensibility* where Elinor and Marianne alike are set apart and mistrusted for possessing "sense," and are thought "satirical" because they are readers, has a dull ring of recurrently felt autobiographical fact conveyed by few other passages in Austen (S&S, 279–80). Austen's observance of a comic felicity that goes beyond the conjugal plot could hold little place outside of conservative apology in the cold decades of the later 1790s or the starving, corrupt 1810s in which Austen was actively writing. To produce "philosophical" novels in her day meant to be counted among the Jacobin novelists of ideas giving passionate and systematic scrutiny to the repressive structures of "things as they are." Embracing such an identification meant to hazard the public visibility of claiming for oneself the status of a philosopher as a woman; it meant to include oneself in a group focused on radical writers, including Mary Wollstonecraft and Mary Hays, vilified by the Anti-Jacobin press in the 1790s and satirized from a middle-class perspective by their fellow female novelist Elizabeth Hamilton in *Memoirs of Modern Philosophers* (1800).

Austen realizes philosophical subjectivity not through building systematic structures or making polemical statements, but through the enacted, multilevel intelligence of her prose, which becomes her comic mode of thinking about the conduct of "intelligent behavior."[16] Henry Austen's "Biographical Notice" has often and understandably been read as a document anxious to establish Jane Austen's good standing as a pious Christian and a contented member of the immediate family—an author withdrawn from the public spotlight, "unpretending" of any claim to fame, and of almost any claim to due monetary reward for her writings. Gender and the professional standing of Austen's authorship are everywhere at stake in this characterization of her diffidence toward claiming a public figure. By the Victorian era, however, the domesticity and apparent confinement of Austen's figure and scope had become vehicles of a broadly philosophical interest amongst her first canonizing male reviewers. In 1859, G. H. Lewes, the critic (and partner of George Eliot, Austen's only rival in this art), said of Austen that she "has made herself known without making herself public."[17] The focus of the Jacobin Romantic novel on the injustice of gender confinement—including the incarceration of women—is refigured by Lewes as a matter of intimacy and disclosure in a context that understands domestic life as above all an epistemological space.

In the present essay it is also a writerly space. If Austen is made known through her prose rather than her person, the writerly character of that disclosure by her sentences upends, against all the ever-mounting subsequent historical evidence to the contrary, the celebration of Austen as a form of personal access.[18] Lewes's formulation of Austen's talent for *being* known without institutional publicity constitutes a philosophical claim for a knowledge construed otherwise than traditional epistemology, and elicits comparison with Cavell's career-long theme of knowing versus acknowledgment. Though I think Austen's philosophical resonance also has potentially tragic modes in connection to what Cavell identifies as the insistence of her prose "to minimize (hence maintain) the expression of distress in everyday existence,"[19] the present essay has enough to handle in treating comedy. It contends that Jane Austen remains underappreciated as a philosophical writer to just the extent, and also in the same way, that comedy is undervalued as a mode of philosophical discourse. Most fundamentally, comic modes of thought do not see truth as a structure of adequation, but in the play of excess and lack. This play not only can relieve some of the heaviness of reading novels as philosophical work(s), but disrupts the very conceptual frame of the assumption that philosophical issues bear their metaphysical freight upon a single, dualistic axis. Ryle's theory of mind in *The Concept of Mind*—though expressed this way only incidentally and not systematically—is comic, insofar as it opposes the two-part mental schematic of an act of introspection sutured to a separate level of action that is manifested in outer behavior or performance. Ryle's framing of this defective scheme critically pinpoints the "mythical bifurcation of unwitnessable mental causes and their witnessable physical effects."[20] "So the practice of humour is not a client of its theory."[21] The philosophical project found in Austen's fiction is not to establish and present a "stock of truths" but to test concern with "intellectual excellencies and deficiencies."[22]

Specific comic possibilities follow from Ryle's boldly drawn critique of the dual picture of mind as composed of a scene of introspection and a scene of behavior tacked together. For instance, Ryle makes the crucial sociolinguistic point that learning to talk with others precedes learning to talk to ourselves. He also posits that we learn to talk to ourselves at a level prior to solitary introspection. "This trick of talking to oneself in silence is acquired neither quickly nor without effort; and it is a necessary condition of our acquiring it that we should have previously learned to talk intelligently aloud and have heard and understood other people doing so." Permitting comic emphasis on the word *silent*, Ryle maintains that "special schooling is required to inculcate the trick of reasoning in silent soliloquy."[23] The argument reaches a subversively comic conclusion by upending the introverted self-involvement of Hamlet-like soliloquy. By the same measure the embarrassment of talking to oneself (akin to reading silently yet moving one's lips?) is repaired of its stigma in being socialized. In generic terms, the convention that a "soliloquy" be understood as referring to a condition of silence, even as it is voiced and heard aloud on stage, is shared in tragedy but not in comedy. In comedy, the performance of a character soliloquizing aloud usually plays off the idea that she is in fact doing what she is doing: talking to herself, addressing the audience; both at once. In *Emma*, the novel's uproarious monologues of Miss Bates on Knightley's apples and Mrs. Elton on Donwell strawberries indeed do just this, without presenting the reader with even a tempting illusion to hold the thought picture in which introspection and socialized thinking are separate, where thought is presumed to occur in an occult or secret place kept in reserve. Though not protagonists, Miss Bates and even Mrs. Elton are paradigmatic Austen characters because they cannot keep their minds to themselves.

In volume 3 of *Emma*, Mr. Knightley's thinking shares this comic theory of mind but is rendered as judicious rather than compulsory practice. He reads silently but comments aloud as he examines Frank Churchill's long revelatory letter of explanation, excuse and apology regarding the secret engagement with Jane Fairfax. Knightley's practice of interjecting comments as he reads combines the older historical practice of reading out loud with a different sort of behavior, that of forming—and venting—an evaluative opinion aloud as he reads: "'It will be natural for me,' he added shortly afterward, 'to speak my opinion aloud as I read. By doing it, I shall feel that I am near you.'"[24] Knightley's mode of shared reading opposes what the historian of the book Alberto Manguel calls the "unrestricted relationship" of "interior space" and offers a counter to the picture of a self-directed, indeed secret reserve of "intimate knowledge."[25] (The only secret reserved in this final section of the book is Emma's awareness of Harriet Smith's fantastic but real hope of marrying Knightley. Emma must look away from him at a key point to preserve this information: her broadly smiling face, precisely, being too true an indication of her thought [E, 516]). Reading silently—but also thinking in silence— is the sophisticated product of a prior conduct of reading (and thinking) aloud in company, one evocative in the present context of Austen's novelistic practice of writing for the ear and of performing her novels orally before family audiences.

Austen's felicitous comic timing hence offers a compelling illustration of Ryle's distinction between knowing *how* and knowing *that* in *The Concept of Mind*. According to Ryle's argument, the inability to recognize "the clown's trippings and tumblings" as "the workings of his mind"—to account for the mental interwrought with the physical, the body in cognition—should be traced back to "Descartes' Myth."[26] For Ryle, that myth locates the foundations of philosophy solely in introspection or in what he calls an "occulted" scene of cognition.[27] This category mistake, for Ryle, lays much of the foundation of modern skepticism and is the key philosophical instantiation of the problem of other minds. In the most rigid and perplexed of "other minds" philosophizing, a metaphysical quest is launched upon Adam Smith's essentially physiological concession on the first page of *A Theory of Moral Sentiments* that we cannot directly experience what another is feeling, sense another's sensation, suffer another's pain (a prior and enabling condition being the finitude of our own bodies).[28] In the Box Hill scene of *Emma*, as rereaders learn, Frank Churchill's command to each group member to say "what you are all thinking of" is not a direct query of the other minds question, but a kind of satire upon that question (E, 402). It is a screen on behavior, not epistemology.[29] Nevertheless, Adam Smith's paradoxically enabling concession becomes the mythic source of an epistemological and ontological fixation for philosophers. In Ryle's account, the move attributed to Descartes leads to more than the notorious picture of the thinking self as the ghost in the machine. It precipitates a theory of mind in which "minds are not merely ghosts harnessed to machines, they are themselves just spectral machines."[30] By contrast, in a fruitful reading of Ryle's essay "Jane Austen and the Moralists," Alice Crary points to the imbrication of Austen's vocabularies of cognition with the novelist's multilevel rendering of human emotional capacities, of "capacities that are simultaneously affective and cognitive."[31] What Ryle shows in that essay, according to Crary, "is that Austen's moral vocabulary reflects a conception of human cognitive capacities and capacities for feeling as essentially tied together. . . . Ryle argues that Jane Austen's conception of human understanding leaves room for the possibility of forms of instruction that persuade in that they engage our feelings and that contribute directly to understanding in so far as they do so."[32] Ryle's own examination of Austen (both in the book *The Concept of Mind* and in his well-known essay) shows how the "moral thought her novels contain is tied to various elements of their narrative form—to ways in which they elicit emotional responses from us specifically as novels."[33]

Not narrative form alone, but also prose style, features as the medium of this elicitation. In a 1950 *Times Literary Supplement* article reviewing *The Concept of Mind*, Austin praises Ryle not only for his intellectual shrewdness at identifying worthwhile philosophical problems and offering strong ideas, but for a "manner of writing" that is "racy, untechnical and idiosyncratic." Austin concludes that piece by evincing such flair on his own: "The jokes of a clown, says the professor, *are* the workings of his mind; and certainly his own wisecracks and epigrams (though far from clowning) go to bear out his theory in his own case. *Le style, c'est Ryle*."[34] To date, there have been excellent studies of the body that relate to the comedic aspects of Jane Austen's novels, and studies of the subversive dimension of Austen's outbursts of comedy. The moment seems ripe for a retheorization of prose as such, which Franco Moretti has nominated the real hero of the nineteenth-century novel.[35] Recently in the subfield of digital humanities, the Stanford Literary Lab has synthesized and published its exploratory group research on the interfacing of linguistic choice and style at levels other than the paragraph—the unit traditionally functioning as a carrier of formal narrative style.[36] A main goal of this essay is to begin to extend the widespread understanding of the novel as a medium of such multilayered narrative training (at once cognitive, affective, and social) to the theory of prose, stylistics, and philosophical poetics. The present essay's approach to a comic, cognitive stylistics in Austen aims to develop as from the other side Simon Jarvis's recent assessment of Austin's achievement in twentieth-century English comic prose.[37] As I have undertaken this larger project over the past several years, I have been struck by a trajectory found in D. W. Harding's career, in which the presentation of Austen's multivalent social intelligence precedes subsequent efforts to map a critical poetics of rhythm, including the poetics of prose.[38]

3

Channeling eighteenth-century social doxa, Peter Sabor characterizes as an "oxymoron" the title of Austen's "The female philosopher," which he annotates in *The Cambridge Edition of the Works of Jane Austen* (J, 477). Would Austen have viewed the identity of female philosopher—and proto-novelistic philosopher—as oxymoronic too? If that is where Austen must start as an enthusiastic young writer in at least one of her ventures, what does such an opening position entail, especially as it all but forces us to assent in advance to the idea of that career as a nonstarter? The logical-semantic relation of an oxymoron is based upon contradiction and conjunction, but in practice it is usually read simply as a self-contradiction, even as an impossibility. In the *Juvenilia* manuscript, Austen translates the "oxymoronic" standing of her title figure away from its logical role as a self-contradictory structure, carried aprioristically by the logic of self-contradiction, and onto a partial association with a character that identifies with a "philosophy" with no interest or future. By the same token, in terms of genre and mood, Austen turns moral didacticism to exuberant satire. If to exist as an oxymoron means more than to state a contradiction, but to experience contradiction, the boisterous mockery that signals the irony to come in Austen's work opens a possible future.[39] Rather than collapse into identification, the title's philosopher applies to the level of the writing subject who performs a variety of positions and tonalities toward knowing. I register "female philosopher" not as an oxymoron, but as an ironized, perhaps even disavowed, ideal—though not for that an attenuated performance.

"The female philosopher—a Letter" might well summon one of Jane Austen's many descriptive recountings to her sister Cassandra of paying a social call. It anticipates the original epistolary first drafts of *Sense and Sensibility* and *Pride and Prejudice*. The text presents a familiar structure of contrastively paired sisters. In fact, there are two pairings of sisters: the two present daughters of the visiting Mr. Millar: Julia, age eighteen; and her sixteen-year-old sister, Charlotte (the eldest, the official Miss Millar, remains with her mother); as well as the pairing made by the letter writer who signs Arabella Smythe with her sister Louisa Clarke, the letter's recipient. (The different surnames indicate one of them is married.)

Julia Millar is the first character described in the text, and her description positions her as the necessary first candidate for the title figure. She has "a countenance in which Modesty, Sense and Dignity are happily blended" and a "form" of "Grace, Elegance, and Symmetry" to match (J, 216). This physical characterization of Julia serves as more than a description of her manners and comportment. Notice how it also defines a conduct in prose. The younger Charlotte is offered as the "humorous" figure in this rapid character sketch. Her energy and style of expression cannot be pulled apart from her physical characterization, and indeed her wit supersedes external appearance in representational terms:

> She is fair and her face is expressive sometimes of softness the most bewitching, and at others of Vivacity the most striking. She appears to have infinite Wit and a good humour unalterable; her conversation

during the half hour they set with us, was replete with humorous Sal-
lies, Bonmots and repartées, while the sensible, the amiable Julia uttered
Sentiments of Morality worthy of a heart like her own. (J, 216)

Prompted by a banal conversation in which the fathers kiss in French fashion and
exchange inevitable truisms about the change of "various circumstances" over a
twenty-year "interval of time" since they last met, "the lovely Julia" draws on the
occasion to make

> most sensible reflections on the many changes in their situation which
> so long a period had occasioned, on the advantages of some, and the
> disadvantages of others. From this subject she made a short digression to
> the instability of human pleasures and the uncertainty of their dura-
> tion, which led her to observe that all earthly Joys must be imperfect.
> She was proceeding to illustrate this doctrine by examples from the
> Lives of great Men when the Carriage came to the Door and the amia-
> ble Moralist with her Father and Sister was obliged to depart, but not
> without a promise of spending five or six months with us on their return.
> (J, 217)

As Sabor points out, these "sensible reflections" are commonplace. They are the
"extracts" of a Mary Bennet arranging her moral *idees reçues*, rather than the "exer-
cising [of] independent thought" (J, 477). When Mr. Bennet turns (already
somewhat derisively) to Mary for her thoughts on the one subject that interests
him—the critical anatomy of "nonsense"—Mary "kn[ows] not how" to respond
and is left "adjusting her ideas," in Mr. Bennet's cutting words (P&P, 7).

The content-free, hydraulically balanced sententiae given to the female philosopher Julia to mouth ("the advantages of some, and the disadvantage of others")
reproduce the parallel Johnsonian sentence shape with all its turgid weight and
none of its asymmetrically decisive judgment power.[40] The sentiments here pass
with an increasingly marked satirical intensity from statements of moral philosophy gleaned from the conduct manuals into a comic vein of verbal and social mannerism that displays Julia's inattentiveness and even her boorishness: "A short
digression to the instability of human pleasures and the uncertainty of their dura-
tion"; a promised visit of many months too long—or its threat! If Julia is to be
equated with the title's "female philosopher" (and her surname's allusion to
Scottish jurist and friend to the philosophers, John Millar, further underlines this
equation as a starting place), then clearly young Jane Austen has no use for
translating the identity of being a philosopher to the subjectivity of the female
comic writer. The twist, in gender and power, of Mr. Bennet's specific kind of

patriarchal indolence seems required to elicit the philosophical purview in Austen's world, to laugh at our neighbors and to be laughed at ourselves in turn.

The text assuredly brings that judgment to mind against Julia Millar's sententiousness (and even against Charlotte's mere amiability). But then, the way Austen's narrator mockingly adverts to all the younger sister's decidedly lacking and dysphoric traits indeed suggests a thinking subjectivity—one found both in the satirical observer and in the letter's recipient—inferred not from the Millars but from *these* sisters embedded in the frame:

> We of course mentioned You, and I assure you that ample Justice was done to your Merits by all. 'Louisa Clarke (said I) is in general a very pleasant Girl, yet sometimes her good humour is clouded by Peevishness, Envy and Spite. She neither wants Understanding nor is without some pretensions to Beauty, but these are so very trifling, that the value she sets on her personal charms, and the adoration she expects them to be afforded are at once a striking example of her vanity, her pride, and her folly.' So said I, and to my opinion every one added weight by the concurrence of their own.
>
> your affecte. Arabella Smythe (J, 217)

In passages like this Virginia Woolf heard the impersonality of the true artist already in the teenager laughing at the world from a co(s)mic distance.[41] Pictures of perfection make Austen feel sick and wicked especially where they are markers of a settled identification with a virtuous character in preformulated possession of concurred-upon virtuous traits. Exuberant comic style distributes the thinker's authority across the many variegated and moving surfaces of the writing.[42]

4

To reach this conclusion is to ask again the question—long under investigation with regard to free indirect style—of whether Austen's comedic style performs a socially regulative function. Most strikingly, William Hazlitt makes just this argument concerning all comedy in the expanded print-public sphere. His 1813 essay "On Modern Comedy" decries the public sphere's "insipid sameness" and laments the decline of wit to "wisdom at second hand" recirculated in a "nation of authors and readers." Hazlitt, by contrast, affirms the vital role served by the peculiarity of prejudice over the "common stock," the "general form." With a kind of perverse acumen, his caustic outburst at generality uses Locke's famous metaphor to target both the idea of a cultural blank slate, and to offer a disruptive figure of sexual embodiment: "We all follow the same profession, which is criticism, each individual is every thing but himself, not one but all mankind's epitome, and the gradations of vice and virtue, of sense and folly, of refinement and grossness of character, seem lost in a kind of intellectual *hermaphroditism*. But on this *tabula rasa*, according to your Correspondent, the most lively and sparkling hues of comedy may be laid."[43]

It is hard to say exactly why Hazlitt chooses the archaic *hermaphroditism* as a figure for modern homogeneity and leveling. Whatever response one might offer, the gendered markings of stylistic identity and the most radical scenarios of disembodied narrative voice similarly witness each other, in the case of Austen. "What we took for Style," writes D. A. Miller in *Jane Austen, or The Secret of Style*, "everyone else took for Woman."[44] Miller's stylish account of style as a "fantasy of unconditioned being," the impersonal mode of style itself, registers an implicit and writerly rejection of the Comte de Buffon's well-known personification of style as the man himself. Miller's rendition of style may also be linked to the psychoanalytic discourse on comedy. What aligns Austen's irony with that particularly English, decorously sangfroid—and male—brand of stoic comedy? On this matter, Freud (preceding pun intended) shares an insight to build from. His paper on "Humour" (1927) distinguishes from jokes the "grandeur and elevation" of humor, which Freud classes the "triumph of narcissism." Through humor, Freud claims, the ego is able to assert its invulnerability, its refusal to be distressed and impacted by trauma. Through the successful display of humor, "the ego refuses to be distressed by the provocations of reality, to let itself be compelled to suffer."[45] Thus *Mansfield Park*, with Fanny Price, Austen's most inwardly wary and distressed protagonist, needs Mary Crawford's almost impervious style and her knowing quip about rears and vices. And thus *Persuasion*, the novel in which Austen is most concerned with the suffering, aging, and traumatized body, is also the novel in which Austen's humor jumps furthest off the page in high-spirited (if not always generous) relief.[46] If Freud finds links to psychopathology in this positive achievement to refuse compulsory distress, there are also ties to the practice of fiction, in "the rejection of the claims of reality and the putting through of the pleasure principle."[47]

The opening passage of *Pride and Prejudice* does indeed seek and supply the counterfactual well-being that Freud ascribes to humor at the end of his essay in paraphrasing its effect through performative ventriloquy—"Look! Here is the world, which seems so dangerous!"[48] Especially on the heels of the perilous exile of the Dashwood sisters in Austen's only preceding book, *Sense and Sensibility*, Freud's exclamation of the ego's refusal to admit suffering seems like an apt rendering of the function of *Pride and Prejudice*'s famous beginning: "It is a truth universally acknowledged, that a single man in possession of a good fortune, must be in want of a wife" (P&P, 3). Miller's reading of this moment as the pinnacle of impersonal Austen Style shows attunement to the triumph of an unperturbed comic irony over the social forces that determine embodied vulnerability. In a reading that aligns with and also queers (neuters or neutralizes) Freud's, Austen "enact[s] a fantasy of divine authority" according to Miller: "Of that godlike authority which we think of as the default mode of narration in the traditional novel, Jane Austen may well be the *only* English example."[49] This impervious, impersonal vantage refuses the demand of exigent social desires. "We last left the secret of Style at this: that the stylothete harbors a hidden wish—of whose impossible fulfillment she has made an absolute refusal—to renounce the renunciation that makes her one."[50]

Austen's most famous sentence is charismatically counterfactual. Its triumphant economy is culled from a psychology of need and the social doxa of gossip. This social voice is rendered clearly in the humor of the following sentence of "ironic or comic addendum."[51] "However little known the feelings or view of such a man may be on his first entering into a neighborhood, this truth is fixed in the minds of the surrounding families, that he is considered as the rightful property of some one or other of their daughters" (P&P, 3). Formed into something resembling a joke—a joke whose production of knowledge, I want to say, is best and perhaps only rendered as a performance of *know how*—a philosophy of the subject is in play and at stake in this purportedly godlike instance of impersonal narration. Miller's dazzlingly intricate, dense, and quick reading of the stylist's "hidden wish . . . to renounce the renunciation *that makes her one*" (embodied, human, and finite), through its virtuosic action as prose, may help to reframe how other human dynamics assume partly revisable forms within the novel's structured political and gender fields: to mark, for instance, the precarity and exchangeability of "*some one or other* of their daughters" (a disempowerment that also conveys vibrancy and health in the collective) in terms of the false autonomy and illusory free choice of the "*single*" young man of means (an empowerment that may at the same time suggest a young man outnumbered). The joke Austen delivers stems *not* from the notion that the neighborhood hasn't yet had a chance to get to know the newly arrived single man's "feelings or view" (though that is true), but works against the assumption that it is the prerogative of the single man—if he is like Bingley—not yet to know his mind in all the "ductility of his temper" (P&P, 17); or that—like Darcy—he knows his mind quite firmly as composed of a different truth. Then so brilliantly, with a success prefigured here due to the compressed, still somehow light, energy of this prose if by nothing else, neither of these kinds of resistance based on the privilege of male cluelessness is allowed to matter. Interestingly, Miller locates the perilously social feat of style at the level of a character's language

(Elizabeth Bennet's), rather than in the creator Austen's: "From the start Elizabeth's style presumes all the freedom from need, the severance from vulgarity, that it eventually secures her in fact as mistress of Pemberley" once she has taught Mr. Darcy to laugh at himself.[52] Yet those invulnerable high spirits would be corrected downward in the less famous, contraveningly dour, statement in the expository opening chapter of *Mansfield Park*: "But there certainly are not so many men of large fortune in the world, as there are pretty women to deserve them" (MP, 3). It is as if the ebulliently counterfactual comedian had read nothing but Malthus for research in the interval between these two novels.

Within Austen's lifetime we can see a shift from moral philosophy to political economy as the dominant framework of social understanding.[53] This shift places a philosophical pressure on the expenditure of stylistic energy.[54] Ryle asserts that "Jane Austen the Moralist quickly outgrew Jane Austen the burlesquer."[55] But did she? Not if we follow upon Ryle, and refuse to separate Austen's engagement with moral philosophy from her commitment to style. In her splendid Introduction to the Oxford World's Classics edition of *Catharine and Other Writings*, Margaret Anne Doody presents the author of the *Juvenilia* as a comic stylist whose signature effect was "female exuberance," a Wife of Bath who also is her own Chaucer, before admitting to the curtailment of this persona as a viable option in the publication culture of the 1790s:

> That Austen can—and should—be placed on a line which runs from Rabelais to Dickens seems to me right. Or at least, Chesterton's statement points to the line to which Austen *could* have belonged—had the world and the publishers allowed such a thing. Female exuberance, a female 'buffoon' convulsed with laughter like the Wife of Bath—but the Wife of Bath as her own Chaucer, not as a character—this is a disturbing idea indeed. The public is not ready for the 'female buffoon' inspired by gigantic and seemingly heartless laughter—not in the 1790s.[56]

Yet recently, Doody has returned to and radically modified her view of Austen's development as a comic artist. In *Jane Austen's Names*, she no longer posits a decisive shift between the dynamic comic energies of the *Juvenilia* and the marriage plots of the six published novels:

> Jane Austen's earliest known works defy realism. They deploy the rhetoric and tropes of conventional fiction in order to set narrative on its ear. These early fictions are brilliantly discordant and nonrealistic, sometimes merely parodic but more often pushing through the parodic into the fantastic and splendid. Jane [Austen] is a mistress of the surreal. Austen, so it seemed to me, had sacrificed a great deal not only of her original humour

and wit but of her vision of the world, in order to please the circulating libraries and get published at last.

I have now ceased my lamentations. At that point I had not realized the full magnificence of Austen's achievement. She had not let go of the surreal and fantastic and edgy elements so wonderfully present in the first works. Instead, she combined these elements with the decorum of and concerns of the courtship novel. Her daring pretence to be *only* realistic is as good as a masquerade.[57]

The critical arc shown in these two passages of Doody's work from the 1990s and the present demonstrates a shift from the view of Austen's style as a policing mechanism to a perspective in which style may perform functions of both identity and critique. This approach renders style not as the symbol of the man himself, but as a "self-different emanation."[58]

I want to treat and accept as an invitation Doody's conclusion to find in the mature Austen a "daring pretence to be *only* realistic," and apply this assessment to her comic philosophical mode with respect to the register of the ordinary. The ordinary is both available to Austen (to no one else so much), and formalized in twentieth-century Ordinary Language philosophy, estranged from her—or at risk of being unavailing—as ahistorical and anachronistic. It is not that empirical source research on what Austen actually read does not matter, or fails to enrich our understanding of the novels. There are numerous philosophically oriented individual essays on Austen. But in the most developed account of Austen's intellectual background, Peter Knox-Shaw's survey essay on Austen and Philosophy and his study *Jane Austen and the Enlightenment*, the play of philosophical energies in the novels tends oddly to be dampened. By referring her approach to the mixed motives of the common sense school—a professed "low road" laid down by the trio of Adam Smith, David Hume, and Samuel Johnson—Knox-Shaw takes a sensible line on what we can reconstruct on balance about Austen's philosophical temperament.[59] Indeed, Knox-Shaw's broadly Aristotelian understanding of Austen compares directly to Ryle's approach in "Jane Austen and the Moralists," which sees Austen as an Aristotelian moral thinker rather than as a Calvinist. Austen's alignment with realism, probability, and the "mixed" character model would leave Julia Millar well behind, but nonetheless suggests the moral dynamics of plotting that give us *Sense and Sensibility*'s Lucy Steele and Lady Catherine de Bourgh in *Pride and Prejudice*: characters whose bad behavior, self-interest, or resentful pique ultimately open a way through the blocked marriage plots these characters themselves had previously frustrated. Knox-Shaw does not entertain the idea that connections right under our nose in Austen's native use of her natural language (though less historically determined by the example of a mitigated British skepticism and

Enlightenment) can be of any account of philosophical standing with the novels.[60] In contrast to the plurality of the ordinary-language method, Knox-Shaw's account of Austen's relation to enlightenment thought justifiably, but reductively, takes its headings one faculty at a time. For instance, he pairs *Sense and Sensibility* with the sympathetic investments of empiricist thought; *Mansfield Park* with religious historiography; *Emma* with political sovereignty. By contrast to such an isolating and serial methodology, Ryle says about Austen and *Pride and Prejudice* in *The Concept of Mind*: "When Jane Austen wished to show the specific kind of pride which characterized the heroine of *Pride and Prejudice*, she had to represent her actions, words, thoughts, and feelings in a thousand different situations. There is no one standard type of action or reaction such that Jane Austen could say 'My heroine's kind of pride was just the tendency to do this, whenever a situation of that sort arose.'"[61]

5

Austen's practice of comedy may rely on scripts for closure, but these narrative and psychological turns nonetheless felicitously renounce the lure to think of the provision of closure in terms of omniscience. A philosophical implication of that happy dismissal of omniscience and certainty is that thought about action supersedes the obsessive dimension sometimes found in pursuing classic problems of knowledge. In the context of the later nineteenth-century British novel, Adela Pinch argues in *Thinking About Other People in Nineteenth-Century British Writing* that "viewing the forms of nineteenth-century literature from the point of view of theories of thinking as action, rather than from the point of view of the problem of representing other minds, can illuminate crucial aspects of these forms. A focus on thinking as action will allow us . . . to question whether omniscience is the most salient term for understanding representations of thinking in the Victorian novel."[62] The Austen that emerges from a consideration of her novels in the company of Ordinary Language philosophers is not just a moral thinker, nor just a critic on epistemological questions of (mis)perception, but a resourceful and profoundly comic thinker on the philosophy of action.

Though the games played on Box Hill in *Emma* designedly aim the reader's attention at the problem of other minds—Frank Churchill mocks this problem, and Austen allegorizes its thinking-inside-the box mentality as a dysphoric demand, a compulsion—the real stakes in play relate to Frank's Austinian linguistic acts of pretending and making excuses. His conduct may be referred to "the long-term project of classifying and clarifying all possible ways and varieties of *not exactly doing things*, which has to be carried through if we are ever to understand properly what doing things is."[63] Getting to know Frank Churchill provides a lesson that we should not come to expect demystification from the excuse as a speech-act genre. Indeed, a principle achievement of free indirect style lies in its renunciation, which is not one, of omniscience. In *Emma*, excuses tend to be explicitly, or mischievously and surreptitiously, kept inseparable from undisavowed pleasure. The subject of excuses affords Austin amusement, instruction, and pleasure. His essay "A Plea for Excuses" starts off with a great deal of *admitted* pleasure. This is both pleasure for the thinker at work and in wit, and a satisfaction communicative and public:

> Much, of course, of the amusement, and of the instruction, comes in drawing the coverts of the microglot, in hounding down minutiae, and to this I can do no more here than incite you. But I owe it to the subject to say, that it has long afforded me what philosophy is so often thought, and made, barren of—the fun of discovery, the pleasures of co-operation, and the satisfaction of reaching agreement.
> What, then, is the subject?[64]

We know from the title already that the subject of Austin's paper is excuses. Austin in the written version of his paper is reveling in the "amusement" and "instruction" he cannot help feel, extending the interest of a subject matter whose typically ascribed function as a speech act is to demarcate liability. (Thus Ryle's view of the word "voluntarily," which for Cavell defines a "clash" between Ryle and Austin, and makes Austin the more specific, pluralistic, labile—and comic—philosopher.[65]) The paper opposes a mode of inquiry that presents metaphysical dichotomies as philosophical "dummies," through bizarrely leveled "actions" that are made to stand in for verbs with a personal subject.[66] For Austin the subject of excuses in ordinary language philosophy offers a rare chance to experience "the pleasures of co-operation, and the satisfaction of reaching agreement." This is just the kind of "microglot," tonally ironic, answerable and happy "union" on which Austen's *Emma* ends as a performance of our unending exposure to and through language.

NOTES

1. Gilbert Ryle, *The Concept of Mind* (London and New York: Hutchinson's University Library, 1949; London: Penguin, 1990), 32, 33.
2. Jane Austen, "Volume the Second," notebook compiled between June 1790 and June 1793, British Library.
3. Jane Austen, *Juvenilia*, ed. Peter Sabor, in *The Cambridge Edition of the Works of Jane Austen* (Cambridge: Cambridge University Press, 2006), 216–21 (hereafter cited as J).

4. In thinking about Austen's comic practice as a dimension of her prose rather than as an aspect of mode or genre as traditionally conceived, my argument aligns with major points in Lauren Berlant and Sianne Ngai's introduction, "Comedy Has Issues," to their recent special issue of *Critical Inquiry* on the subject of comedy (*Critical Inquiry* 43, no. 2 [Winter 2017], 233–49). Berlant and Ngai pose the question of comedy as an expression of post-Fordist labor when they ask: "How should we understand comedy differently, and how does comedy stage its own anxiety-producing/ alleviating, social-distance-gauging missions differently, if people are increasingly supposed to be funny all the time" (236)? "Related to this interpenetration of comedy as art and as life is a sense we have that it is no longer clear what the 'opposite' of comedy is" (238).

5. Though it lacks a single print source, the anecdote about Ryle is in common circulation, and has been cited most recently by Deidre Shauna Lynch in *Loving Literature: A Cultural History* (Chicago: University of Chicago Press, 2015), 155.

6. J. L. Austin, *Sense and Sensibilia* (London: Oxford University Press, 1962), 4. This title is the foremost instance of the jaunty allusive habit that Christopher Ricks calls "Austin's Swink." Ricks remarks of Austin that "his witticism is not cheaply at the expense of Jane Austen, being itself a tribute to the wit that she was and that she mustered. *Sensibilia* emends *Sensibility* as little, and yet as much, as Austin emends Austen" (*Essays in Appreciation* [Oxford: Oxford University Press, 1996], 260).

7. Stanley Cavell, *Philosophy the Day After Tomorrow* (Cambridge, MA: Harvard University Press, 2005), 188.

8. Slavoj Zizek, *The Sublime Object of Ideology* (London: Verso, 1989), 62.

9. Redirecting his point, I owe the language of this sentence to Walter Pater, "Style," in *Appreciations, With an Essay on Style* (London: Macmillan, 1944), 1.

10. Henry Thomas Austen, "Biographical Notice of the Author," in *Northanger Abbey*, ed. Susan Fraiman (New York: Norton, 2004), 191.

11. On syllepsis in particular—also with reference to Ryle and Cavell—see Garrett Stewart, *The Deed of Reading: Literature, Writing, Language, Philosophy* (Ithaca, NY: Cornell University Press, 2015).

12. Ryle, *Concept of Mind* (1990), 23.

13. See Stewart, *Deed of Reading*, 122, for discussion of Ryle with Dickens and the "[] comic heritage" of the figure of syllepsis; see 142–144 for a discussion of Ryle with Pope.

14. Jane Austen, *Sense and Sensibility*, ed. Edward Copeland, in *The Cambridge Edition of the Works of Jane Austen* (Cambridge: Cambridge: University Press, 2006), 402 (hereafter cited as S&S).

15. Gilbert Ryle writes in "Jane Austen and the Moralists": "I am not going to try to make out that Jane Austen was a philosopher or even a philosopher *manquée*. But I am going to argue that she was interested from the south side in some quite general or theoretical problems about human nature and conduct in which philosophers proper were and are interested from the north side" (*Oxford Review* 1 [1966]:5).

16. I take this phrase from J. L. Austin's review of Gilbert Ryle in "Intelligent Behavior: A Critical Review of *The Concept of Mind*," in *Ryle*, ed. Oscar P. Wood and George Pitcher (London: Macmillan, 1970), 45–51; first published in the *Times Literary Supplement*, April 1950.

17. *Jane Austen the Critical Heritage*, ed. B. C. Southam (London: Routledge & Kegan Paul, 1968), vol. 1, 150.

18. For an analysis of the writerly Austen known "at the level of the sentences," see Ian Balfour, "Free Indirect Filmmaking: Jane Austen and the Renditions (On *Emma* among Its Others)," in *Constellations of a Contemporary Romanticism*, ed. Jacques Khalip and Forest Pyle (New York: Fordham University Press, 2016), 249.

19. Cavell, *Philosophy the Day After Tomorrow*, 124.

20. Ryle, *Concept of Mind* (1990), 34.

21. Ryle, *Concept of Mind* (1990), 30.

22. Ryle, *Concept of Mind* (1990), 28–29.

23. Ryle, *Concept of Mind* (1990), 27, 47; for Erving Goffman, "Felicity's Condition" is that we seek to communicate and are not insane (*The Goffman Reader*, ed. Charles Lemert and Ann Branaman (Malden, MA: Blackwell, 1997), 167–92.

24. Jane Austen, *Emma*, ed. Richard Cronin and Dorothy McMillan in *The Cambridge Edition of the Works of Jane Austen* (Cambridge: Cambridge: University Press, 2005), 485 (hereafter cited E).

25. Alberto Manguel, *A History of Reading* (New York: Penguin, 1996), 50–51.

26. To the extent that Ryle's argument offers a wholescale critique of mind/body dualism and the derivation of that view from Descartes, its application to Austen comes with a great debt to the tradition of first-generation feminist scholarship on Austen. Responding to feminist critics of Austen "who interpret her as endorsing only one possible outcome for her heroines: marriage," Jillian Heydt-Stevenson argues (through the example of Anne Elliot and Captain Wentworth in *Persuasion*) that "the basis of a happy marriage arises from the affirmation of a woman's physicality and mind—her body-consciousness," in *Austen's Unbecoming Conjunctions: Subversive Laughter, Embodied History* (New York: Palgrave Macmillan, 2005), 203–4.

27. See *Concept of Mind*, 16, for one instance of Ryle's repeated argument that the mind/body split renders the workings of mind a private space of privileged access, hence "inevitably occult to everyone else." Yet Ryle's position should not be confused with the argument that the mind is immanently related to the body. In his writing on syllepsis, Ryle, and nineteenth-century fiction, Stewart is shrewd to maintain that though "disembodied Cartesian subjectivity . . . puts otherness in hiding and in doubt," the mind and the body as figured by the two nondualistic predicates of syllepsis are "neither commensurable nor wholly separate and unavailable to each other. Concerning bodily motion vis-à-vis cognition, there is neither pure disjunction nor pure conjunction between them. But access there is" (*Deed of Reading*, 122).

28. Adam Smith, *A Theory of Moral Sentiments*, ed. D. D. Raphael and A. L. MacFie, in *The Glasgow Edition of the Works and Correspondence of Adam Smith*, gen. ed. A. S. Skinner (Oxford: Clarendon Press, 1976–1983), vol. 1, 1.

29. The philosopher Jason Stanley argues that thinking and action are not distinct capacities governed by different cognitive states (*Know How* [Oxford: Oxford University Press, 2011], 1–35). Stanley builds upon Ryle's argument in *The Concept of Mind*, yet counters Ryle's fundamental position that "knowing how" (that is, intelligent action manifested in ability or disposition) is *not* a species of "knowing that" (knowledge determined or guided by propositional truth). Stanley views Ryle as a behaviorist in *The Concept of Mind*. The central argument of Stanley's *Know How* is "that knowing how to do something is the same as knowing a fact" (vii).

30. Ryle, *Concept of Mind* (1990), 21.

31. Alice Crary, *Beyond Moral Judgment* (Cambridge, MA: Harvard University Press, 2007), 139.

32. Was it news to Austin that "the 'tone' of an utterance gets stuck to the utterance," Cavell wonders in *Philosophy the Day After Tomorrow*? (163).

33. Ryle, *Concept of Mind* (1990), 44; Crary, *Beyond Moral Judgment*, 138–39.

34. Austin's formulation on Ryle appears to play on the saying of Buffon, "Style is the man himself" ("Intelligent Behavior," 51).

35. Franco Moretti, *The Bourgeois: Between History and Literature* (London: Verso, 2013).

36. Sarah Allison et al., "Style at the Scale of the Sentence"; *Literary Lab* 5 (June 2013). https://litlab.stanford.edu/LiteraryLabPamphlet5.pdf (accessed May 4, 2016).

37. Simon Jarvis, "How to Do Things with Tunes," *ELH* 82, no. 2 (2015): 365–83.

38. D. W. Harding's development of interests can be seen by comparing his oft-cited study of Jane Austen's practice of social judgment, in *Regulated Hatred and Other Essays on Jane Austen* (London and Atlantic Highlands, NJ: The Athlone Press, 1998), to his collection *Words into Rhythm: English Speech Rhythm in Verse and Prose* (London: Cambridge University Press, 1976). Harding's notorious essay, "Regulated Hatred: An Aspect of the Work of Jane Austen," was first published in *Scrutiny* 8 (March 1940): 346–62.

39. My emphasis on the possible rather than the probable in Austen draws from William H. Galperin's important work in *The Historical Austen* (Philadelphia: University of Pennsylvania Press, 2003).

40. By contrast, Mary Lascelles identifies Austen's "familiarity with, and love of" Johnson's work in "her aptitude for coining pregnant abstractions": "Miss Bates's *desultory good-will*"; Mrs. Elton's *apparatus of happiness*"; see Lascelles, *Jane Austen and Her Art* (London: Oxford University Press, 1939), 109.

41. Virginia Woolf, "Austen," in *The Common Reader: First Series*, ed. Andrew McNeillie (New York: Harcourt, 1925), 136.

42. Thus my approach to Austen's comic style differs broadly from the formative account of her "proper" feminine style as an inscription of constraining and conventional social forces. For that argument, see Mary Poovey, *The Proper Lady and the Woman Writer: Ideology as Style in the Works of Mary Wollstonecraft, Mary Shelley, and Jane Austen* (Chicago and London: University of Chicago Press, 1984), esp. chaps. 6 and 7.

43. William Hazlitt, "On Modern Comedy," in *Selected Writings*, ed. Jon Cook (Oxford: Oxford University Press, 1991), 101.

44. D. A. Miller, *Jane Austen, or The Secret of Style* (Princeton: Princeton University Press, 2003), 2.

45. Sigmund Freud, "Humour," in *The Standard Edition of the Complete Psychological Works of Sigmund Freud*, trans. James Strachey (London: Hogarth Press, 1961), vol. 21, 162.

46. Heydt-Stevenson terms this effect the "comic mourning" of *Persuasion*; see *Austen's Unbecoming Conjunctions*, 181–205. If comedy is a "classic body genre," the novel, it has been argued, absorbs the comic genre's intensities as a mode but then exiles comedy's full disruptive force from "realist causality" (Berlant and Ngai, "Comedy Has Issues," 239).

47. Freud, "Humour," 163. Heydt-Stevenson discusses Freud's treatise on jokes as an illustration of "the limits of applying male-oriented critiques to women's humor, especially for Austen's bawdy humor" (*Austen's Unbecoming Conjunctions*, 207).

48. Freud, "Humour," 166.

49. Miller, *Jane Austen*, 31; emphasis in the original.

50. Miller, *Jane Austen*, 59.

51. The phrase is Harding's, on Austen, in *Words into Rhythm*, 138. Particularly with regard to the question of free indirect style, the opening sentence of *Pride and Prejudice* exhibits Alenka Zupančič's Hegelian-Lacanian psychoanalytic "definition of comedy as the expression of the universal in the concrete," as summarized by Berlant and Ngai, "Comedy Has Issues," 234.

52. Miller, *Jane Austen*, 44.

53. In *Utopia, Limited: Romanticism and Adjustment* (Cambridge, MA: Harvard University Press, 2015), Anahid Nersessian argues in the context of a reading of Harriet Martineau's *Illustrations of Political Economy*, that "in the *Illustrations*, free indirect discourse turns out to be the voice of a third term between character and narration called political economy, or even just capitalism," and, "it is through free indirect discourse that political economy becomes 'immanent to language'" (192, 195).

54. Compare Harding in *Words into Rhythm*: "These [rhythmic effects] are modes of energy expenditure (or of preparedness for expending it). . . . We need not wonder how the rhythm comes to 'express' them; it is part of them," 154. More generally, Harding concludes his chapter on "Expressive Effects of Prose Rhythm": "The approach I have suggested towards elucidating the expressive value of prose rhythm depends on viewing the movement of prose as analogous to gait and gesture and other bodily movements, with the constant transition from one posture to another that everyday activity presents," 150.

55. Ryle, "Jane Austen and the Moralists," 12.

56. Margaret Anne Doody, "Introduction," in *Catherine and Other Writings*, by Jane Austen, ed. Margaret Anne Doody and Douglas Murray (Oxford: Oxford University Press, 1993), xxxiv. Doody traces the view of Austen's "naturally exuberant" comic power to G. K. Chesterton (qtd. xxxiii).

57. Margaret Anne Doody, *Jane Austen's Names: Riddles, Persons, Places* (Chicago: University of Chicago Press, 2015), 387–88; emphasis in the original.

58. See Barbara Johnson, "The Alchemy of Style and Law," in *The Feminist Difference: Literature, Psychoanalysis, Race, and Gender* (Cambridge, MA: Harvard University Press, 1998), 166–67.

59. Peter Knox-Shaw, "Philosophy," in *Jane Austen in Context*, ed. Janet Todd (Cambridge: Cambridge Univ. Press, 2005), 332.

60. This sentence draws from Stanley Cavell's language and concerns in "Must We Mean What We Say," in *Must We Mean What We Say? A Book of Essays* (Cambridge: Cambridge University Press, 1976), 4–5. Cavell is not complacent about the reliance on natural language without further empirical grounds, and later offers this judgment on his criteria: "If I am wrong about what he does (they do), that may be no great surprise; but if I am wrong about what I (we) do, that is liable, where it is not comic, to be tragic" (14).

61. Ryle, *Concept of Mind* (1990), 44.

62. Adela Pinch, *Thinking About Other People in Nineteenth-Century British Writing* (Cambridge: Cambridge University Press, 2010), 15.

63. J. L. Austin, "Pretending," *Philosophical Papers*, 2nd ed., ed. J. O. Urmson and G. J. Warnock (London: Oxford University Press, 1970), 271.

64. Austin, "A Plea for Excuses"; in *Philosophical Papers*, 175.

65. Cavell, "Must We Mean What We Say?" 3, 4, 6.

66. Austin, "A Plea for Excuses"; in *Philosophical Papers*, 178–79.

JANE AUSTEN

Comedy against Happiness

DAVID SIGLER

THIS ESSAY EXAMINES THREE OF Jane Austen's jokes to theorize the ideological function of comedy in her work as it builds but undermines community: first, the narrator's fat-shaming dismissal of Mrs. Musgrove in *Persuasion*; second, the unexpected emergence of a narrator in *Lady Susan* as Austen curtly dismisses the epistolary mode; and third, Mrs. Bennet's inquiries, in *Pride and Prejudice*, about preparations under way for Charles Bingley's return to Netherfield, a situation rife with double entendre about butchers and ducks. These examples complicate current notions about the normative and comic dimensions of Austen's writing. A psychoanalytic approach can help us see how, even as Austen's comic structures assist ideologically in the consolidation of wealth, privilege, and heteronormativity under way in the Regency period, they also reckon with a gap at the heart of these hegemonic structures that unsettles Austen's notions of happiness, community, and social cohesion. Austen very often reveals that gap in her jokes, a procedure that suggests her proto-psychoanalytic sensibilities.

Joel Faflak has recently lamented the absence of psychoanalytic impulse in Austen. In an era, he says, when male writers were basically "*invent*[ing] psychoanalysis" in their contestations of philosophy, Austen was developing a normative discourse of mandatory happiness that, in suturing the subject into the hegemonic social order, averts meaningful cultural critique—effectively generating a nineteenth-century version of cognitive behavioral therapy.[1] He finds that "Austen's novels seem immune to psychoanalysis."[2] Others concur, noting how "the volume and quality of psychological studies of Austen lags significantly behind work done from other perspectives" and has "hardly affected critical opinion of her work."[3] Yet her jokes have a vaguely Freudian air that has sometimes been noted but seldom scrutinized in the voluminous criticism. The two most important studies of Austen-as-humorist suggest connections to Freud only in passing: Patricia

Meyer Spacks, as part of a longer comparison of Austen to Hobbes, momentarily observes that Austen's "view of laughter foretells Freud's theory of jokes" but doesn't elaborate, while Jillian Heydt-Stevenson cites Freud in calling Austen's comedy "tendentious" but immediately backs away from the connection, because it only "illustrates the limits of applying male-oriented critiques to women's humor, especially for Austen's bawdy humor."[4] Yet Austen and Freud seem to think about comedy quite similarly. Such a hypothesis will enable us to see how Austen exploits the comic register for ambiguous ideological purposes, namely, to track the social and ideological consequences of the splitting of the subject across and through the unconscious. Hers is comedy against happiness, but that situates itself within the ideological regime of happiness to trouble its affordances.

Northrop Frye would have classified Austen's oeuvre as Aristotelian "New Comedy," meaning that Austen wrote comedies of sexual desire, very often with Oedipal undertones, and functioning by "social integration," in which "the general atmosphere of conciliation . . . makes the final marriage possible."[5] Her comedic technique aspires toward community and social cohesion. Yet it enforces consensus by revealing the split in the subject and the gap, that is, the nothing or No One, that occasions it. Consequently, happiness and social integration are very often at odds in Austen's work, having been sewn together insecurely through her comic techniques.

For Heydt-Stevenson, Austen's comedy functions mostly through unexpected comparison, as "when two ideas or images or people, set side by side, reveal unforeseen similarities."[6] Yet the examples examined here indicate that Austen uses comedy not to highlight similarities and thus engender synthesis, but rather to enfold heterogeneous material into normative social structures without assimilating them. To employ the terms of Alenka Zupančič's study *The Odd One In: On Comedy*, Austen's comedy "stages the impossible," offering a way of "tarrying with a foreign object" within tightly controlled communities regulated by intensely normative gender and class pressures.[7] By "foreign object," I mean, here, primarily the unconscious. I have written elsewhere about the changing meaning of "the unconscious" in Austen's time, and the function of that concept in her fiction.[8] Basically, by "unconscious" I mean a nexus of repressed material, which, being totally inaccessible to the subject, seeks discharge in language, coded wishes, and jokes; specifically, jokes reconnoiter this realm as a way of reclaiming the enjoyments of early childhood.[9] There is something social about investigating the unconscious: to apprehend it, Freud says, one must learn to see oneself as one sees "other people" and identify with them rather than oneself.[10] As Austen, through comedy, folds this foreign material into the order of things to create a "short circuit," her demand for happiness is intermittently disrupted.[11] Thus Austen's fixation on happiness, which has become a controversial aspect of her work, is mitigated from within by the mechanisms of her jokes. As the jokes incorporate inaccessible material into normative communities premised on happiness, Austen's supposedly absent psychoanalytic side asserts itself.

Austen's jokes are often disquieting and ambiguous. So much of the interest in Austen's texts inheres in the subtle reversals opening within the diegesis, as she elaborates a complex and multivalent form of irony that can disrupt jokes even in the process of their own development. Spacks even concedes that "one can never be sure, reading Jane Austen, where the next joke is coming from—or what, exactly, it means."[12] Freud's models for reading comedy are well suited for such an author, given their astonishing responsiveness to undecidability and their eagerness to seek out their own interpretive limits and collapse. Classifying jokes multiply, by comic technique, then subject matter, and then by motivation, Freud develops overlapping models so that each approach can upend and supplement the others. He traverses form and content, to analyze the ambiguous ways that "the substance of the joke" can be tucked into "the joking envelope."[13] He establishes classifications for jokes, such as "tendentious jokes," which deserve their own special forms of analysis, but then goes on to find that all jokes actually belong to the subcategory.[14] He tries to distinguish comedy from jokes but refuses to distinguish these from irony, explaining that jokes and comedy employ the techniques of irony and vice versa.[15] The primary difference between jokes and comedy, he explains, is that the former draws on the unconscious while the latter does not, and so a distinction becomes impracticable: "I cannot come to a decision on the basis of my feeling."[16] "None of this precisely suggests that the relations between jokes and the comic are very simple," Freud acknowledges, as "it is quite impracticable to deal with jokes otherwise than in connection to the comic."[17] And whereas Henri Bergson, Freud's contemporary, devotes three essays to the social motivation for laughter, Freud pursues the more radical premise that "strictly speaking, we do not know what we are laughing at."[18] That is why Freud's *Jokes and Their Relation to the Unconscious*, when combined with derivative psychoanalytic models such as Zupančič's, is able to grasp the constitutive oddness of Austen's comedy without explaining it away.[19]

PERSUASION'S "LARGE FAT SIGHINGS"

Austen's joking reaches its moral nadir when, in *Persuasion*, the narrator ridicules Mrs. Musgrove for being fat while she mourns her son's death. The scene proceeds as follows: "They were divided only by Mrs. Musgrove. It was no insignificant barrier, indeed. Mrs. Musgrove was of a comfortable, substantial size, . . . and while the agitations of Anne's slender form, and pensive face, may be considered as very completely screened, Captain Wentworth should be allowed some credit for the self-command with which he attended to her large fat sighings over the destiny of a son, whom alive nobody had cared for."[20] It is an abominable criticism to offer. The passage, in its elucidation of these supposedly "unbecoming conjunctions," has been central to recent discussions of Austen and comedy, most notably Heydt-Stevenson's book *Austen's Unbecoming Conjunctions*, which emphasizes the bawdy and bodily nature of Austen's jokes.[21] This "infamous proclamation," Heydt-Stevenson observes, is "dangerous, because sacrilegious," given the easily recognized assault on taste and decorum that arises when mocking people for looking bad as they mourn the deaths of their children.[22] The comedy functions through the enthusiastic violation of cultural taboos, according to which "bewailing the lost becomes an aesthetic exercise."[23] Yet, notes Heydt-Stevenson, this transgressive joke develops a comparison between Anne Elliot and Mrs. Musgrove, as both are shown to be "in serious danger of looking ridiculous" as they "look preposterous mourning."[24] The scene also contains echoes of a sexual scandal involving Lord Nelson and his mistress Lady Hamilton, as Jocelyn Harris has suggested.[25]

The thing I want to note about this passage—and what complicates current understandings of Austen's comedy as a protest against cultural scripts—is its ambivalence toward its own comic operations. The narrator continues: "Personal size and mental sorrow have certainly no necessary proportions. A large bulky figure has as good a right to be in deep affliction, as the most graceful set of limbs in the world. But, fair or not fair, there are unbecoming conjunctions, which reason will patronize in vain—which taste cannot tolerate—which ridicule will seize" (P, 73–74). To whom is the narrator responding here? The narrator admonishes itself for its cruelty, acknowledging the "right" of all people to "affliction," regardless of their attractiveness or the shape of their body. The narrator even adds "certainly," to make this right seem uncontested. Yet the narrator then dismisses this objection, claiming, "Ridicule will seize" on the unfortunate, be that "fair or not fair." Mrs. Musgrove "certainly" has a "right" to mourn her son, but the narrator has no choice not to respect that right. A debate about sympathy has broken out from within the monologue, a debate made more complicated by the way that the narrator, having brutally mocked Mrs. Musgrove, immediately commends Captain Wentworth for his "self-command" and concern for her.

The narrating consciousness has split internally, with "reason" taking issue with "taste" and "ridicule." Taste and ridicule acknowledge their wrongness but can't seem to help themselves. Reason, even though it rightly respects Mrs. Musgrove on the basis of her rights, is being upbraided by some sort of superegoic meta-narrator for its ineffectiveness. The meta-narrator is acting not as subjectiv-ized "old maid" (as D. A. Miller has said of this scene) but as an inhuman reposi-tory of cultural meanings.[26] What is the purpose of this super-narrator if it was only going to supplant the first one and justify its cruelty as inevitable? Austen is doubly cruel here: first, the narrator mocks Mrs. Musgrove, and then the super-narrator mocks the cruelty of the narrator, even claiming that it violates human rights, only then to reaffirm the judgments of the original narrator. Such a double structure is the very essence of the comic in psychoanalytic terms, as Zupančič has theorized it: "the ego-ideal itself [here, the narrator] turns out to be the par-tial (comical) object . . . [and so] directly *is* a human weakness."[27]

"The comedy of bodily shapes and facial features" at root mocks inefficiency, Freud supposes, and so depends upon wasted movement for its comic effects.[28] In Austen's passage such mockery happens three times: the narrator mocks the inef-ficient movement ("large fat sighings") of Mrs. Musgrove, but immediately also notes Anne Eliot's own wasted movement ("completely screened") and its own inef-ficient operations ("will patronize in vain," and the double whammy of "large fat"). In that way, the narrator takes the place of Mrs. Musgrove to become the butt of its own joke. Yet it does this without letting Mrs. Musgrove, Anne, or the reader, off the hook. This is, to extend Spacks's analysis, one of the "intricate ways in which laughter and judgment relate to one another in Austen's novels."[29]

The conflicted tone here throws the reader into a state of uncertainty, or divided attachments. The narrator is mocking itself for mocking Mrs. Musgrove, while Wentworth and Anne are "probably looking on," trying to manage a deli-cate situation.[30] If jokes, for Freud, are about reclaimed pleasure, and if insult jokes tend to generate their own further incentive bonus, then jokes that mix their reclaimed pleasure (and incentive bonus) with self-admonishment are particularly vexing and in need of theoretical explanation, and "the case of tendentious jokes is a special one among these possibilities." He asks: "What happens in general, if, in a combination, determinants of pleasure and determinants of unpleasure con-verge? On what does the outcome depend, and what decides whether the outcome is in pleasure or unpleasure?"[31] And, to connect this line of questioning to psy-choanalytic ideas about community and ideology, we might specifically ask how a tendentious joke like Austen's can form the basis of a community, if it seems to refract even individual voices, as Miller suggests the narrator has here become, instead of producing collectivities.

Obviously, a complicated comic structure is needed if a moment of dread-ful fat shaming can become a lesson in sympathy from someone who suddenly believes that human bodies, even fictional ones, have "no necessary proportions." To better understand this reversal, and how it creates community in Austen's fiction, we might take a small further detour into *Jokes and Their Relation to the Unconscious*. The hinge of the mechanism is often, for Austen, self-recognition, suggests E. M. Dadlez: "Austen's people, even the bad ones, are too much like us not to engage at least a modicum of understanding."[32] But how can self-recognition emerge in a case in which Austen treats her narrator with alarm and her diegetic characters with disdain? How could a joke so cruel as "large fat sighings" possibly build community or train the reader to approach Mrs. Musgrove with "a modicum of understanding"? Although jokes, like dreams, stem from the unconscious in disturbingly personal ways, they depend upon, as Freud calls it, a "social process."[33] That process is performative—it does not simply and mechanically depend upon others, as Bergson supposes, but rather creates community through its very operations. Austen's joke helps us theorize the operations of that performative structure as it incorporates unconscious material into the community and builds community around unconscious material.

At work here are what Freud calls "ideational mimetics," which enforce social norms but are also a form of sympathy, requiring the reader's (or listener's) ability to insert oneself into the fiction.[34] "A joke," explains Freud, "is the most social of all the mental functions that aim at a yield of pleasure. It often calls for three persons and its completion requires the participation of someone else in the mental process it starts."[35] The tripartite structure creates and maintains an intricate and eroticized interplay of desires and inhibitions, one that readers today, in a world improved by the thought of Eve Kosofsky Sedgwick, will recognize as homosocial.[36] The three positions are the joke teller, the object (or butt) of the joke, and the person to whom it is told. In tendentious jokes, joke teller and listener bond in and through their cruelty to the butt of the joke. Yet it is really the listener (or reader) who is most vulnerable, as they have to be ready to change personalities entirely, and as a matter of habit. The listener/reader must match the psychic disposition of the teller: "He must be able as a matter of habit to erect in himself the same inhibition which the first person's joke has overcome," demonstrating a "readiness for inhibition, which I must regard as a real expenditure, analogous to mobilization in military affairs."[37] Although Freud's interest usually primarily lies in the skill of telling jokes, via "the technical methods of the joke-work,"[38] here he considers the anterior skill of listening and laughing: listening to jokes well requires both *ability* and *readiness* "as a matter of habit." The listener/reader has to be ready, through habitual training, to turn against the butt of the joke or else the joke will fail—and in that sense a joke is always something the listener must "collaborate" in.[39] In a kind of Hobbesian register, one needs to be inured, then, to cruelty, in order to build a community. Inhibition, meanwhile, is both necessary and superfluous to the process: it must be created and maintained just so it can be undone and lifted. The third party creates "a postponement," which, as if by a Lacanian stroke of logical time, is a necessary absence foundational to the structure of the joke as it relays between its three poles.[40] The skill of listening to jokes requires "real" military-grade expenditure, even if both the military affairs and the expenditure itself are metaphorical.

Jokes about "bodily shapes" have a special intersubjective structure, as such jokes additionally put the listener/reader into the place of the object of the joke. To make sense of such a joke, Freud says, we have to measure the body in question against a norm, and that norm, for any listener, is measured in relation to oneself.[41] So for such jokes as "unbecoming conjunctions" to work, readers are required to measure themselves against Mrs. Musgrove's "large bulky figure." The joke is funny, presumably, because Mrs. Musgrove is bigger and less elegant, presumably, than the reader, who is expected to uphold the normative dimension of the joke. Austen encourages the reader to think in such a way by writing another female body into the scene for comparison: "Anne's slender form, and pensive face" are "screened" by Musgrove's body for Wentworth. The reader becomes caught between an ideal ego and an ego ideal, having been asked to identify with the joke teller and butt of the joke at one and the same time. Readers of this passage must, then, be ready to turn against themselves in multiple ways at once.

Here we confront, as Freud did, the impossibility of disentangling jokes from the comic, as Austen's humor toggles between these modes. In comedy, explains Freud, the joke teller and butt of the joke are necessary, but a listener is optional, whereas jokes require all three—which is to say that jokes, unlike comedy, need an audience. Freud adds two twists, though, to complicate the structure beyond any usefulness: the butt of the joke, despite being necessary, is unnecessary—it "adds nothing new"—and the teller and listener are fused together, until "the joke and the comic are combined" and "the same remark can be both things at once," even if "socially the comic behaves differently from jokes."[42] Unlike comedy, jokes partake of the unconscious: they work like dreams, while the comic does not, and so one must be surprised by jokes, but must expect comedy.[43] Because the distinction is unconscious, we cannot ever really know where or why these lines are drawn, making the categories practically meaningless. This indeterminacy between jokes and the comic muddies the "sighings" joke in *Persuasion*, rendering ambiguous its import. It's a joke about the indeterminacy between jokes and comedy, in a way, as Mrs. Musgrove functions in both the unconscious and the conscious realms at once: in one sense, we expect the narrator to make fun of her to uphold the norms shaping femininity throughout the novel, in the same way we expect Louisa to be mocked for her overdependence on Wentworth[44] or Anne for her suggestibility; in another, though, the reader is expected both to identify with Mrs. Musgrove and feel subjected to those same normative judgments all while laughing, which entails identifying with the narrator. And meanwhile the process is working in reverse, as the narrator's self-castigations signify its identification with the reader all the while. At the level of the comic, the comment maintains an ideological regime based on fat-shaming, while at the level of the joke, we become concerned with rights (that is, Mrs. Musgrove's "right to be in deep affliction"). This splitting of the subject across the register of the unconscious is a psychoanalytic structure, one that necessitates the superego as a regulatory mechanism. The reader, having already been asked to identify with both Anne and Mrs. Musgrove, is now encouraged to identify with the superego itself. Such an identification, Jacques Lacan reminds us, *is* the foundation of community per Freud's totem myth.[45] These "fat sighings" split the subject through their ambivalence and multivalence, calling a world of social expectation into being.

Freud says that insulting jokes, taken as a comic subspecies, have a special capacity for pleasure, as they generate a unique surplus enjoyment: "The insult takes place, because the joke is thus made possible. But the enjoyment obtained is not only that produced by the joke: it is incomparably greater."[46] The listener gets the pleasure of the joke *and* the pleasure from the lifting of a prohibition against cruelty. This is what Freud calls "the *incentive bonus*" for insulting jokes, the ineffable and useless thing that, according to Zupančič, aligns comedy with love.[47] In comedy and love, she argues, "Not only do we not get what we asked for, on top of that (and not instead) we get something we haven't even asked for. The nonrelation is supplemented by another nonrelation, which uses the thing obstructing the relation as its very condition."[48] The two are sustained as two by the impasse between them and the incentive bonus thus generated. *Persuasion*'s insulting joke and *Pride and Prejudice*'s duck joke, as we will soon see, are similarly built around an obstacle, made of nothing quantifiable, that establishes intersubjective connections, and through that commonality we can see how love, in Austen, might take the shape of transgressive cruelty. The nonrelation between the participants becomes, paradoxically or dialectically, the basis of their relationship, such that *Pride and Prejudice* can develop flirtatious rapport out of Darcy's total incompatibility with Elizabeth, *Persuasion* can build its central courtship around the previous failure of that same courtship, and *Mansfield Park* can develop a love relationship around Edmund's thoughtlessness as it intersects with Fanny's unpleasantness. The incentive bonus derived from comic insults, *Persuasion* reveals, similarly operates in the world of the quantifiable and yet resists being tallied—hence the oxymoronic formulation of Freud's, "incomparably greater."

The "fat sighings" decried in *Persuasion* jump across several psychic levels and several modes of humor to bring people together. As Zupančič recognizes:

"Comedy thrives on all kinds of short circuits that establish an immediate connection between heterogeneous orders . . . . [its operations are] not that of a smooth,
imperceptible passing of one into another, but that of a material *cut* between
them . . . [in which] the only genuine immediate link between these two things is
the very cut between them."[49] In *Persuasion*, the gap between the reader and
narrator, which as we have seen is opened, sutured, and then reopened in the
"unbecoming conjunctions" scene, depends upon the novel's ironic capacity to be
taken aback at its own commentary.

"POST OFFICE REVENUE" IN *LADY SUSAN*

The starkest example of such movement in Austen's oeuvre occurs at the end of
Lady Susan, in which the arrival of the omniscient narrator "brings in . . . a comic
note" to a cynical and subversive fiction.[50] Miller shows, in his analyses of *Persuasion* and *Pride and Prejudice*, what happens when an Austen narrative temporarily
suspends that otherworldly narratorial voice, which he aptly calls No One.[51] In
Lady Susan we find the reverse situation, the sudden arrival of No One, or what
William H. Galperin calls "the sudden audibility of the hitherto silent narrator."[52]
The result is an even more pronounced version of the splitting, and consequent
self-castigation, that *Persuasion* comically exploits with Mrs. Musgrove. The
example can help us understand the significance of this structure for Austen's
interrogations of community and happiness, which will enable us next to track
the operations of the duck joke in *Pride and Prejudice*.

    The ending of *Lady Susan*, notes Sandie Byrne, is unlike that of other Aus-
ten novels, as it is unconcerned with property.[53] It focuses instead on its own form.
No One unexpectedly appears, or is rather invented, to criticize the epistolary
nature of the novel so far on the grounds of its stylistic excessiveness and imprac-
ticality: "This Correspondence, by a meeting between some of the parties, & a
separation between the others, could not, to the great detriment of the Post office
Revenue, be continued longer. Very little assistance to the State could be derived
from the Epistolary Intercourse of Mrs. Vernon & her neice; for the former soon
perceived, by the style of Frederica's letters, that they were written under her
Mother's inspection, & therefore deferring all particular inquiry till she could make
it personally in Town, ceased writing minutely or often."[54] If Austen Style is always,
as Miller promises, "a truly out-of-body voice" making a "thrillingly inhuman
utterance," this one is an extreme case for disrupting the epistolary structure of
the fiction.[55] Like the "fat sighings" joke from *Persuasion*, this one manipulates
the reader's expectations, positioning him or her uncomfortably, and it does so by

objecting to an emotionally fraught situation on aesthetic grounds. It proceeds, as Freud recommends for analysts, by "emotional coldness," which, like a telephone receiver, "must turn [its] own unconscious like a receptive organ towards the transmitting unconscious of the patient."[56] We discover that there has apparently always been a narrator, if only a silent and very unobtrusive one; it is simply that the reader, like the characters who have been writing letters, has not been aware of it. In making the narrator apparent, this intrusion highlights the materiality of the text, the labor of writing, and the intricate psychical apparatuses of the fiction: we are shown that writing this manuscript, in an epistolary format or not, demands fortitude and patience which "could not . . . be continued longer." No One's concerns, like those of a psychoanalyst, are here "arrangements about *time* and *money*": once the characters have overspent their account for postage and taken up their allotment of the author's time, No One sharply and without sympathy intervenes, breaking its long silence to end the narrative session.[57] At the moment that the joke introduces this new level, it immediately and performatively crosses that level, positioning No One within the fictional world. The very obstacle or gap between the levels becomes a bridge between them, much as we saw with the rapport broken and built in *Persuasion*.

Through the joke, Austen's writing of the novel becomes inseparable, conceptually, from the characters' writing of their letters—in formalist terms, Austen eliminates any difference between fabula and syuzhet in the very moment of the latter's appearance. The reader is thus forced to share the position of the butt of the joke, which here is the novel itself: Austen teases the epistles in this epistolary novel for not being aware that they have been part of a novel. Yet the joke has another side, too, in that the narrator is meanwhile pretending to be unaware that the letters comprising the manuscript have been fictional, and thus have not been contributing to the national coffers. And when No One appears, pretending that the fiction has not been a fiction, it does so by alerting us that even the letters we had been reading had likely been *themselves* governed and directed by a superegoic overseer, as Frederica's letters "were written under her Mother's inspection." At stake are the novel's repressed knowledge and the participants' intentions, both of which are unreadable.[58] Here, then, comedy and jokes intersect and cannot finally be disentangled, per the Freudian model. The joke from *Lady Susan* works along exactly these lines: by pretending that the world of the fiction is real, as if the entrance of a narrator would save money on postage, No One disavows the novel's status as such at the moment when it becomes most novelistic. The moment of metadiscourse actually dispels the possibility of metadiscourse.

Spacks astutely if cynically observes that an Austen reader's desire for "happiness" is a desire for novelistic convention, because happiness is a property specifically of fiction.[59] Similarly, a joke about the form of the novella is also, necessarily, a joke about its own form, in that, as Freud says, inevitably we take pleasure in the form of the joke as well as its content.[60] Yet the content of the narrator's interjection demands consideration too, given its thematic connections to comedy as such. No One enforces a comic shift in perspective, ensuring that the reader takes a fresh distance from the proceedings. As Austen establishes distance with this joke, she also dialectically pulls No One back onto the same plane as the letters. Hegel can show us what is going on here. In the Culture section of *The Phenomenology of Spirit*, he disentangles the levels of irony that can attend wit when wit begins to double, or layer, consciousness. When consciousness becomes "disrupted consciousness," he says, in a "nihilistic game which it plays with itself," the witty upper level of the consciousness is at the advantage because it is aware that what it is saying is ironic. This is the situation with the fledgling narrator in *Lady Susan*. Having spoken snidely, its mind, such as it is, is fully cognizant of its advantage over its seemingly naïve counterparts in the letters. It uses this advantage for comic purposes, much as occurs in Hegel when the Notion appears, and "its language is therefore clever and witty."[61] The ironic gap that opens between the two levels—here, between the novel's epistolary storyworld and its dismissive narrator—has an unintended consequence: "It merely condensed into a trivial form the content of Spirit's utterance; in making the *opposite* of the noble and good into the *condition* and *necessity* of the noble and good, it thoughtlessly supposes itself to be saying something else." Its advantage of self-knowledge is squandered, advises Hegel, as it has become "in its essence the reverse of itself."[62] It is, unlike "the plain mind," "a mixture compounded of a complete perversion of sentiment, of absolute shamefulness, and of perfect frankness and truth," and it "will be a tinge of ridicule which spoils them."[63] "Thus," we might say, extrapolating from Hegel, the advantaged narrator is compromised by its own elevation over the fabula. *Lady Susan* thus plumbs the reverse side of Hegel's warning that "what Enlightenment declares to be an error and a fiction is the very same thing as Enlightenment itself is"—here, the elevated narrator becomes, through its own shock tactics, part of the erroneous fiction it disavows.[64]

Along these lines, the narrator's appearance in *Lady Susan* connotes a splitting of the novel's consciousness. Ironically, it does so through unification: Austen Style (to borrow Miller's term) collects and accounts for the decentralized polyphony of the letters. In opening an ironic gap between itself and the characters' voices, and in smugly knowing its own advantage, the voice is doomed to become just one more character in a long line to present their thoughts on Susan to the reader. In Hegelian terms, we might say that the substance has become the subject—the defining trait of what Zupančič, in her own reading of Hegel, calls "true comedy."[65] As Miller advises, "Negation has always been the prime mover of Absolute Style" in Austen.[66]

As the narrator's thoughts are caught within the dialectical spiral, the ideology of happiness is caught within its churning mechanisms. The narrator, now forcefully interceding, does so to emphasize how happiness cannot ever be known from the outside: "Whether Lady Susan was or was not happy in her second Choice—I do not see how it can ever be ascertained—for who would take her assurance of it on either side of the question? The World must judge from Probability" (LM, 76). Here Austen formulates the central link, through the unknowable, from comedy to love to happiness, that orients her fiction generally. The ideological condition called happiness is radically unknowable from outside, yet we are only "outside" of the happy consciousness because of the intrusion of the narrator. Free indirect discourse, being privy to the thoughts of characters, seems perhaps uniquely poised to "ascertain" Susan's degree of happiness, but even then, we are confronted with the question of whether happiness is even ever attainable or if people can be trusted to know it for themselves. The narrator rightly notes that the letters would not necessarily clarify things, given the rhetorical strategies Susan has been using to persuade everyone in her circle. Yet it is the presence of the narratorial "I"—really Style itself whose identity seems so otherworldly and antisubjective—that interferes. "To narrate is already to explain," as Paul Ricoeur says, and so the narrator's apparent refusal to explain is both a self-defeating act and an expression of bad faith, and commits the very transgression it is trying to prosecute against Susan with regard to Frederica.[67]

At the level of its content, the passage from *Lady Susan* explicitly addresses the questions posed, implicitly, by the fact of narrator's comic intervention. The narrator becomes immediately concerned with Susan's self-serving "maternal fears" for Frederica's health given "the lucky alarm of an Influenza" (LM, 75). Susan's supposed fear of influenza, which no one believes, is effectively a fear of other people and their proximity—a pretended fear, then, of community. One irony here is that, not a moment after the narrator has declared an end to the correspondence, during which various characters had been expressing more or less directly their skepticism about Susan's motives, the narrator itself begins to write to *us*, the reader, in a similar way. The narrator, far from establishing itself as a narrator, rather inscribes itself into the chain of letters and interpellates the reader into the novel as, effectively, a character, thereby eliminating the distance apparently established a moment before. The narrator dispels itself as narrator in the very moment of its arrival. Far from enabling us to see, at last, that this series of letters has been fiction rather than real life—albeit backhandedly, through the ironic suggestion that the novel *has* been real life, such that its letters might enrich the nation—this narrative self-dispersal implies that our real life as readers, such as it is, exists as part of the fictional storyworld. As Zupančič says, "We do not get to the Real by eliminating the symbolic fiction, the mask, and looking behind it, but by *redoubling* the symbolic fiction, the mask, by putting another on top of the already existing one."[68] Exactly so, we have found, at the end of *Lady Susan*, and will again in *Pride and Prejudice*, "her most comic novel," but one in which "laughter can become dangerous self-indulgence."[69]

"THREE COUPLE OF DUCKS" IN *PRIDE AND PREJUDICE*

As Eric C. Walker observes, being single in Regency culture (as in our own) suggests a state of incompleteness or transition that awaits its culmination in marriage.[70] The couple was the basic unit of subjectivity in early nineteenth-century Britain, especially and aggressively so in Austen, who of course would remain voluntarily unmarried herself. Austen exploits the ideology of coupledom as *Pride and Prejudice* begins to conclude, developing a grim joke about ducks counted by the couple at the butcher's. Freud cautions that marriage jokes are generally "cynical jokes and what they disguise are cynicisms"; this one undoubtedly, if one may use the expression for a duck joke, fits that bill.[71] The joke functions somewhat differently from the previous two examples, operating not by positioning the reader ambivalently in relation to a shifting or emergent narrator, but by allowing the reader to connect the utterances of two different characters, without narratorial interference. The joke restlessly substitutes friends for food and reversals of hospitality, and with the technique of comically treating metonymies as metaphors.

The setup of the joke occurs when Elizabeth rather pedantically chides her mother for being, as the narrator puts it, "very dull for several days" in the aftermath of Lydia's union with Wickham: "This is the consequence, you see, Madam, of marrying a daughter," said Elizabeth, "it must make you better satisfied that your other four are single" (P&P 366). The talk of conjugality enables Mrs. Bennet to imagine that courtship might resume between Jane and Charles Bingley, thereby lifting, for a moment, her "dullness." After all, Bingley shall soon be returning to Netherfield, putting the Bennet matriarch "quite in the fidgets" even as she disclaims any interest in the wealthy former suitor of her daughter. She asks Mrs. Phillips, her sister: "Is it quite certain he is coming?" (P&P 366–67) The punchline comes in Phillips's reply: "You may depend on it, . . . for Mrs. Nicholls was in Meryton last night; I saw her passing by, and went out myself on purpose to know the truth of it; and she told me that it was certain true. He comes down on Thursday at the latest, very likely on Wednesday. She was going to the butcher's, she told me, on purpose to order in some meat on Wednesday, and she has got three couple of ducks just fit to be killed" (P&P 366). The joke is bleak and subtle, undermining the novel's conjugal acts of wish fulfillment. No sooner has Mrs. Bennet finally begun to reckon with the emotional costs of exogamy than Mrs. Phillips presents, through this offhand reference to ducks, the violent consequences of meting out meat by the couple. Although Bingley is coming to hunt, he still (knowingly or through blithe entitlement) has his hunting already done in advance, through the combined efforts of his domestic workers and a butcher (P&P 366). The joke further develops through Mrs. Phillips's tone, both matter-of-fact and atwitter, and in her strategies for amassing and counting fowl. It unfolds in Mrs. Bennet's strained attempt to match that tone and employ the same counting mechanisms for her daughters, having garnered inside information about how to attract and please Bingley.

To measure ducks by the couple is to see the world as Austen can tend to, with the married couple as "the smallest unit," to quote Mary Poovey, by which we can understand subjectivity.[72] The joke is all the cleverer because ducks really do come in couples and can be counted (on) as such: the monogamy of the duck implies that the novel's human marriage market expresses a base animal drive that ends with the couple on display for our consumption. It is apparently immaterial whether the ducks are from his Netherfield reserve or from the butcher: the "and" conjoining "order in some meat" and "just fit to be killed" obscures any difference between ducks raised, ducks hunted, or duck meat purchased: the point is that Bingley will be hunting and will be eating duck, and that's all that actually matters. The "and" is also additive, though, demarcating the butcher's ducks as essential to the operation but supernumerary to the tally. The butcher's ducks are the extra element, the surplus that makes possible the smooth operation of Bingley's hunting trip. This is in itself comic, as "comedy and comic satisfaction thrive on things that do not exactly add up," given their dependence on "a heteronomous addition, a supplement that brings with it a logic of its own."[73]

The joke finds its support in two of Austen's letters, which give the quip special resonance as an inside joke and outline its context. In a letter to her sister Cassandra dated September 15, 1795, Austen writes: "Edward and Fly went out yesterday very early in a couple of shooting jackets, and came home like a couple of bad shots, for they killed nothing at all. They are out again to-day, and are not yet returned. Delightful sport! They are just come home, Edward with his two brace, Frank with his two and a half. What amiable young men!"[74] The second letter, also to Cassandra, was written from Chawton and dated May 31, 1811: "I will not say that your mulberry-trees are dead, but I am afraid they are not alive. We shall have pease soon. I mean to have them with a couple of ducks from Wood

Barn, and Maria Middleton, towards the end of next week" (L, 199). The letters, taken together, resonate multiply with this "couple of ducks" scene. In the first letter, which was written in the period when Austen was writing "First Impressions," her early draft of *Pride and Prejudice*, we find a humorous acknowledgment of the fruitlessness of duck hunting, something pursued not for its spoils but for its ability to signal amiability between men, while resulting in "nothing at all." Indeed, the amiability of the men seems to depend on their having "killed nothing" and their "bad shots." In the 1811 letter, composed while Austen was writing *Pride and Prejudice*, Austen counts ducks by the couple. She does so to make a joke about cannibalism and hospitality, suggesting through her syntax that her guest, Maria Middleton, will be on the menu along with ducks and peas. She insinuates that she will be having a friend for dinner, and then further blurs lines between life and death, hospitality and violence, care and neglect, by treating the act of cannibalism as an extension of her comments on the suffering mulberry trees.

Mrs. Phillips, taking after Austen's letters, tallies ducks by the couple, making effectively a body count—it's three couple of ducks rather than six or a half dozen. She makes a grouping of couples, which is alarming given Mrs. Bennet's meditations just then about Lydia with Wickham and the prospect of Bingley for Jane. Mrs. Phillips's enthusiasm that the ducks are "just fit to be killed" associates matrimony with death in a way that might disturb Jane, especially given her aunt's role in directing Lydia toward Wickham originally. The tropes layer onto each other and become complicated: the ducks metonymically signify to Mrs. Phillips the return of Bingley to Netherfield, which in turn metonymically signifies to Mrs. Bennet Bingley's continuing eligibility for marriage. The compound metonymies next slide into metaphor because of the discussion, immediately previous, of the Bennet daughters' varying states of singlehood and couplehood. Thus Jane is figured as "some meat" for Bingley's eventual consumption. Austen is demonstrating what Freud would call comedy's "tendency to compression, or rather to saving."[75]

The joke takes an even darker turn once Mrs. Bennet begins making overtures to Bingley: "When you have killed all of your own birds, Mr. Bingley," she urges him, "I beg you will come down here, and shoot as many as you please" (P&P, 373). Mrs. Bennet here is treating Bingley rather "famillionairely," that is, without recognizing the obvious ways that capital differences are structuring their interactions.[76] She ignores how she is in no position to play the beneficent host, given Bingley's economic leverage. Although she asserts, however unconvincingly, that "he is nothing to us, you know, and I am sure *I* never want to see him again," she is ready to prepare a couple of ducks from Netherfield, and Jane Bennet, for Bingley's visit toward the end of next week (P&P, 366).

Bingley appears here not a venerated sportsman but as an inept hunter willing to quietly, and through surrogates, buy what he imagines having done himself. He is the only unimportant part of this scenario: the real joke is that Mrs. Bennet is *correct* to say that "he is nothing to us" and "that is nothing to us." Bingley is being awaited as a void, the occasion for everyone's preparations but inessential in himself, a hunter who is certainly entitled to hunt for sport but from whom we might not expect much without the invisible labor supporting his fantasy. Bingley is thus the joke here, for a joke, in Freud's definition, is an "*absence*" "clothed in words."[77] Hence the extra dimension of the joke, when Mrs. Bennet says, "I beg you will come down here, and shoot as many as you please"—the tables have turned, and it is *she* who is treating Bingley, who is "nothing," with admirable famillionairity.

As Freud says of his potentially misogynist marriage-broker jokes, which might seem to mock a woman for being unattractive, the jokes are actually attacking the ideological infrastructure of marriage, not the bride or the broker.[78] Austen's jokes, like Freud's, risk reifying social hierarchies as natural, mocking fat or economically disadvantaged people for not knowing their place; yet in doing so they create alliances out of obstacles or create convergences out of tropes, persistently destabilizing these same hierarchies through her comic structures. Mrs. Phillips's account of the butcher enables Mrs. Bennet to substitute ducks for daughters until she can disavow her desire for her neighbor's desire.

COMEDY AGAINST HAPPINESS

Not only does Austen write comedy, but psychoanalytic definitions of comedy can seem to require an Austen plot—comedy, in one memorable definition, being "a legitimacy crisis followed by the sudden appearance of a cornucopia."[79] The "cornucopia" tendered in Austen usually takes the form of anticipated happiness, a ubiquitous but controversial aspect of her work. *Pride and Prejudice* is, for example, "in its readiness to ratify and grant our happiness . . . almost shamelessly wish fulfilling," argues Claudia L. Johnson, although it "vindicates personal happiness as a liberal moral category, rescuing it from the suspicion into which it had fallen."[80] Mary Favret has found Austen's readers in the United States to be obsessed with happiness, while Stefanie Markovits maintains that Austen's drive toward happiness is powerful but "kinetic," such that "it forces much present happiness beyond the parameters of the action of the novel, which instead concentrates on the promise of happiness in marriage."[81] As Faflak sees it, happiness for Austen is an expression of social cohesion, to the extent that her novels can be said to perform a "monstrous" ideological task, "polishing the social veneer that sustains . . . illusions as illusions" and enforcing a structure that "makes the enmeshment palpable."[82] Happiness, Faflak argues, is Austen's "full-blown pathology, a viral affective attack" with "catastrophic effects" in *Persuasion*.[83]

It would appear that laughter is the wooden horse through which this "affective attack" is launched. Jokes remain Austen's "main resource, her most basic attitude," and, through so being, become the substratum of the world's most exquisite three-decker happiness-producing and happiness-enjoining machines.[84] It has often been assumed, perhaps too readily, that comedy is subversive in Austen's hands, being "an outlet for her hostility toward ideologies that dominate women" and a way of "criticizing . . . eighteenth-century gender politics."[85] A critical stance, though, is not always anti-ideological. Even when comedy seems subversive, it can often grant its audience the requisite distance from hegemonic structures so that ideology can operate the better. It expects the audience's happiness, and as Zupančič warns, "The imperative of happiness, positive thinking, and cheerfulness is one of the key means of expanding and solidifying . . . ideological hegemony."[86] Hence we should worry about the alliance of comedy and happiness in Austen, given their propensity to work in league to ensure political inaction.

Yet jokes are "double-dealing rascals," as Freud advises—the Willoughby and Wickham of rhetoric.[87] The relationship between jokes, happiness, ideology, and the community is dynamic and often precarious in Austen. This instability may itself partially redeem Austen from what Miller has called the "cultural *valence*" of her voice, by which he means how Austen's narration tends to "combine with central ideological elements of a culture invested in such an image for itself" even as it provides a refuge for marginalized readers.[88] Although I readily recognize her embeddedness in these discourses, her comic structures, I hope to have suggested, frequently deform such formations from within, especially as she reckons with the splitting of the subject and what Lacan would call the agency of the letter in the unconscious. Such reckoning happens, for instance, in the alignment of community and happiness in her jokes. Even if her comedy produces community through enforced consensus, that community, through the process, must incorporate a destabilizing blankness. It happens because of the performative dimension of her comedy, a function that links the three examples explored in this paper.

Freud cautions that "every joke calls for a public of its own, and laughing at the same jokes is evidence of far-reaching psychical conformity."[89] Here he goes further than Bergson's claims that laughter is a "social gesture" and that "you would hardly appreciate the comic if you felt yourself isolated from others," as Freud sees comedy as both constitutive of the social order and as an engine for ideology.[90] It is an important observation for a psychoanalytic tradition often all too eager to think about psychic structures in individual terms, by comparing joke-work to dream-work or analyzing the traumatic sexual roots of comic expression. What Freud is offering is an almost dystopian perspective: to share a laugh, people have to share a way of thinking. Not only are jokes (and, by extension, comedy) ideological state apparatuses, enforcing social norms and depending upon them, but also they performatively "call for a public," summoning communities into existence on the basis of the "far-reaching psychical conformity" they manufacture. If the ideological name for such conformity is "happiness," then we might see comedy as a happiness-producing apparatus designed for the production, and not merely the maintenance, of social cohesion.

Hence it is important for us to observe the unspoken flip side of Faflak's observation about happiness, which is that Austen, as a comic writer, can be understood as a novelist of community. Recent scholarship has emphasized not only the cohesion of Austen's world, but the ways in which Austen's fiction itself creates a kind of "Austen community" around the world.[91] Freud can help us understand this dynamic, given his claim that the comic depends on "social relations" and "is found in people."[92] Happiness, construed as a normative requirement that the subject fit in to a community, depends upon comic structures that make it their aim to jump social levels and incorporate heterogeneous material into the community without assimilating it. If, as Frye has maintained, "the natural tendency of comedy is to include as many as possible in its final festival," Austen's comedy does so by emphasizing rather than flattening out differences.[93]

As we have seen, this involves not only the differences between characters or classes or genders, but also differences internal to the subject: ego happiness is different, as Zupančič notes, from id happiness, superego happiness, or (indeed) the happiness of the phallus.[94] Austen's approach to comedy entails that the very gap separating social levels or personalities becomes its own source of unexpected satisfaction. Her work can be seen to be inclusive and exclusive at the same time, often operating at different levels and then collapsing these differences, with the gates to Pemberley guarded by and through comedy. If comedy, as Zupančič asserts, is the "radicalization" of a norm rather than a rejection or supportive iteration of it, then Austen's ambivalence, even when unconscious, can perform ideological codes even while dismembering them.[95]

Austen's jokes create publics, and these include the reader and narrator, who are interpellated into the comedy. For Austen, this often means accruing layers of irony or figuration and then disassembling them in a volatile way, to ensure that the social and fictional structures are premised on their own undecidability. This creates community through its enforced consensus building. Some have worried that this aspect of Austen's work ensures her complicity with cultural norms. Yet in building and expanding its triangular structure, Austen works across the gap that is the unconscious, ensuring a "nothing" at the heart of social arrangements as the occasion for its refraction and thus expansion. In so doing, Austen enfolds heterogeneous, unsynthesizable material into the community and lets it do its disquieting work. Austen shows how ideological scripts contain gaps and even carves out space to ensure that those gaps can continue to be accommodated within those scripts even after their discovery. It is not that Austen can be said to reinforce or unsettle hegemonic cultural paradigms, but rather that her comedy reveals the structural reasons for the persistence of these paradigms despite and through their malfunction.

NOTES

1. Joel Faflak, *Romantic Psychoanalysis: The Burden of the Mystery* (Albany: State University of New York Press, 2008), 7; emphasis in the original; and his "Jane Austen and the Persuasion of Happiness," in *Romanticism and the Emotions*, ed. Joel Faflak and Richard C. Sha (Cambridge: Cambridge University Press, 2014), 117.

2. Faflak, "Jane Austen," 100.

3. Laurence W. Mazzeno, *Jane Austen: Two Centuries of Criticism* (Rochester, NY: Camden House, 2011), 202.

4. Patricia Meyer Spacks, "Austen's Laughter," *Women's Studies* 15, nos. 1–3 (1988): 80; Jillian Heydt-Stevenson, *Austen's Unbecoming Conjunctions: Subversive Laughter, Embodied History* (New York: Palgrave Macmillan, 2005), 207.

5. Northrop Frye, "The Argument of Comedy," in *Narrative Dynamics: Essays on Time, Plot, Closure, and Frames*, ed. Brian Richardson (Columbus: Ohio State University Press, 2002), 104, 103.

6. Heydt-Stevenson, *Austen's Unbecoming Conjunctions*, 25.

7. Alenka Zupančič, *The Odd One In: On Comedy* (Cambridge, MA: MIT Press, 2008), 83.

8. David Sigler, *Sexual Enjoyment in British Romanticism: Gender and Psychoanalysis, 1753–1835* (Montreal: McGill-Queen's University Press, 2015), 22–28, 59–62.

9. Sigmund Freud, *The Standard Edition of the Complete Psychological Works of Sigmund Freud*, trans. James Strachey (London: Hogarth Press, 1964), vol. 14, 186; vol. 8, 170.

10. Freud, *Works*, vol. 14, 169. See also Jacques Lacan, *Écrits: The First Complete Edition in English*, trans. Bruce Fink (New York: Norton, 2006), 392.

11. Zupančič, *Odd One In*, 83, 91.

12. Spacks, "Austen's Laughter," 84.

13. Freud, *Works*, vol. 8, 92.

14. Freud, *Works*, vol. 8, 132.

15. Freud, *Works*, vol. 8, 73.

16. Freud, *Works*, vol. 8, 206, 208.

17. Freud, *Works*, vol. 8, 181, 9.

18. Freud, *Works*, vol. 8, 102.

19. Sigmund Freud, *Jokes and Their Relation to the Unconscious*, trans. James Strachey (New York: Norton, 1960).

20. Jane Austen, *Persuasion*, ed. Janet Todd and Antje Blank, in *The Cambridge Edition of the Works of Jane Austen* (Cambridge: Cambridge: University Press, 2006), 73 (hereafter cited as P).

21. Heydt-Stevenson, *Austen's Unbecoming Conjunctions*.
22. Heydt-Stevenson, *Austen's Unbecoming Conjunctions*, 183–84.
23. Heydt-Stevenson, *Austen's Unbecoming Conjunctions*, 183.
24. Heydt-Stevenson, *Austen's Unbecoming Conjunctions*, 184.
25. Jocelyn Harris, *A Revolution Almost beyond Expression: Jane Austen's* Persuasion (Newark: University of Delaware Press, 2007), 97–99.
26. D. A. Miller, *Jane Austen, or The Secret of Style* (Princeton: Princeton University Press, 2003), 69.
27. Zupančič, *Odd One In*, 32.
28. Freud, *Works*, vol. 8, 190.
29. Spacks, "Austen's Laughter," 71.
30. Freud, *Works*, vol. 17, 186.
31. Freud, *Works*, vol. 8, 135.
32. E. M. Dadlez, "Form Affects Content: Reading Jane Austen," *Philosophy and Literature* 32, no. 2 (2008): 328.
33. Freud, *Works*, vol. 8, 140–58.
34. Freud, *Works*, vol. 8, 195.
35. Freud, *Works*, vol. 8, 179.
36. Eve Kosofsky Sedgwick, *Between Men: English Literature and Male Homosocial Desire* (New York: Columbia University Press, 1985).
37. Freud, *Works*, vol. 8, 151.
38. Freud, *Works*, vol. 8, 88.
39. Freud, *Works*, vol. 8, 145.
40. Freud, *Works*, vol. 8, 99.
41. Freud, *Works*, vol. 8, 191.
42. Freud, *Works*, vol. 8, 181, 203.
43. Freud, *Works*, vol. 8, 181, 219.
44. Peter Knox-Shaw, *Jane Austen and the Enlightenment* (Cambridge: Cambridge University Press, 2004), 236.
45. Lacan, *Écrits*, 95.
46. Freud, *Works*, vol. 8, 136.
47. Freud, *Works*, vol. 8, 137; emphasis in the original.
48. Zupančič, *Odd One In*, 135.
49. Zupančič, *Odd One In*, 8.
50. Sandie Byrne, *Jane Austen's Possessions and Dispossessions: The Significance of Objects* (Basingstoke: Palgrave Macmillan, 2014), 203.
51. Miller, *Jane Austen*, 68–69, 45–48, 25.
52. William H. Galperin, *The Historical Austen* (Philadelphia: University of Pennsylvania Press, 2003), 123.
53. Byrne, *Jane Austen's Possessions*, 248.
54. Jane Austen, *Later Manuscripts*, ed. Janet Todd and Linda Bree, in *The Cambridge Edition of the Works of Jane Austen* (Cambridge: Cambridge: University Press, 2008), 75 (hereafter cited as LM).
55. Miller, *Jane Austen*, 1–2.
56. Freud, *Works*, vol. 12, 115.
57. Freud, *Works*, vol. 12, 126; emphasis in the original.
58. Freud, *Works*, vol. 8, 182–83.
59. Spacks, "Austen's Laughter," 84.
60. Freud, *Works*, vol. 8, 92.
61. Georg W. F. Hegel, *Phenomenology of Spirit*, ed. J. N. Findlay, trans. A. V. Miller (Oxford: Oxford University Press, 1977), para. 521.

62. Hegel, *Phenomenology of Spirit*, para. 523; emphasis in the original.
63. Hegel, *Phenomenology of Spirit*, para. 522.
64. Hegel, *Phenomenology of Spirit*, para. 549.
65. Zupančič, *Odd One In*, 34.
66. Miller, *Jane Austen*, 76.
67. Paul Ricoeur, *Time and Narrative*, trans. Kathleen McLaughlin and David Pellauer, vol. 1 (Chicago: University of Chicago Press, 1984), 178.
68. Zupančič, *Odd One In*, 105; emphasis in the original.
69. Audrey Bilger, *Laughing Feminism: Subversive Comedy in Frances Burney, Maria Edgeworth, and Jane Austen* (Detroit: Wayne State University Press, 1998), 71; Spacks, "Austen's Laughter," 74.
70. Eric C. Walker, *Marriage, Writing, and Romanticism: Wordsworth and Austen after War* (Stanford: Stanford University Press, 2009), 19.
71. Freud, *Works*, vol. 8, 110.
72. Mary Poovey, *The Proper Lady and the Woman Writer: Ideology as Style in the Works of Mary Wollstonecraft, Mary Shelley, and Jane Austen* (Chicago: University of Chicago Press, 1985), 203.
73. Zupančič, *Odd One In*, 130, 189.
74. *Jane Austen's Letters*, ed. Deirdre Le Faye, 3rd ed. (Oxford: Oxford University Press, 1995), 11 (hereafter cited as L).
75. Freud, *Works*, vol. 8, 42.
76. Freud, *Works*, vol. 8, 12–20, 140–42.
77. Freud, *Works*, vol. 8, 167, emphasis in the original.
78. Freud, *Works*, vol. 8, 108.
79. Momus, "Afterword," in *Žižek's Jokes*, by Slavoj Žižek, ed. Audun Mortensen (Cambridge, MA: MIT Press, 2014), 142.
80. Claudia L. Johnson, *Jane Austen: Women, Politics, and the Novel* (Chicago: University of Chicago Press, 1988), 73, 78.
81. Mary Favret, "Free and Happy: Jane Austen in America," in *Janeites: Austen's Disciples and Devotees*, ed. Deidre Lynch (Princeton: Princeton University Press, 2000), 166–87; Stefanie Markovits, "Jane Austen and the Happy Fall," *SEL: Studies in English Literature 1500–1900* 47, no. 4 (2007): 781.
82. Faflak, "Jane Austen," 118–20.
83. Faflak, "Jane Austen," 115.
84. Gabriela Castellanos, *Laughter, War and Feminism: Elements of Carnival in Three of Jane Austen's Novels*, Writing About Women (New York: Peter Lang, 1994), 1.
85. Heydt-Stevenson, *Austen's Unbecoming Conjunctions*, 207; Bilger, *Laughing Feminism*, 9.
86. Zupančič, *Odd One In*, 4–5, 7.
87. Freud, *Works*, vol. 8, 155.
88. Miller, *Jane Austen*, 39; emphasis in the original.
89. Freud, *Works*, vol. 8, 151.
90. Henri Bergson, *Laughter: An Essay on the Meaning of the Comic*, trans. Cloudesley Brereton and Fred Rothwell (New York: Macmillan, 1914), 20, 5.
91. Laurence Raw and Robert G. Dryden, "Introduction," in *Global Jane Austen: Pleasure, Passion, and Possessiveness in the Jane Austen Community*, ed. Laurence Raw and Robert G. Dryden (New York: Palgrave Macmillan, 2013), 3–14.
92. Freud, *Works*, vol. 8, 189.
93. Frye, "Argument," 104.
94. Zupančič, *Odd One In*, 64.
95. Zupančič, *Odd One In*, 193.

3

"OPEN-HEARTED"

Persuasion and the Cultivation of Good Humor

SEAN DEMPSEY

AUSTEN, LIKE SHAKESPEARE, taps into the "biological-mythical roots of comedy,"[1] a genre in both writers' hands that always ends in marriage. However, marriage is never simply a matter of individual preference nor a simple submitting to the way things are; rather, marriage marks a moment when the form one will take within a given social set is decided. Marriage lends itself to comedy so easily because both are built through "interruptions and breaks, a continuity that constructs with discontinuity."[2] Comedy, like marriage, is concerned with how things are joined together, and it is in *Persuasion* that we find the most mature version of Austen's comic vision.

Although *Persuasion* as a whole may represent for the reader a "reality thickened with retrospection,"[3] it is particularly in the second half of the novel during moments of "high-wrought nervous tension" that readers are exposed to an intimate view of Anne Elliot's external "reality." In these moments of intensity, the felt presence of Anne's sensorium is suggested by the author's textual "distortion of the two 'normal' outward dimensions: time is recklessly speeded up, space grotesquely contracted."[4] What interests me most about *Persuasion* is the way these intense moments of dislocation can enable readers to witness and vicariously participate in both Anne and Captain Wentworth's gradual realization of an "open-hearted" good humor (P, 175). Such humor can be understood in at least three ways: as the cultivated ability to appreciate what is funny or comical, as recalling older understandings of the bodily humors, or as referencing a temporary state of mind or feeling (a posture of attention). Humor takes its place with wit and irony as one of the key components of comedy and the comic, and this essay will explore the way that it can be variously understood through attention to Austen's *Persuasion*.

Part of what makes *Persuasion*'s lead romantic characters' gradual realization of good humor possible is that each key moment of Anne and Captain Wentworth's renewed courtship takes place through intense moments of dislocation. These exceptional instances of close contact are often "accompanied by overwhelming moments of access to the outside world."[5] A key example of such a moment can be found in the party scene when Captain Wentworth and Anne have a conversation that reveals to Anne both Wentworth's lack of attachment to Louisa Musgrove and the depth of his continued feelings for her. Upon hearing his speech, and realizing the potential implications for her own situation, "Anne, who, in spite of the agitated voice in which the latter part had been uttered, and in spite of all the various noises of the room, the almost ceaseless slam of the door, and ceaseless buzz of persons walking through, had distinguished every word, was struck, gratified, confused, and beginning to breathe very quick, and feel a hundred things in a moment" (P, 199). Afterward, in response to this "interesting, almost too interesting conversation," Anne finds herself filled with "exquisite, though agitated sensations," but is nevertheless "in good humour with all," having "received ideas which disposed her to be courteous and kind to all, and to pity every one, as being less happy than herself" (P, 200–201).

Although Anne is admirably rational in many respects, as Alan Richardson notes she is also "highly susceptible to influxes of feeling from sources not always consciously present to Anne herself, registered instead in the body, in ways that at times become so pressing as to overwhelm the conscious subject."[6] When overwhelmed in this way, the illusory unity of a buffered subjectivity is punctured or made permeable by the actions of an embodied mind. Richardson argues that "Austen's famously innovative style for conveying the heroine's impressions in *Persuasion* speaks as much to a new psychological appreciation of unconscious mental life and embodied cognition as to a new esthetic mode for representing the flux of conscious experience." In his reading, these moments of dislocation that are so vividly rendered throughout *Persuasion* are meant to "mark the collision of conscious awareness with unconscious thoughts and feelings and the intense physiological sensations that accompany them." These "invasions of feelings,"[7] as John Wiltshire calls them, are registered in the novel's "rapid and nervous syntax designed to imitate the bombardment of impressions upon the mind."[8] This is why *Persuasion* "is as notable for its hidden throbs as for its external embodiment of desire."[9]

How then are we to understand Anne's "good humour" in this and similar scenes? Jill Heydt-Stevenson argues that Austen's comic irreverence and bawdy humor "announces her 'knowingness,' since laughter, like sexuality, is associated with agency."[10] Invoking such memorable moments as the innuendo implied in *Pride and Prejudice* when Darcy responds to Caroline Bingley's suggestion that he allow her to mend his pen for him since she "mend(s) pens remarkably well" by saying "Thank you—but I always mend my own" (P&P, 51) or the suggestiveness of Mary Crawford's joking reference in *Mansfield Park* to Naval "Rears, and Vices," Heydt-Stevenson offers an intriguing model of the role the comic plays within Austen's work, which is exemplified by Fanny Price's use of the phrase "slipping into the ha-ha" within *Mansfield Park* (MP, 116). Although "imperceptible from a distance, the ha-ha was a 'sunk fence' that prevented livestock from crossing from the park into the garden, while also allowing the viewer to maintain the fiction that the grounds were seamlessly connected." The ha-ha receives its name for the sudden surprise and laughter that might erupt when one recognizes they have been duped by a *trompe l'oeil*. Heydt-Stevenson convincingly argues that Austen's own bawdy "slip" into the ha-ha "extends and expands the space normally allowed to a woman during this period," but implicit in her model is the perhaps even more provocative suggestion that in the comic there is a crisis of coherency wherein the connection between elements is suddenly called into question and where the slipping away of the fiction that things are seamlessly connected is suddenly felt.[11]

Heydt-Stevenson's approach helps us see how Austen's comedy "opens up interstices that prevailing assumptions about women . . . have sutured,"[12] and how Austen announces her "knowingness" through double entendres or "unbecoming conjunctions" that are scattered throughout her novels. These conjunctions can be useful because they are "elastic" structures that can "allow for the simultaneous apprehension of paradoxical responses." However, although this emphasis on unbecoming conjunctions is helpful, it also comes with certain limitations. An "unbecoming conjunction" is "what happens when two ideas or images or people, set side by side, reveal unforeseen similarities,"[13] and these suddenly seen similarities can surprise, shake up conventions, and even provide an "outlet" for pent-up "hostility toward ideologies that dominate women."[14] Nevertheless, I argue that the heights of "good humour" that Anne achieves at several key moments in *Persuasion* can take us a step further still.

There is, I argue, a therapeutic dimension to the forms of experience that the second courtship, and the novel as a whole, taps into, which helps assuage those resentments that are too readily "insinuated into the pores of experience" and threaten to calcify both body and mind. What is needed is some shock that can jolt one off their "grooves of regularity," and thereby expose the artificiality of typical postures of attention, while also suddenly freeing up affective energy, which can then be reinvested into generating and motivating new forms of action.[15] To attend is to stretch toward, "to direct one's faculties toward something or someone."[16] A good-humored posture of attention steps beyond the ironies and biting satire of unbecoming conjunctions because it is attentive "to something that is not present and cannot be attended to by an act of transitive attention." It is "an intransitive, objectless disposition of attentiveness."[17] This is attention as Simone Weil understood it, "one which consists of suspending our thought, leaving it detached, empty and ready to be penetrated by the object . . . [or] in order to receive into itself the being it is looking at, just as he is."[18] In what follows, I will explore the role good humor plays in *Persuasion* by first giving a general overview of my approach to the comic before looking at *Persuasion* more closely and considering how and why good humor is so crucial to understanding the novel as a whole.

A helpful introduction to the mode of comedy I have in mind comes from Henri Bergson, for whom laughter occurs when we see how "some rigidity" or another has been "applied to the mobility of life," but we are ourselves capable of moving beyond this stasis.[19] Often the pleasure produced in a comedic situation erupts when "we have a clear apprehension of this putting the one on the other," but are able to produce a pleasurable friction from "the rubbing together of two alternative perspectives."[20] In *The Odd One In*, Alenka Zupančič similarly argues that the immediacy comedy produces is not that of a smooth, imperceptible passing of one thing into another, but that of a material cut between them. From this perspective, wit is one of the basic building blocks of the comic because it is the pleasurable yoking of two disparate images, and comedy, more generally, helps us see and find pleasure in "the cut" between two or more objects or frames of reference. When the comic is effective, there is "a moment of disorientation, a momentary suspension in which the subject vacillates between [her] being and [her] meaning" so that "it is no longer clear on which side [she is] standing."[21] Although this rhythmic oscillation between being and meaning undermines understanding, it can nevertheless be therapeutic because such moments can overwhelm typical postures of attention so that we lose "recourse to the networks, practices, and relays of attachment that sustain representation," suddenly revisiting the moment prior to the decision about what things mean.[22]

Immanuel Kant argued that what is most significant about a comic response is this sudden shifting of "the mind now to one standpoint and now to the other" that the subject must undergo in order to "contemplate its object."[23] Kant further claims that this moment of disorientation may ultimately correspond to the movement of the body through a "reciprocal straining and slackening of the elastic parts of our viscera, which communicates itself to the diaphragm (and resembles that which is felt by ticklish people), in the course of which the lungs expel the air with rapidly succeeding interruptions." This ticklish exercise in elasticity is "beneficial to health," and like the Burkean sublime, albeit for different reasons, can help clear out blockages that inhibit us from becoming our best selves.[24] For Kant, "laughter is an affect arising from a strained expectation being suddenly reduced to nothing."[25]

In *The World as Will and Representation*, Arthur Schopenhauer similarly argues for incongruity as the basis of the comic, suggesting that "laughter results from nothing but the suddenly perceived incongruity between a concept and the real objects that had been thought through it in some relation. . . . All laughter therefore is occasioned by a paradoxical, and hence unexpected, subsumption."[26] The implication of the incongruity theory is that at the heart of the comic is the recognition of an astonishing misfit between concept and object. This amusing misalignment often takes the form of wit ("when we consciously apply a concept to an object which does not measure up to it") or folly ("when an agent does something that fails to satisfy his concept of what he is about," that is, Don Quixote tilting at windmills).[27] However, I suggest that in Austen's comic vision, as in Kant's, the comic is not only a cognitive but also a physiological experience.

Kant agrees with earlier thinkers like Francis Hutcheson that humor derives from an intellectual recognition of incongruity, but also adds a physiological theory to explain why we have a pleasant reaction to that intellectual recognition. According to Kant, we laugh at absurdities not because the intellect itself finds pleasure in that which frustrates it, but because the intellect's attempt to reconcile an absurd conjunction of ideas causes a physical response that is found to be pleasant. A jest "must have something in it capable of momentarily deceiving us," but "when the semblance vanishes into nothing, the mind looks back in order to try it over again, and thus by a rapidly succeeding tension and relaxation, it is thrown to and fro and put in oscillation."[28] Good humor often enables a moment of wonder, which "is a dizzying, vertiginous, and destabilizing experience" that threatens to upend all prejudices and preconceptions.[29] When the comic approaches wonder in this way, it becomes a potentially potent phenomenon that can help cut, edit, or splice one from conventional attachments and help one attend to those impartialities that interrupt normative forms of common sense through a pleasurable oscillation of losing and finding oneself.

The comic can sometimes stage a disorienting moment of seeing nothing, because "comedy is the moment in which substance, necessity, and essence all lose their immediate—and thus abstract—self-identity or coincidence with themselves."[30] Comedy can help us see that A does not equal A, or that our concepts do not fit the objects we attach them to as securely as we might think. However, this tendency toward misfits is not tragic because although the comic may operate within a secular horizon of immanence that has abandoned reference to anything beyond itself, it nevertheless includes the wondrous possibility of an immanent transcendence that is experienced whenever the expectations of a limiting point of view are popped and the world before us is seen anew.

Comedy puts into practice one crucial point: "We really encounter nonsense only when and where a sense surprises us."[31] Seen in this light, the comic can be compared to what Jacques Rancière has called dissensus, or as Davide Panagia has formulated it, "an aesthetico-political moment that results in the reconfiguration of the regimes of perception that seize our attention, so that we can no longer assume the legislative authority (or logical priority) of any one form of perception." A comic moment of dissensus can momentarily disrupt "the mechanisms that enable the fluidity of the operation" of those regimes of perception that typically mediate the meaning of experience.[32] Doing so may introduce something exceptional into the common world of perceiving and thereby confound habitual postures of attention. This sudden experience of a state of exception can be significant because before a new partition of the sensible can be fashioned or adopted, an interruption of previous forms of relating must occur.

But what, then, are we to make of Anne Elliot's good humor if not as a wise passiveness? How does *Persuasion* offer something beyond the apophatic experiences of wonder detailed in the previous novels—from Catherine Moreland's "motionless wonder" (NA, 167) produced when she, to invoke Byron's critique of Keats,[33] absentmindedly *frigs* her own imagination through habitual misrecognition, to Elizabeth Bennet's wretched perplexity after receiving Darcy's letter, to Emma's "amusement" while gazing outside the door of Ford's while shopping with Harriet, with "a mind lively and at ease, [that] can do with seeing nothing, and can see nothing that does not answer" (E, 251)? Like Emma, Anne is capable of possessing a "mind of winter" so that being nothing herself she "beholds / Nothing that is not there and the nothing that is."[34] This posture of attention of a "mind lively and at ease" that "can do with seeing nothing" and sees "nothing that does not answer" is worthwhile, in part because it can generate new intuitions and restore faith in the world precisely by tapping into the intensity that creates it. To be caught up in wonder is to experience a "moment of pure presence" where thought itself is arrested because the mind is unable to "move on by association to something else."[35] Nevertheless, the wonder felt in these moments of seeing nothing is insufficient in itself. Even though wonder can often consist of a pleasurable loss of perspective, one must nevertheless work to avoid the temptation "to indulge in indecision and indeterminacy, and to retreat into a self-reflexivity that marvels at our capacity to defer judgment endlessly, as though that were itself our end."[36]

Although the potentially infinite possibility of revising reflective judgment can become an excuse to continually delay its exercise, one must recognize that to indulge in a process of infinite deliberation and reflection, as Fanny Price realizes in *Mansfield Park*, is also a refusal to act.

Even at the beginning of the novel, Anne, who at twenty-seven is already far more mature than any of the other Austen heroines, has already learned the lessons the other heroines receive during the course of their own stories. This is made clear early on when Anne is among the Musgroves at Uppercross and she reflects on how the "removal from one set of people to another, though at a distance of only three miles, will often include a total change of conversation, opinion, and idea" (P, 45). She wishes her foolish father and older sister could recognize how "unconsidered" their preoccupations at Kellynch-hall were at Uppercross. For herself, she is surprised that when she came "with a heart full of the subject which had been completely occupying both houses in Kellynch for many weeks," there were only passing remarks on these issues. She is reminded that "she must now submit to feel that another lesson, in the art of knowing our own nothingness beyond our own circle, was become necessary for her" (P, 45).

Clearly, some of the autumnal tone of *Persuasion* can be traced back to this need to learn how to know one's own nothingness, but there is a fanciful facet to this art of knowing as well, because Anne also acknowledges "it to be very fitting, that every little social commonwealth should dictate its own matters of discourse." Furthermore, if she did not want to be an "unworthy member" of the community she has been transplanted into, then "it was highly incumbent on her to clothe her imagination, her memory, and all her ideas in as much of Uppercross as possible" (P, 46). With this recognition of a "camelion-like" need to clothe the imagination in a manner fitting the context of present circumstances, one feels justified in speaking of a Romantic Austen, perhaps one who, like Anne Elliot, "had been forced into prudence in her youth, [but] learned romance as she grew older" (P, 32).

The art of knowing one's own nothingness is needed because as David Hume suggests all appearances are "broken appearances": discontinuous, separate, and interrupted. One's sense of existence is "rooted in movements of assemblage, recollection, projection, splicing, editing, and the like." Images do not "bind" themselves, and so the faculty of the imagination is needed to draw upon causality, contiguity, habit, and resemblance in order to "artifice strategies of composition in the face of ontological discontinuity."[37] In this way, all politics flows from the power and possibilities of assembly, and this is how and why "every little social commonwealth" can stitch together the discourse that will clothe its own imagination.

One's sense of self "comes into existence only as the result of a laborious stitching together of disparate parts" and such acts of *re-ligio* [binding again] affect and are affected by how we see ourselves oriented in the world.[38]

Critics interested in how Austen represents the processes by which sense and sensibility are stitched together and invested with meaning have often been influenced by Michel Foucault. In "The Tittle-Tattle of Highbury," for instance, Casey Finch and Peter Bowen consider how free indirect discourse is itself the language of self-surveillance, in part because it exposes how the language of the private self must be expressed in terms of an always already public language.[39] Similarly, Mark Canuel has suggested that the household of a place like Mansfield Park enables "a technique of social organization that lends persons and their actions a privileged form of legibility."[40] Other critics have explored the ways in which Austen represents the breakdown of these "technologies of classification" and other processes of investiture. David Southward, for example, has investigated those "little zigzags of embarrassment" (E, 143) that are experienced when one is felt to be "doing wrong and being looked at" (MP, 310).[41] These moments of embarrassment are memorable because they incorporate the sensation of "the confused halting of the social machinery, an awkward lack of direction in speech and behavior, the contagious darting from person to person; in short, the 'little zigzags' of a mind looking inward in its sudden self-consciousness and outward as it scurries to rectify the situation."[42]

In order to both offer a somewhat different approach and to further explicate what all of this has to do with humor, I turn to Jonathan H. Grossman's inquiry into how Austen participates in what Norbert Elias has called the "civilizing process."[43] Elias defines "the civilizing process" as the set of practices that result in the pacification of behavior and the control of one's emotions.[44] Part of the labor of the leisured is to give body to social values through the establishment of polite culture. The uncanny socializing force of politeness is due to the fact that "nothing seems more ineffable . . . than the values given body, made body by the transubstantiation achieved by the hidden persuasion of an implicit pedagogy, capable of instilling a whole cosmology."[45] In other words, as in the example of Wordsworth's "Old Cumberland Beggar," when values such as charity become second nature "the mild necessity of use compels." Principles "embodied in this way are placed beyond the grasp of consciousness" because the "body has beliefs" that are "submerged below the level of consciousness—embedded, for example, in the habits of muscle memory or speech patterns, or in manners."[46]

Although Grossman is primarily interested in how good manners subtly make even a weak patriarch like *Emma*'s Mr. Woodhouse compelling, I want to connect this body that has beliefs to earlier notions of the humoral body because doing so helps clarify the implications of Austen's comic vision. Learning the "arts of the self" that can shape these submerged intensities in productive ways is the key to legislating new ways of being in the world, because "to change an intersubjective ethos significantly is to modify the instinctive subjectivities and intersubjectivities in which it is set."[47] Part of the pleasure and power of Austen's writing, and perhaps also of Romanticism more generally, is the way it not only so often offers fleeting glances at these sensations beneath syntax, but also enables occasions for reforming them as well.

In *Humoring the Body: Emotions and the Shakespearean Stage,* Gail Kern Paster delineates a model of an early modern understanding of the humoral body, or the body with beliefs that the civilizing process is thought to affect. In a cosmos permeated by passions, or those "forces that are at once extremely powerful and actually or potentially beyond our control," the humoral body was "characterized not only by its physical openness but also by its emotional instability and volatility, by an internal microclimate knowable, like climates in the outer world, more for changeability than for stasis."[48] To be in good humor required behaving in such a way so as to satisfyingly balance the four qualities of cold, hot, wet, and dry within one's own personal microclimate. These forces "constituted the material basis of any living creature's characteristic appraisals of and responses to its immediate environment; they altered the character of a body's substances and, by doing so, organized its ability to act or even to think."[49] This is an ecological view of subjectivity, rooted in the "dynamic reciprocities between self and environment imagined by the psychophysiology of bodily fluids." There is a porousness felt between circumstance and character because "circumstance engenders humors in the body and humors in the body help to determine circumstance by predisposing the individual subject to a characteristic kind of evaluation and response."[50] In this understanding of the humoral body, "the passions are the winds and waves of the body, producing internal changes that the subject suffers as if they came from the outside," and it is due to these passionate persuasions that the humoral body is "characterized by corporeal fluidity, openness, and porous boundaries."[51]

Like the humoral body, the sense of self that triumphs in *Persuasion* is fluid and dynamic. Throughout the novel Anne is frequently crowded in on and even overcome by her environment. Upon her first reintroduction to Wentworth, for instance, "a thousand feelings" rush in on Anne and her normal rhythms of perception are so affected that "the room seemed full—full of persons and voices" (P, 64). The feelings of porousness Anne frequently experiences in Wentworth's presence are not unlike those Sigmund Freud discusses at the beginning of *Civilization and Its Discontents,* wherein there is a "sensation of 'eternity,' a feeling as of something limitless, unbounded - as it were, 'oceanic.'"[52] The crucial question remaining at the end of *Persuasion* is, given this sense of self, how then should each of us steer "the vital sensorium that supplies the soul's moving vehicle."[53]

This is the crux of the conversation Anne has with Captain Harville concerning whether men or women are more prone to being inconstant in their feelings. Harville puts forward his belief "in a true analogy between our bodily frames and our mental; and that as our bodies are the strongest, so are our feelings; capable of bearing most rough usage, and riding out the heaviest weather." Anne responds by arguing that men's "feelings may be the strongest," but women's are the most tender in part because man may be "more robust than woman, but he is not longer-lived" (P, 253). She continues by suggesting that it would be too hard on men if it were otherwise, because "'You are always labouring and toiling, exposed to every risk and hardship. Your home, country, friends, all quitted. Neither time, nor health, nor life, to be called your own. It would be too hard indeed' (with a faltering voice) 'if woman's feelings were to be added to all this'" (P, 254). It is at this moment of faltering that a "slight noise" calls their attention to Wentworth's side of the room. He had been writing a letter but dropped his pen. When the sentiments and tones of Anne's faltering voice reached him, he had under an "irresistible governance" "seized a sheet of paper, and poured out his feelings" (P, 262). He could now finally fully abandon the "madness of resentment, which had kept him from trying to regain her" (P, 263).

This spontaneous overflow of powerful emotion doesn't fit with the model of subjectivity first advocated by Wentworth early in the novel when he compares Louisa's "character of decision and firmness" to a "beautiful glossy nut," which, "blessed with original strength, has outlived all the storms of autumn." At this point Wentworth's ideal subjectivity is that of a buffered self with "not a puncture, not a weak spot any where" (P, 94). He learns of the limitations of this model at the moment of Louisa's accident. The words Louisa utters just before her fall could serve as the motto for her variation on the Cartesian cogito: "I am determined I will" (P, 118). It is also significant that it is Louisa who is ultimately transformed through her surprising courtship with Captain Benwick "into a person of literary taste, and sentimental reflection" (P, 182).

Anne is different because she is not as "determined" as Louisa, and Anne is able to move beyond the merely sentimental in part because she is constantly in the process of finding herself. The locution Austen frequently deploys when "Anne is addressed by the outside world is 'Anne found herself': in the carriage on the way home from Lyme, Anne 'found herself' being addressed by Wentworth. At Uppercross she 'found herself' having the child removed from her back."[54] The kind of cogito that Anne exemplifies is far closer to the Lacanian model than the Cartesian: "I am not, where I am the plaything of my thought; I think about what

I am where I do not think I am thinking."[55] It is precisely this capacity for oscillating between seeing and knowing and between being and thinking that is the mark of good humor.[56]

One of Anne's moments of wondrous dislocation in *Persuasion* helps further demonstrate the advantages she holds over Austen's other heroines. While talking with Wentworth, Anne discovers "that he had a heart returning to her at last; that anger, resentment, avoidance, were no more," and "He must really love her." When she subsequently walks into a room with her sister Elizabeth, both are "very, very happy," but we are told that "it would be an insult to the nature of Anne's felicity, to draw any comparison between it and her sister's; the origin of one all selfish vanity, of the other all generous attachment." Whereas her sister, like her father, is almost cartoonishly trapped in the aesthetic, so that nothing either wishes for seems to them to be out of reach, Anne's kingdom was within. "Anne saw nothing, thought nothing of the brilliancy of the room. Her happiness was from within" (P, 201). For her, happiness is not the clutching after satisfaction of this or that desire, but a deep openness to the possibility that something good can happen. Such happiness "elicits an 'ambient attention' to one's surroundings, something at once deeply felt, interpersonal, and anonymous."[57] In another moment of romantic happiness, Anne is found "sporting" with her own delightful musings "from Camden-place to Westgate-buildings," and these musings are "almost enough to spread purification and perfume all the way" (P, 208). In the fullness of such moments, Anne is acutely attentive to her ambient environment.

Key facets of good humor are exemplified by two of the secondary characters met in *Persuasion*. The first is Mrs. Smith, a childhood friend Anne reconnects with only after a series of misfortunes had befallen her. Despite the fact that Anne "could scarcely imagine a more cheerless situation in itself than Mrs. Smith's," for she has lost her affluence, her husband, and her health, "Anne had reason to believe that she had moments only of languor and depression, to hours of occupation and enjoyment. How could it be?" Anne watches, observes, and reflects "and finally determined that this was not a case of fortitude or of resignation only," but that Mrs. Smith possessed "the choicest gift of Heaven"—an "elasticity of mind, that disposition to be comforted, that power of turning readily from evil to good, and of finding employment which carried her out of herself, which was from Nature alone" (P, 167). The person possessing it "takes and resigns what they give with equal cheer, and makes her- or himself malleable to their impressions."[58] Such (neuro-)elasticity can be related to notions of disinterest, as long as disinterest is understood not as viewing from an impartial Archimedean perspective, but rather as at least momentarily adopting an apophatic posture of attention—one that recognizes that there can be "no a priori criteria of interest or structures of part-taking that govern why or how one object, organ of perception, or structure of feeling might command our attentions."[59]

However, in addition to elasticity, another element needs to be incorporated in order to make sense of the model of good humor offered in *Persuasion*. This additional ingredient is perhaps most succinctly exemplified in the scene where Anne and the Crofts are traveling by coach and Mrs. Croft seems to praise the Musgrove girls as "very good humoured, unaffected girls, indeed," but does so in such "a tone of calmer praise, such as made Anne suspect that her keener powers might not consider either of them as quite worthy of her brother." Just then Mrs. Croft is alerted to an approaching danger, saying to her husband, "My dear admiral, that post!—we shall certainly take that post." However, "by coolly giving the reins a better direction herself, they happily passed the danger." Anne finds "some amusement at their style of driving, which she imagined no bad representation of the general guidance of their affairs," and in this she is likely correct (P, 62). This scene is notable because it illustrates an almost ideal vehicular consciousness—one alert and attentive to its surroundings and quite capable of skillfully steering "the vital sensorium that supplies the soul's moving vehicle."[60]

Although a good-humored posture of attention may involve "a self-emptying or kenosis," it is not adopted out of a "mindless desire" for novelty but rather as "an achievement, a habit of focused seeing and participating in what gives itself to us."[61] Good humor is good because it cultivates a sensibility in which one becomes an "expert with sail and oar" over one's own particular vehicular consciousness.[62] To attend in this way is to glimpse a realm full of a "yet unconsummated form of the good," but a good "that will be realized only if we unconditionally and habitually bestow our attention on what presents itself to us, and that will be lost if we don't."[63] By encouraging a childlike (or absolving) forgetfulness of the ties between particular events, good humor fosters a capacity to look at any given situation with a renovated eye. Such apophatic postures of attention offer occasions to overcome the fallacy of misplaced concreteness by attending anew to that "crux of embodiment: the turning point where bodies may be said to emerge into our fields of perception, meaning, language—into a world."[64]

Good humor, in this way, can offer us a different understanding of what an experience of porousness might mean in a secular age.[65] Many of Anne Elliot's experiences in *Persuasion* resonate with what Catherine Keller has termed "aporetic probity," wherein "passages blocked in the moment of doubt, of defense, clear and open like pores." In this model the self is still buffered, folded, or distinct, but the folds that make it up "are pores, passages in and out of becoming creatures that have no substantial boundaries. Yet in their singular freedoms they expose endless layers of porous surface, faces of the deep." This new porousness "is an embodying perspective that can give valence to life and meaning, a vertical dimension in which ordinariness incandesces, flaming and flowering."[66] To be a humorist, as both Anne and Wentworth are at the end of *Persuasion*, means becoming open-hearted by cultivating a capacity for losing the plot and finding it again subtly or surprisingly altered. It is by being able to "subdue [our] minds to [our] fortunes" in this way that Austen's readers may also "learn to brook being happier than [we] deserve" (P, 269).

NOTES

1. Julia Prewitt Brown, "The Feminist Depreciation of Austen: A Polemical Reading," *Novel: A Forum on Fiction* 23 (Spring, 1990): 307.
2. Alenka Zupančič, *The Odd One In: On Comedy* (Cambridge, MA: MIT Press, 2008), 140.
3. William H. Galperin, *The Historical Austen* (Philadelphia: University of Pennsylvania Press, 2003), 5.
4. Marilyn Butler, *Jane Austen and the War of Ideas* (New York: Oxford University Press, 1987), 277.
5. Adela Pinch, "Lost in a Book: Jane Austen's *Persuasion*," *Studies in Romanticism* 32, no. 1 (Spring 1993): 108.
6. Alan Richardson, *British Romanticism and the Science of the Mind* (Cambridge: Cambridge University Press, 2001), 102.
7. John Wiltshire, *Jane Austen and the Body: "The picture of health"* (Cambridge: Cambridge University Press, 1992), 177.
8. A. Walton Litz, "Persuasion: Forms of Estrangement," in *Jane Austen: Bicentenary Essays*, ed. John Halperin (Cambridge: Cambridge University Press, 1975), 228.
9. Jocelyn Harris, *A Revolution Almost Beyond Expression: Jane Austen's Persuasion* (Newark: University of Delaware Press, 2007), 144.
10. Jillian Heydt-Stevenson, "'Slipping into the Ha-Ha': Bawdy Humor and Body Politics in Jane Austen's Novels." *Nineteenth-Century Literature* 55, no. 3 (December 2000): 312.
11. Heydt-Stevenson, "Slipping into the Ha-Ha," 311.
12. Jillian Heydt-Stevenson, *Austen's Unbecoming Conjunctions: Subversive Laughter, Embodied History* (New York: Palgrave Macmillan, 2005), 27.
13. Heydt-Stevenson, *Austen's Unbecoming Conjunctions*, 25.
14. Heydt-Stevenson, *Austen's Unbecoming Conjunctions*, 206.
15. William E. Connolly, *A World of Becoming* (Durham, NC: Duke University Press, 2010), 61.
16. David Marno, *Death be Not Proud: The Art of Holy Attention* (Chicago: University of Chicago Press, 2016), 8.
17. Marno, *Death be Not Proud*, 10.
18. Simone Weil, quoted in Thomas Pfau, "The Art and Ethics of Attention," *Hedgehog Review* 16, no. 2 (Summer 2014): 34. Simone Weil, "Reflections on the Right Use of School Studies," in *The Simone Weil Reader*, ed. George A. Panichas (Wakefield, RI: Moyer Bell, 1999), 47–48.
19. Henri Bergson, *Laughter: An Essay on the Meaning of the Comic*, trans. Cloudesley Brereton and Fred Rothwell (New York: Macmillan, 1914), 38.
20. Zupančič, *Odd One In*, 49–50.
21. Zupančič, *Odd One In*, 181.
22. Davide Panagia, *The Political Life of Sensation* (Durham, NC: Duke University Press, 2009), 10.

23. Immanuel Kant, *Critique of Judgement*, trans. Nicholas Walker (Oxford: Oxford University Press, 2007), 162.

24. Pinch argues that "as the novel progresses, Anne's moments of shock and inundation increasingly take a typically sublime turn" ("Lost in a Book," 109). There certainly seems to be a sublime element to Anne's experiences, and the applicability of the sublime has an added resonance when we recall that for Edmund Burke, "the efficient cause of the 'delight' occasioned by the experience of the Sublime is the power of terrible objects to 'clear the parts' of the nervous system of dangerous and debilitating blockages arising from mental lassitude" (Charles Rzepka, "Re-collecting Spontaneous Overflows: Romantic Passions, the Sublime, and Mesmerism," *Romantic Praxis* [Winter 1998], https://www.rc.umd.edu /praxis/passions/rzepka/rzp.html, para. 11). In the Burkean model, the sublime helps clear out the blockages that inhibit us from being good subjects. Both Anne, who becomes "hardened" by the daily affronts she suffered in her own household; and Wentworth, who is affected by the "madness of resentment," could certainly benefit from some of the sublime's delightful agitation (P, 263). Nevertheless, Austen swerves from the Burkean model in important ways, and I propose that the comic rather than the sublime is the better basis for an understanding of what Austen is up to in *Persuasion*.

25. Kant, *Critique of Judgement* (2007), 161.

26. Arthur Schopenhauer, *The World as Will and Representation*, trans. E. F. J. Payne, (New York: Dover Publications, 1966), vol. 1, 59.

27. Ronald F. Atkinson, "Humour in Philosophy," in *Humour and History*, ed. Keith Cameron (Oxford: Intellect, 1993), 17.

28. Kant, *Critique of Judgement* (2007), 162.

29. Mary-Jane Rubenstein, "A Certain Disavowal: The Pathos and Politics of Wonder," *Princeton Theological Review* 12, no. 2 (2006): 12. In the Platonic dialogues, Socratic wonder (*thaumazein*) "arises when the understanding cannot master that which lies closest—when surrounded by utterly ordinary concepts and things, the philosopher suddenly finds himself surrounded on all sides by aporia." Wonder is what strikes Theaetetus in the Platonic dialogue that bears his name, when "he loses his grasp on notions that had seemed utterly self-evident, sending him reeling, his head spinning" (Plato, *Theaetetus*, trans. Harold North Fowler [Cambridge, MA: Harvard University Press, 1996], 155d).

30. Zupančič, *Odd One In*, 34.

31. Zupančič, *Odd One In*, 180.

32. Davide Panagia, *The Political Life of Sensation* (Durham: Duke University Press, 2009), 42.

33. For more on this critique see Marjorie Levinson, *Keats's Life of Allegory* (Oxford: Blackwell, 1988).

34. Wallace Stevens, "The Snow Man," in *The Collected Poems of Wallace Stevens* (New York: Alfred A Knopf, 1971), 9–10.

35. Jane Bennett, *The Enchantment of Modern Life: Attachments, Crossings, and Ethics* (Princeton: Princeton University Press, 2001), 5. See also Philip Fisher, *Wonder, the Rainbow, and the Aesthetics of Rare Experiences* (Cambridge, MA: Harvard University Press, 1998); Robert Mitchell, "Suspended Animation, Slow Time, and the. Poetics of Trance," *PMLA* 126, no. 1 (January 2011), 107–22; and Michael W. Clune, *Writing against Time* (Stanford: Stanford University Press, 2013). For a helpful discussion of the role of wonder in Austen, see Sonia Hofkosh, "The Illusionist: *Northanger Abbey* and Austen's Uses Of Enchantment," in *A Companion to Jane Austen*, ed. Claudia L. Johnson (Chichester, U.K.: Wiley-Blackwell, 2009), 101–11.

36. Vivasvan Soni, "Committing Freedom: The Cultivation of Judgment in Rousseau's *Emile* and Austen's *Pride and Prejudice*," *Eighteenth Century: Theory & Interpretation* 51, no. 3 (Fall 2010): 380.

37. Davide Panagia, *Impressions of Hume: Cinematic Thinking and the Politics of Discontinuity* (Lanham, MD: Rowman & Littlefield, 2013), 2.

38. Kaja Silverman, *The Threshold of the Visible World* (New York and London: Routledge, 1996), 17.

39. Casey Finch and Peter Bowen, "'The Tittle-Tattle of Highbury': Gossip and the Free Indirect Style in *Emma*," *Representations* 31 (Summer 1990), 1–18.

40. Mark Canuel, "Jane Austen and the Importance of Being Wrong," *Studies in Romanticism* 44, no. 2 (Summer 2005): 128.

41. This is the fate Fanny Price anxiously imagines awaits her at an upcoming ball.

42. David Southward, "Jane Austen and the Riches of Embarrassment," *Studies in English Literature, 1500–1900* 36, no. 4 (Autumn 1996): 764–65.

43. Jonathan H. Grossman "The Labor of the Leisured in *Emma*: Class, Manners, and Austen," *Nineteenth-Century Literature* 54, no. 2 (Fall 1999): 143–64.

44. See Norbert Elias, *The History of Manners. The Civilizing Process*, trans. Edmund Jephcott (New York: Pantheon, 1978), vol. 1.

45. Pierre Bourdieu, *Outline of a Theory of Practice*, trans. Richard Nice. (Cambridge: Cambridge University Press, 1997), 94.

46. Grossman, "Labor of the Leisured in *Emma*," 153.

47. William E. Connolly, *Why I Am Not a Secularist* (Minneapolis: University of Minnesota Press, 1999), 28.

48. Gail Kern Paster, *Humoring the Body: Emotions and the Shakespearean Stage* (Chicago: University of Chicago Press, 2004), 19.

49. Paster, *Humoring the Body*, 13.

50. Paster, *Humoring the Body*, 14.

51. Paster, *Humoring the Body*, 19.

52. Sigmund Freud, *Civilization and Its Discontents*, ed. James Strachey (New York: W. W. Norton, 1989), 11.

53. James Chandler, *An Archaeology of Sympathy: The Sentimental Mode in Literature and Cinema* (Chicago: University of Chicago Press, 2013), 203. Chandler observes how the word "sensorium" was coined by Henry More in the late 1640s in an attempt to salvage key Christian tenets—such as the immortality of the soul—from materialist critique. More was willing to concede to the new mechanistic materialism that the soul was distinct from the body, but he nevertheless argued that the soul was "housed or 'carried' in a highly subtilized form of matter that registered perceptual vibration and effected locomotion" (190). The sensorium was this "subtilized body" that served as the soul's "vehicle," which More believed could survive the death of the gross body. For someone like More, "sensibility is the essential quickness, the vital sensorium that supplies the soul's moving vehicle" (180). Emerging out of and evolving from this legacy of Latitudinarian theology, Chandler argues that from the rise of the novel through contemporary cinema, "the sentimental spectator proves to be a figure in motion." Such a figure can "assume multiple locations in narrative space, [and] this figure is defined in no small part by its capacity to pass virtually into other points of view" (176). This capacity to move and be moved is sensibility.

54. Pinch, "Lost in a Book," 106.

55. Jacques Lacan, *Écrits: The First Complete Edition in English*, trans. Bruce Fink (New York: Norton, 2006), 430.

56. For a suggestive Lacanian approach to the role of the comic in Austen, see Molly Anne Rothenberg's "Jane Austen's wit-craft" in *Lacan, Psychoanalysis and Comedy*, ed. Patricia Gherovici and Manya Steinkoler (New York: Cambridge University Press, 2016), 184–205.

57. Joel Faflak, "Jane Austen and the Persuasion of Happiness." in *Romanticism and the Emotions*, ed. Joel Faflak and Richard C. Sha (Cambridge: Cambridge University Press, 2014), 116.

58. Claudia L. Johnson. "Persuasion: The Unfeudal Tone of the Present Day," in *Persuasion (Norton Critical Editions)*, ed. Patricia Meyer Spacks (New York: W. W. Norton, 1994), 303.

59. Panagia, *Impressions of Hume*, 7.

60. Chandler, *Archaeology of Sympathy*, 203.

61. Pfau, "Art and Ethics of Attention," 38.

62. T. S. Eliot, *The Waste Land*, line 420.

63. Pfau, "Art and Ethics of Attention," 37.

64. Catherine Keller and Chris Boesel, *Apophatic Bodies: Negative Theology, Incarnation, and Relationality* (New York: Fordham University Press, 2009), 10.

65. Here I am referring to Charles Taylor's influential description of our secular age as being both the cause and the consequence of a general shift from a porous to a buffered consciousness, which took place from around 1500 until the present day. For the porous self, "the source of its most powerful and important emotions are outside the 'mind'; [and] the very notion that there is a clear boundary, allowing us to define an inner base area, grounded in which we can disengage from the rest, has no sense" (*A Secular Age* [Cambridge, MA: Harvard University Press, 2007], 38). In contrast, the buffered self has developed a radical reflexivity that recognizes a boundary between inside and outside, and in which the things outside don't necessarily affect the real "me" that resides inside the buffer of my self-enclosure. Although there are obvious advantages in this new constitution of subjectivity, modern mobility comes at the cost of a feeling of alienation that manifests as a dissociation of sensibility. The challenge for the buffered self is finding how to regain access to the feeling of fullness previously enjoyed by the porous self while maintaining the rights that the modern subject enjoys.

66. Keller and Boesel, *Apophatic Bodies*, 146.

Part Two

(*EMMA'S*) LAUGHTER WITH A PURPOSE

4

AFTER THE LAUGHTER

Seeking Perfect Happiness in *Emma*

SOHA CHUNG

> The letter which I have this moment received from you has diverted me
> beyond moderation. I could die of laughter at it, as they used to say at
> school. You are indeed the finest comic writer of the present age.
> —Jane Austen, to Cassandra (L, 6)

JANE AUSTEN, WHO HERSELF WAS one of the finest comic writers of her age, indeed enjoyed laughing at her sister Cassandra's entertaining, pleasant letters and responding with her own. In the above letter written in 1796, Austen reveals the delight of being "diverted beyond moderation" and also the pleasure of sharing laughter with her sister. Although they are not laughing at the same moment, their exchange of laughter and amusement becomes a source of their intimacy. Vivien Jones points out that the humorous correspondence between the sisters suggests their deep understanding of each other's feelings. Jones argues that because laughter and humor were stigmatized for women, Austen's ironic letters and her affirmation of her excessively laughing self reflect how "Cassandra offers an intimacy beyond politeness which provides relief from the emotional exhaustion of otherwise inescapable, and often empty, social obligations."[1] Especially because laughing could cause her to be an object of misinterpretation and censure, Austen is expressing her trust in her sister through the candid description of her laughter.

As a well-known humorist as well as a public female writer, Austen faces a difficult struggle between her relish for a big, cheerful laugh and her sense of propriety. Her letter undoubtedly shows how willingly she enjoyed a happy laugh, but at the same time, it reveals her awareness of the "moderation" expected from her laughter. She cannot describe herself as dying of laughter without mentioning that she knows she is crossing a line. This delicacy she retains as a writer is what ultimately allows her to keep her propriety while playing with the boundary of proper manners. Moreover, her free expression of excitement and laughter in the letter suggests the nature of the intimacy she shares with her sister. For Austen, true intimacy involves appreciating and sharing laughter. This is rare intimacy in light of the multilayered prejudice and intolerance against women's laughter during Austen's time. Unlike most conduct book writers who only emphasize the harmful social effect of laughter, Austen seeks the possibility of intimacy that derives from laughter. Becoming a writer famous for her wit, Austen dares to move beyond the private space between sisters to express her love for laughter and pursue her search for a reader who could possibly be another "Cassandra." In fact, Austen's awareness of contemporary discourses restricting women's laughter and her attempt to find a balance between a desire for pleasure and a sense of propriety are most distinctly illuminated through her own fictional creation, a female protagonist who continually falls into troubles because of her excessive laughter: Emma Woodhouse.

It is well known that Austen referred to Emma as "a heroine whom no one but myself will much like."[2] The first sentence of the novel introduces Emma as gifted with "the best blessings of existence," in that she is "handsome, clever, and rich, with a comfortable home and happy disposition" (E, 5). Readers more used to sympathizing with unfortunate characters suffering from all kinds of economic or domestic travails might find it hard to feel friendly toward this perfect, well-off heroine who has "lived nearly twenty-one years in the world with very little to distress or vex her" (E, 5). Moreover, Emma enjoys "the power of having rather too much her own way, and a disposition to think a little too well of herself" (E, 5). It is no wonder that Austen thought nobody would much like this heroine. As Emily Auerbach points out, *Emma* "centers on a woman who centers on herself,"[3] and many agree that *Emma* is a reformation story of an errant heroine who gradually must learn modesty, generosity, and self-knowledge.[4] Interestingly, her lack of virtue is most visible when she laughs.

Emma is notorious for her heartless laughter in the Box Hill scene where she publicly mocks Miss Bates. Not only does she expose herself to the severe criticism of her admired Mr. Knightley, but her morality becomes seriously weak in the wary eyes of a reader as well. Since the opening sentences of the novel, Emma's inner quality has constantly appeared questionable, and her laughter at this scene only seems to confirm negative views of her character. Despite her subsequent deep regret, Emma's laughter indicates her lack of compassion, consideration, and humility, which makes some view the entire scene as a "descen[t] into the spiritual and emotional chaos."[5] Following discourses on laughter that emphasize its antisocial function, Emma's laughter in this scene suggests her lack of virtue and aligns her with a Hobbesian sense of her own superiority or with what Henri Bergson will later identify as emotional detachment.[6]

Austen herself has received much criticism on account of her laughter. Her witty, satirical descriptions led Marvin Mudrick, for example, to call her "almost inhumanely cold and penetrating."[7] For some critics, Austen's laughter, like Emma's, raises doubts regarding her virtue. Sarah Emsley reports that "despite Austen's reputation as light, bright, and sparkling, she has been accused on more than one occasion of intolerance, insensitivity, and a general lack of charity."[8] If Austen's laughter is subject to censure, it seems to be on the same ground as Emma's. Both are guilty of a lightness and brightness that may lead them to laugh where some would wish they did something else. Such a wish, however, risks misunderstanding the laughter of both the character and the author, and attending more carefully to Emma's laughter may help us to develop a more nuanced understanding of Austen's own.

Emma certainly laughs a lot, more than any other Austen heroine, and her laughter has generally been read as holding very simple, straightforward meanings. Patricia Meyer Spacks, one of the few critics to discuss Emma's laughter as an important factor of her character, focuses on how Emma's laughter functions as "a momentary declaration of control or of superiority" in the Box Hill scene.[9] However, closer examination of the narrative reveals that her laughter rarely carries a sense of control or superiority. More often than not, Emma's laughter is accompanied by vexation, mortification, and even guilt as she follows her laughter with a process of self-examination and self-correction. Austen clearly points to the gap between how Emma's laughter is read by others and how it is understood by herself, showing that what to others may appear a bit too light and sparkling is actually accompanied by painful introspection and reverie. While Emma's life is a series of seekings and plottings of amusements, and her laughter does reflect her desire for pleasure, over the course of the narrative, she has to learn how hard it is to attain moments of perfect happiness and joy. For Austen, the important question is not how to subdue laughter, but how to achieve a perfectly happy laughter that is not followed by shame, repentance, or harsh judgments.

As a physical and visible indication of one's inner state, laughter becomes a useful site for investigating how pleasure is expressed and judged. As laughter involves physical expression, it easily becomes the object of others' judgment. Since Emma is always aware that her laughter is being watched, she sometimes tries to be alone before she lets out her laugh. Therefore, whenever she laughs, we can learn something about her relationship with others and how her expression of pleasure works in her society. *Emma* is full of laughter, not just Emma's, yet her laughter is more critically judged than any other character's. Her social position and, most of all, her gender, make her the central object of others' observations. As a daughter who needs to serve her overly anxious father and as a mistress of Hartfield who has to care for the entire Highbury community, Emma's every move is closely examined. Despite her independent situation, Emma cannot be the one who decides the proper moments for pleasure. Her feeling and expression of pleasure inevitably work within the intricate social network, and to laugh with "true happiness," Emma needs to find a balance between personal and communal happiness.

Thus, when examining Austen's portrayal of laughter, we need to consider not just the social function of laughter but also its personal value. Austen clearly highlights the positive value of Emma's laughter while demonstrating how hard it is for women to achieve a moment of happy laughter. Emma laughs in many different scenes in many different ways, but regardless of the variations on display, most of her laughter makes her feel uncomfortable afterward. Emma's successive "faulty" laughs suggest the heavy restriction put on women's experience of pleasure. When contemporary conduct literature teaches women not to laugh and instead only to serve the pleasure of others, Austen's portrayal of the beauty of an individual woman's laughter is quite outstanding.

Some feminist critics have worked to emphasize the strength and value of female laughter by claiming its subversive power. For example, Regina Barreca, Audrey Bilger, and Eileen Gillooly show how Austen uses laughter to ridicule and attack the dominant patriarchal system and the unreasonable portrayal of ideal femininity.[10] Although their work addresses the positive virtue of female laughter, their study has been limited to a narrow meaning and function of laughter. To these critics, laughing is still always laughing "at" something, and it remains confined to the Hobbesian function of ridicule. With regard to Austen, this approach is inadequate, since even though Austen often uses laughter to mock absurdity, she also makes clear that the basic role of laughter is to express one's own state of pleasure, satisfaction, and happiness. To understand the value of laughter Austen portrays, we first need to see it as a part of our everyday emotional experience. The subversive power of female laughter, for Austen, comes from its lively demonstration of individual female happiness. Even after showing the many hardships and considerable uneasiness that Emma often experiences after laughing, Austen makes Emma keep her laughter until the end and allows her to enjoy the perfectly happy laughter that marks the finale. While conscious of the critical views on female laughter, Austen actively illuminates the value of women's happy laughter. As a writer of comedy as well as a fan of laughter, Austen celebrates the joy of laughing and guides us to the wise ways to achieve that joy.

Emma is undoubtedly a fortunate woman who has not much to worry about, and pleasure is a vital motivation for her everyday activities. Emma's only concern is her father's temper, but she usually knows how to appease it. When Emma is not tending to her father's moods, she has freedom to look after her own pleasure. Once she arranges a card table for Mr. Woodhouse, Emma spends time to plan and anticipate dinner parties and picnics that will amuse herself, and most of all, to prove her skill as a matchmaker. Believing that Miss Taylor and Mr. Weston's marriage was possible because of her assistance, she describes matchmaking as "the greatest amusement in the world" (E, 10). When, after Miss Taylor's marriage, she decides to be an arbiter of a match between Mr. Elton and Harriet Smith, she does so both for charity and for pleasure. Although Emma highlights that her matchmaking is for others—"this is the only way I have of doing [Mr. Elton] a service" (E, 12),—she finds much pleasure in the work. She enjoys the feeling of being a generous friend and a competent prophet, and she loves the activities she performs for her plan: organizing dinner parties, drawing a portrait of Harriet, and helping her to collect riddles. In fact, doing good deeds for others and enjoying pleasure are inseparable for Emma, as she finds great satisfaction from seeing herself as promoting other's happiness.

Although Emma's comfortable situation, naturally happy disposition, and active seeking of pleasure all seem to guarantee her a happy fate, Emma's guaranteed happiness does not come easily, as she must continually confront the social view that judges and reprimands both her desire for, and her experience of, pleasure. Unlike other Austen heroines, because her material condition is not an obstacle in her way to happiness, we can see more clearly the social restraints and gender norms that work against her individual happiness. In the first few chapters of the novel, Emma's happy disposition and desire for pleasure are introduced as defects she needs to overcome. The narrator points out that she is used to "doing just what she like[s] . . . directed chiefly by her own [judgment]" (E, 3), and Mr. Knightley believes that the ability to do anything she wants has worked against Emma's proper maturity. While discussing Emma with Mrs. Weston, he comments that Emma is "spoiled by being the cleverest of her family," and laments that through her mother's early death, she "lost the only person able to cope with her" (E, 37–38). Mr. Knightley even hopes to see Emma disappointed or frustrated: "It would not be a bad thing for her to be very much in love with a proper object. I should like to see Emma in love, and in some doubt of a return; it would do her good" (E, 41).

Having an active, happy, and willful mind unbound by any serious restraints, Emma seems to enjoy an easy life. Mr. Knightley, who will of course emerge as the "proper object" of Emma's love, judges this ease as a threat to Emma's character and wants her to experience some rejection and dissatisfaction. Throughout the narrative, Mr. Knightley intervenes at Emma's moments of pleasure to comment on its inappropriateness and sometimes even cruelty. At his direction, Emma repeatedly experiences a discomfort and anxiety about what she does for the happiness of herself and others. While readers often criticize her for being self-centered, narcissistic, arrogant, and controlling,[11] it is questionable how much agency Emma holds in her own experience of pleasure and happiness. Despite Mr. Knightley's concern for Emma, it seems that her life is already filled with disappointments and uncomfortable sentiments.

Emma's laughter is generally viewed as a sign of her sense of superiority or her self-centered mind, but in reality it is more often a sign of her unease and frustration. Emma laughs for the first time when she quarrels with Mr. Knightley about Harriet's refusal of Mr. Martin's proposal. The whole event is a source of pleasure to Emma since she firmly believes that Harriet will soon earn the love of Mr. Elton, whom she deems much superior to Mr. Martin. When Knightley tells Emma that Robert Martin is going to propose to Harriet, Emma, who already knows about the proposal and its unfortunate result, "smil[es] to herself through a great part of this speech" (E, 63). Here, her inward smile signals her pleasure at her own superior knowledge. For some time, she enjoys this delight of superiority. But her happy moments come to an end as Knightley becomes "red with surprize and displeasure" after knowing Harriet's refusal and exclaims, "Emma, this is your doing" (E, 64). Since Emma does not want to keep the uncomfortable atmosphere with Mr. Knightley, she tries to laugh off his retort. But her laughter is no longer a sign of her controlling, superior position.

Rather, she now laughs because she is uncomfortable: "Emma made no answer, and tried to look cheerfully unconcerned, but was really feeling uncomfortable and wanting him very much to be gone" (E, 69). For Emma, having Knightley "sitting just opposite to her in angry state, was very disagreeable" (E, 69). Even though she responds to Mr. Knightley with laughter, that laughter now suggests her thwarted pleasure and her inability to express her vexation, rather than her actual enjoyment. Unlike Mr. Knightley, who naturally expresses his displeasure to Emma, she cannot respond with the same liberty. In fact, we continually see Emma struggling to hide her distress in front of others. As "she dreaded being quarrelsome" (E, 122), she strains to remain silent when she disagrees with her brother-in-law's feelings. Even when Mr. Elton upsets her with his improper attention, she can only laugh it off or "give him a look" (E, 136). Emma's laughter and playful manner are the armor that she wears when she finds herself unable to deal directly with an unpleasant situation.

What Emma most desires to feel is pleasure, satisfaction, and happiness. However, pleasure is always something that will come, not something she enjoys at the moment. In most cases, she only gives the appearance of feeling pleased rather than experiencing actual enjoyment. Her life focuses more on expecting and planning amusements than on enjoying them. We often see her expectation turning into disappointment, and, at those moments, she laughs. When she determines to "enjoy all that was enjoyable to the utmost" (E, 40) as she enters the party at Randalls, for example, her night is ruined by Mr. Elton's annoying flirtation and his most unwelcome confession of love. Likewise, both picnics to Donwell and Box Hill excite much expectation of merriment, but they end with vexation and mortification. Even when she has a good time at the Coles' party, she later feels uneasy remembering the things she did wrong there. As the narrator says, "Perfect happiness, even in memory, is not common" (E, 249). Hence, contrary to Mr. Knightley's assessment, Emma seems quite familiar with disappointment and frustration. This continual experience of dissatisfaction suggests Emma's limited power in her pursuit of pleasure. Regardless of her will, things happen to thwart her expectation. Thus, Emma's greatest goal is to find the moment of "perfect happiness" where she can be truly happy and pleased without alloy.

Before she reaches that perfect moment, Emma has to learn that, unlike many of those who surround her, she cannot fully determine her own pleasure. The novel presents various male characters who stick to their own principles of pleasure and decide what is good for themselves and for others according to their own view. Mr. Woodhouse, to take the first example, always judges others' comfort and pleasure based on his own feeling, "being never able to suppose that other people could feel differently from himself" (E, 6). In his pursuit of pleasure similarly, Frank Churchill may receive the censure of characters like Mr. Knightley, but he never goes through the process of self-examination and regret that Emma does. The sudden whim that takes him to London disrespects Mrs. Weston's feelings and position, but he simply "laugh[s] at himself with a very good grace, . . . without seeming really at all ashamed of what he had done" (E, 229). His laughter, unlike Emma's, is not followed by mortified musings, and we can see that it merely reflects a mind at pleasure.

Mr. Knightley, the unquestionable representation of the true British gentleman, not only claims his right to decide his own pleasure, but he also tries to define the proper pleasure for Emma. He uses phrases that restrict Emma's free experience of feelings. Talking about Miss Taylor's wedding, he says that Emma "*must be* glad" and "*cannot allow* herself to feel so much pain as pleasure" (E, 10; emphasis mine). In the momentous Box Hill scene, similarly, his reproach announces a definition of Emma's feelings: "This is not pleasant to you, Emma—and it is very far from pleasant to me" (E, 408). Like Mr. Woodhouse's, Knightley's rhetoric consistently sets his own judgment as a standard. Besides, even though Mr. Knightley judges the proper pleasure for Emma, he firmly states his own right to decide his own pleasure. While everybody else is excited about the dance party, he alone remains uninterested and aloof. He is "determined against its exciting any present curiosity, or affording him any future amusement" (E, 277). When Emma urges him to participate, he claims, "They shall not choose pleasures for me" (E, 277–78), insisting that no one can be a better judge of his actions and feelings than he himself.

Mr. Knightley's defining of the proper feelings for Emma echoes the rhetoric of contemporary conduct manuals that aim to construct the right manner and feelings of ideal femininity. Penelope Joan Fritzer analyzes the effect of eighteenth-century conduct literature on Austen's novels and argues that conduct books do not merely teach the proper outer manners for women, but also emphasize manners as reflections of one's inner virtue. She states that "[b]oth [Austen's] novels and the courtesy books stress 'deep' manners over 'surface' ones—that is, social manifestations of character over fashion."[12] What Fritzer fails to notice is that Austen often attacks the imperatives of conduct manuals that unconditionally link certain manners with certain virtues or lack of virtues. In most conduct books, laughter is not recommended to women, as it is known to suggest one's selfish, thoughtless mind. In James Fordyce's *Sermons to Young Women* (1766), for example, used so famously by Mr. Collins to educate the Bennet girls, laughter appears as a sign of one's enjoying the "wrong" kinds of pleasure. For Fordyce, laughter, whether the "loud laugh, or childish titter, or foolish simper" provides an "indication of a light mind,"[13] and "the loud bursts of unmeaning laughter" directly counter "the sigh of compassion" that he insists is more musical to men's ears.[14] Clearly, Fordyce uses laughter as a mark that one both lacks and fails to deserve sympathy.

One of Fordyce's primary purposes is to define true happiness for women to come solely from the provision of happiness for others. "Ah! my young friends," he writes, " what pleasure can be compared to that of conferring felicity?"[15] And the provision of pleasure to others, Fordyce claims, is best effected at home, as women will find there "the truest pleasures, and the fairest prospects, that humanity knows."[16] Without considering that there might be differences among women, or that women might have pleasure of their own, Fordyce asserts that every woman should have the same standard for the truest pleasures and that that standard must involve the sacrifice of one's own claims to pleasure. In this context, Emma's seeking pleasure outside of her domestic duty cannot but be a bad model of femininity. Also, to emphasize the need for women's self-denial, Fordyce highlights the importance of their self-command and suggests that laughter is a result of its failure: "When the heart overflows with gaiety, is there no danger of its *bursting* the proper bounds? Is not extreme vivacity a near borderer on folly? To prevent its breaking loose, and throwing itself into very serious inconveniences, into a very hurtful conduct, will surely require the check of self-command" (my italics).[17] Fordyce earlier uses the word "burst" when he describes "the loud bursts of unmeaning laughter" and uses it here again to denote an overflowing gaiety that violates the proper bounds. The "bursting" of laughter is equal to the "bursting" of proper bounds, which marks the failure of self-command. Fordyce claims that "she that cannot distinguish between laughter and happiness, never knew what the latter means."[18] As he never describes laughter as a positive, allowable act, it is always loud, inappropriate, and bad. On her way to true happiness, according to Fordyce, a proper woman should control one's laughter and pay attention to serving others' needs and pleasure. From this view, Austen's burst of laughter at her sister's letter, an act she herself describes as "beyond moderation," is undeniably excessive and thus unfeminine. That Austen makes Mr. Collins, of all people, the proponent of Fordyce's views, indicates her position on his ideas.

Fordyce's sermon was not alone in attempting to dissuade women from laughter; in embracing laughter, Austen placed herself in opposition to a larger body of mid-eighteenth-century conduct literature. *The Lady's Preceptor* (1743), for example, warns its female reader against being the first to laugh in company: "should it happen to be of a humorous and diverting Cast, don't be the first to laugh at it yourself. . . . This is a Behavior too unguarded and indelicate, and betrays a want of Judgment as well as good Education."[19] The book argues that to laugh along with others is pardonable, but "to set up a Laugh in Company, without everyone present being acquainted with the Occasion, is inexcusable."[20] This lesson, like Fordyce's, implies that women's foremost role is to serve and comply with others' feelings. Any personal urge to laugh, not accordant with others' feelings, is highly censured. *The Whole Duty of Woman* (1753) describes a complaisant woman as "she [who] weepeth with those who weep [and she who] laugheth with those who laugh."[21] Many writers propose the art of pleasing, which is basically "to appear pleased with others"[22] or to "mak[e] the company pleased with themselves,"[23] but they are indifferent to the ways of pleasing oneself. It is assumed that to seek one's own pleasure is selfish and detrimental to one's femininity, and it seems extremely difficult for women to hold agency in their laughter, to laugh simply in the ways they want, when there are always others' feelings to consider first. Laughter is mostly associated with negative virtue, and the proper repression of laughter is required in one's path to "true happiness." While Austen, too, is concerned with identifying the proper bounds of laughter, she questions the norm that requires women to neglect their own pleasure. Austen definitely provides an education on laughter in *Emma*, but her lesson is very different from the ones we find in the conduct literature.

Austen clearly points to the unequal position of woman in the search for pleasure. In *Emma*, the heroine's laughter and pursuit of pleasure are similarly censured, but male characters enjoy the liberty of choosing their own standard for pleasure. Mr. Knightley has a firm belief in the man's scope of agency. When he quarrels with Emma about Frank not visiting his father and Mrs. Weston earlier, he states his idea of mature masculinity:

> If Frank Churchill had wanted to see his father, he would have contrived it between September and January. A man at his age—what is he?—three or four-and-twenty—cannot be without the means of doing as much as that. It is impossible.
>
> That's easily said, and easily felt by you, who have always been your own master. You are the worst judge in the world, Mr. Knightley, of the difficulties of dependence. You do not know what it is to have tempers to manage.
>
> It is not to be conceived that a man of three or four-and-twenty should not have liberty of mind or limb to that amount. (E, 157)

The point of this conversation is not who is right. Emma does think that Mr. Knightley is right about Frank and "to her great amusement perceive[s] that she [i]s taking the other side of the question from her real opinion" (E, 156). But Emma is doing more than just making up excuses for Frank. Emma knows much about having "tempers to manage," and she knows the hardship of being "your own master." Emma is saying what she can never say about herself by projecting herself into Frank's position, whose living depends on his selfish, willful, and redoubtable aunt. Mr. Knightley, on the other hand, upholds man's right to have agency. Repeating that Frank is "a man of three or four-and-twenty," he shows his belief in what a mature man can do. Moreover, although he disapproves of Frank's behavior, he knows he has no right to confront him. Emma, a woman of one-and-twenty, cannot enjoy such "liberty of mind." Despite some similarities in their situation, Frank and Emma's scopes of agency are widely different, and the laughter in which they both engage reveals those differences.

Emma's most problematic laughs in the novel occur when Emma teams up with Frank to seek amusements, but their gender difference singles Emma out to be the one who deserves criticism and guilt. Frank's easygoing, pleasant manner allows Emma to be more lax with the sense of propriety that usually restrains her social behavior, and Emma's laughter with Frank reflects both Emma's desire for pleasure and the difficulty of enjoying that pleasure as a woman. The intimacy between Emma and Frank grows rapidly after Emma confides to him her suspicion of Jane Fairfax's relationship with Mr. Dixon, and when they play a puzzle together, Knightley recognizes that Frank and Emma mutually enjoy an "eager laughing mirth" that displeases Jane (E, 378). Later, Mr. Knightley gravely says to Emma, "I am curious to know how [something] could be so very entertaining to the one, and so very distressing to the other" (E, 379), indicating his disapproval of the act. The truth is that Emma already felt guilty about her joke before this scene, right after she first mentioned her suspicion to Frank and worried "whether she had not transgressed the duty of woman by woman" (E, 249). That Emma keeps the content of their inside joke from Mr. Knightley suggests her awareness of the joke's inappropriateness.

Emma is fully aware of the social decorum expected from her, but the new taste of mutually shared pleasure and laughter is too strong to resist. For Emma, who believes that "one half of the world cannot understand the pleasures of the other" (E, 87), it is a great delight to have someone who can understand and participate in her pleasure. Although Mr. Knightley regards Frank as a fellow only concerned with his own pleasure and "ha[s] no English delicacy towards the feelings of other people" (E, 161), Emma feels like her sentiments are approved and respected by Frank. When talking about Jane with Frank, Emma experiences the moment in which her own sense of humor is immediately reciprocated without censure, and it is a rare occasion on which Emma can say, "Your countenance testifies that your thoughts on this subject are very much like mine" (E, 234). Although Frank is deceiving Emma about his feelings and intention, Emma, unaware, enjoys his company. Since Emma feels surrounded by people who disavow or criticize her feeling, Frank's easy manners allow her to be honest with her pleasure, and consequently, she ignores her inner inhibition and enjoys the guilty pleasure. She laughs not because she lacks a proper moral sense but because her desire for pleasure at the moment prevails over her moral sense.

However, in the Box Hill scene, Austen shows that even this seemingly equal and reciprocal relationship is controlled by the man, as Emma finds herself laughing with no joy. At this scene, Emma crosses the line of propriety by again disregarding her inner scruples. Emma had high hopes about the picnic and the joy it would bring, but "there was a languor, a want of spirits, a want of union, which could not be got over" (E, 399). To dispel this discord and dullness of the day, Emma gladly responds when Frank starts to flirt and joke with her and laughs "because she was disappointed" (E, 400). Actually, Frank is using Emma to provoke Jane, his secret fiancée, and by "making [Emma] his first object" (E, 400), he makes Emma the center of everybody's attention. He even requests the entire party to say something entertaining for Emma and announces that she will "laugh heartily at them all" (E, 402–3). Susan Rogers argues that even though "the fine views and open landscape should create a sense of greater space, of larger possibilities," the opposite occurs, and "there is a sense of confinement in the arrangement."[24] This confinement occurs inside Emma's mind as she is "trapped" in a situation in which she must laugh at jokes from Frank that she does not really find amusing. This is where her illusion of mutuality in the pleasure she shared with Frank gets broken, and now Frank's raillery distresses rather than pleases her. However, as she cannot reveal her true mind as always, she tries to "laug[h] as carelessly as she could" (E, 402), and in this careless manner, attacks Miss Bates, the poor, old spinster. Emma's frustrated desire for pleasure, Frank's public demand for her response, and above all, her total lack of control over the entire situation becomes a pressure that forces her to laugh, regardless of her actual feelings, and to mock the one person she should not mock.

Miss Bates is a character whose feelings Emma has been expected to attend to, and because of her low social standing, Miss Bates's presence works as a test for one's social virtue in Highbury society. She is a woman "nobody is afraid of" (E, 91), and whom everybody knows better than to neglect. The first thing Frank learns upon his arrival to Highbury is that "any want of attention to [Miss Bates] *here* should be carefully avoided" (E, 209). Although Emma is deeply aware of the symbolic position of Miss Bates, she cannot deny the displeasure she finds in her company. Emma hates Miss Bates's endless, pointless chatter, unbearable praising of Jane, and overflowing expression of gratitude. Because Emma knows well that she does not deserve her gratitude, she feels uncomfortable in front of her. Whenever she converses with Miss Bates, Emma cannot be honest with her feelings and feels like "much had been forced on her against her will" (E, 173). Even though Emma usually manages to maintain her proper manner in front of her as a social duty, at the Box Hill picnic, the pressure she feels to laugh and her need to be pleased lead to a neglect of her moral sense, and she ends up hurting Miss Bates.

In fact, since Emma's laugh is directed toward another, it becomes much more than a matter of her own morality or Miss Bates's feelings. When she laughs at Miss Bates or jokes with Frank targeting Jane, her laughter becomes a weapon that victimizes others. Especially because of her social position, Emma's laugh makes Miss Bates and Jane's already vulnerable position more visible. Frank, who stimulates Emma's laughter, is also at fault in affronting those whom he should respect and for whom he should care the most. Even though Emma's laugh is not a product of her sense of superiority or pride, it nevertheless displays her superiority and power to others' eyes. Mr. Knightley critiques Emma on both occasions, as he understands that Emma's behavior could risk the communal virtue that Highbury society tries to uphold. Conscious of Emma's social influence,

Mr. Knightley states that to laugh at Miss Bates in front of others is a serious matter as "many of whom (certainly *some,*) would be entirely guided by [Emma's] treatment of her" (E, 408). As the lady of Hartfield, Emma's conduct takes great social meaning, and Emma has to realize that social duty should be respected as much as her own desire for pleasure. Austen understands that if "laughing with" can create intimacy, "laughing at" can break it.

Throughout the narrative, Austen shows how one's desire for pleasure can be a pressure or pain for another to bear, and Emma sorely realizes this through her own errant laughter. Emma has to learn that as much as she loves her own pleasure, she has to respect others' feelings and consider the social weight of her behavior as well. Yet Austen suggests that this lesson is not just for women. Repeatedly, in the novel, Austen delivers her critical view on the social norms that strictly teach women to serve men's needs by representing how men's active, often selfish, pursuit of pleasure becomes a physical and emotional burden for women. When Frank and Mr. Weston mindlessly suggest impractical plans for the dance party, for example, it is Mrs. Weston who has to work hard to accommodate their wants, believing, "to do what would be most generally pleasing must be our object—if one could but tell what that would be" (E, 274). Emma thinks of her friend as "always over-careful for every body's comfort but [her] own" (E, 204). Also, whenever Mr. John Knightley freely expresses the ill temper that distresses Mr. Woodhouse, Emma has to find ways to appease both men while hiding her own distress. Women are frequently represented as sacrificing their own ease to promote men's pleasure; and ironically, Isabella Woodhouse, who has no desire of her own and always thinks and feels as her husband does, is described as the happiest creature in the world and "a model of right feminine happiness" (E, 151). Austen clearly points to the burden of an ideal femininity that has to comply with others' needs; and even Emma, often deemed as selfish, endures her prior duty to serve others. Thus, even if Emma is the only one who actually goes through the painful lesson about the wrongness of her laughter, Austen indicates that this should not be a gendered instruction and that Emma is not the only one who needs it. When Frank still "laugh[s] so heartily at the recollection" (E, 522) of his past conduct at the end, it is clear that he did not properly learn his lessons.

Austen portrays Emma's education on laughter as a result of her self-examination and self-understanding, rather than of strict masculine regulation. Although Mr. Knightley intervenes to criticize Emma's laughs, Emma goes through the process to "feel" the wrong of her action in isolation and understands that as long as her pleasure harms the happiness of others, she cannot enjoy real pleasure. If Mr. Knightley speaks for the social norms that Emma has to regard, Austen shows that for Emma, laughter is also an issue of individual happiness. The wretchedness and "true contrition" (E, 410) that she experiences after the Box Hill picnic teaches her how inconsiderate laughter will only give her pain. At the same time, however, Emma's lesson does not make her give up all her desire for pleasure and simply adhere to the expectations of ideal femininity. Rather, Austen differentiates herself from the conduct-book writers by showing how wonderful the moment of perfectly happy laughter can be, if it does not have to be followed by guilt and shame. At the very end of the novel, Emma finally gets her reward and enjoys her "true happiness."

The novel ends with Emma and Knightley's wedding, but the moment when Emma is described as most happy is when she laughs with joy, alone. In a way, what concludes Austen's comedy is laughter itself, not a wedding. After Emma finds out about her love for Mr. Knightley and his love for herself, she feels the "exquisite flutter of happiness" (E, 473). Yet this happiness still has some alloy: her concern for her father who would be left alone after her marriage and her guilt about Harriet who confessed her love for Mr. Knightley to Emma. Emma's pleasure again seems to come at the expense of others' pleasure. But soon, these problems are resolved: Mr. Knightley proposes to live at Hartfield, and Harriet will be happily married to Mr. Martin. Finally, Emma's rare moment of perfect happiness arrives, and she cannot help feeling "a most unreasonable degree of happiness" (E, 515). There is no more alloy in her pleasure, no regret to follow her laughter.

> She wanted to be alone. Her mind was in a state of flutter and wonder, which made it impossible for her to be collected. She was in dancing, singing, exclaiming spirits; and till she had moved about, and talked to herself, and laughed and reflected, she could be fit for nothing rational.
> . . .
> Serious she was, very serious in her thankfulness, and in her resolutions; and yet there was no preventing a laugh, sometimes in the very midst of them. *She must laugh* at such a close! (E, 518–19; emphasis mine)

The narrator emphasizes that Emma is serious. Her laughter is not another momentary, careless slip or a disguise to cover up her displeasure. She thinks that she "must laugh" even in, or perhaps because of, her seriousness. After the distress that has accompanied her laughter before, she can now appreciate the value of this perfect moment.

Emma laughs this last laugh alone. There is no Mr. Knightley to judge her and no one to get harmed by her laugh. As her laughter is described as wild and unreasonable, there is no doubt that it would appear wrong to Mr. Knightley. Emma is laughing with dancing and singing, but Austen does not describe this as "loud" laughter that should be suppressed. Emma's happiness is more evident and complete in this scene even than in the brief description of her marriage ceremony. Emma does not need Mr. Knightley to judge the appropriateness of her laughter, as she well knows it herself. She finally appears to be the best judge of her own pleasure. Marking the conclusion of Emma's trial with her happiest laughter, Austen demonstrates that her lesson was for Emma to achieve that moment. After all the troubles Emma went through with her laughter, Emma's final, ecstatic laugh carries a sense of liberation.

At this scene, the reader, instead of Mr. Knightley, is driven to decide the value of Emma's laughter. The narrator, after noting that Emma's laughter was "serious," steps aside and refrains from making a judgment. Caroline Austin-Bolt indicates that the mingling of the voice of the first-person character with the third-person narrator's voice creates a sense of sympathy between the reader and the first-person thoughts of a character.[25] Emma once says in the novel, "It is very unfair to judge of anybody's conduct, without an intimate knowledge of their situation" (E, 157). This principle should be applied as well to our judgment of others' feelings. To understand Emma's excessive delight and happiness at the end, we need to know all the previous occasions in which her laughter was stifled, blocked, and criticized. To enable her readers to make fair judgment of her heroine, Austen allows us to have access to Emma's mind. Emma is everywhere in the novel, and through the technique of free indirect discourse, readers can closely follow Emma's feelings before and after her laughter. It is hard to call her insensitive, selfish, or arrogant when her repentant, mortified heart is exposed to our view. As Wayne C. Booth says, "We know her too intimately to take her conscious thoughts at face value."[26]

Through the intimate knowledge of a laughing woman that *Emma* allows, we achieve a much more complex view of women's laughter than the one offered in conduct literature. The intimacy formed between Emma and the reader is even greater than the intimacy that exists between Emma and Mr. Knightley. Even though Emma loves him, she cannot betray Harriet's secret to Mr. Knightley and, thus, cannot share her merriment with him at the end. Moreover, Mr. Knightley is not familiar enough with Emma's past musings and feelings to appreciate the value of her laughter that reaches the point of being unreasonable. On the other hand, readers have intimately known her secrets. Now, it is up to the readers to decide if Emma's laughter is understandable and pleasant. After all, Austen implies that the education Emma went through in the novel was also for the readers. As she did with her sister, Austen attempts to build intimacy with her readers by inviting us to laugh at her comic, entertaining narrative and, at the same time, teaches us the risk of careless laughter and the ways for a truly happy laugh.

For Austen, women's laughter is a complex issue. If Fordyce's sermon condemns laughter as a loud bursting of propriety, and feminist critics praise female laughter as a powerful attack on masculine norms, Austen explores the various aspects of laughter: laughter as disguise, as defense, as a vehicle for self-reflection, and as an expression of pleasure. Maintaining both the virtue and the pleasure of laughter and finding a balance between personal and communal happiness cannot be realized in a simple manner. Knowing the danger of laughter that could distress or oppress others and understanding the morality that should not be abandoned in one's laughter, Austen shows the need to examine what comes after our laughter. Emma's search for the perfectly happy laughter is only achieved at the end once she learns the displeasure of her errant laughter. Laughing, after all, can be a joyful, positive experience, even for women. In *Emma*, Austen succeeds in revealing the beauty of perfectly happy laughter by exploring how difficult it is to achieve that moment.

NOTES

1. Vivien Jones, Introduction to *Selected Letters*, by Jane Austen, ed. Jones (New York: Oxford University Press, 2004), xxii.
2. James Edward Austen-Leigh, A *Memoir of Jane Austen: And Other Family Recollections*, ed. Kathryn Sutherland (Oxford: Oxford University Press, 2008), 119.
3. Emily Auerbach, *Searching for Jane Austen* (Madison: University of Wisconsin Press, 2004), 202.
4. For an example of this view, see Wayne C. Booth, "Control of Distance in Jane Austen's *Emma*," in *Jane Austen's "Emma": A Casebook*, ed. Fiona Stafford (New York: Oxford University Press, 2007), 102.
5. Penny Gay, "*Emma* and *Persuasion*," in *The Cambridge Companion to Jane Austen*, ed. Edward Copeland and Juliet McMaster, 2nd ed. (Cambridge: Cambridge University Press, 2001), 61.
6. For Hobbes and Bergson's ideas of laughter, see Thomas Hobbes, *The Elements of Law, Natural and Politic*, ed. J. C. A. Gaskin (Oxford: Oxford University Press, 1994); and Henri Bergson, *Laughter: An Essay on the Meaning of the Comic*, trans. Cloudesley Brereton and Fred Rothwell (New York: Macmillan, 1914). In Hobbes's view, laughter is nothing but an expression of our sudden glory when we realize that in some way we are superior to someone else (54–55); and Henri Bergson claims that laughter is totally devoid of feelings, that "laughter has no greater foe than emotion" (4).
7. Marvin Mudrick, *Jane Austen: Irony as Defense and Discovery* (Princeton: Princeton University Press, 1952), 1.
8. Sarah Emsley, "Laughing at Our Neighbors: Jane Austen and the Problem of Charity," *Persuasions On-Line* 26, no. 1 (Winter 2005), http://jasna.org/persuasions/on-line/vol26no1/emsley.htm (accessed May 20, 2018).
9. Patricia Meyer Spacks, "Austen's Laughter," *Women's Studies* 15, nos. 1–3 (1988): 83.
10. For each of their views, see Regina Barreca, *Untamed and Unabashed: Essays on Women and Humor in British Literature* (Detroit: Wayne State University Press, 1994); Audrey Bilger, *Laughing Feminism: Subversive Comedy in Frances Burney, Maria Edgeworth, and Jane Austen* (Detroit: Wayne State University Press, 1998); and Eileen Gillooly, *Smile of*

Discontent: Humor, Gender, and Nineteenth-Century British Fiction (Chicago: University of Chicago Press, 1999).

11. For an example of this view, see Claudia L. Johnson, *Jane Austen: Women, Politics, and the Novel* (Chicago: University of Chicago Press, 1988), 122.

12. Penelope Joan Fritzer, *Jane Austen and Eighteenth-Century Courtesy Books* (Westport, CT: Greenwood Press, 1997), 6.

13. James Fordyce, *Sermons to Young Women* (New York: M. Carey, 1809), 67.

14. Fordyce, *Sermons*, 94.

15. Fordyce, *Sermons*, 17.

16. Fordyce, *Sermons*, 56.

17. Fordyce, *Sermons*, 87–88.

18. Fordyce, *Sermons*, 93.

19. *The Lady's Preceptor: Or, a Letter to a Young Lady of Distinction upon Politeness Taken from the French of the Abbe D'Ancourt, and Adapted to the Religion, Customs, and Manners of the English Nation. By a Gentleman of Cambridge* (London, 1745), 11.

20. *Lady's Preceptor*, 20.

21. *The Whole Duty of Woman, By a Lady, Written at the Desire of a Noble Lord* (London, 1753), 43.

22. Lady Sarah Pennington, *An Unfortunate Mother's Advice to Her Absent Daughters; in a Letter to Miss Pennington* (London, 1761), 44.

23. John Gregory, *A Father's Legacy to His Daughters*, ed. Gina Luria (New York: Garland Publishing, Inc., 1974), 32.

24. Susan Rogers, "Emma at Box Hill: A Very Questionable Day of Pleasure," *Persuasions Online* 25, no. 1 (2004), http://www.jasna.org/persuasions/on-line/vol25no1/rogers.html (accessed October 5, 2016).

25. Caroline Austin-Bolt, "Mediating Happiness: Performances of Jane Austen's Narrators," *Studies in Eighteenth Century Culture* 42 (2013): 274.

26. Booth, "Control of Distance," 104.

5

THE COMIC VISIONS OF EMMA WOODHOUSE

Timothy Erwin

Pictures of perfection . . . make me sick and wicked.
—Jane Austen to Fanny Knight, March 23, 1817[1]

MORE THAN TWO DECADES AGO, Hollywood had the idea of updating *Emma* for a mixed audience. The calculated gamble depended upon a couple of crucial elements. For one thing, the story of a high school student playing Cupid for her teachers and friends before abruptly falling in love herself would have to stand on its own. A decade earlier, director John Hughes had shown with *The Breakfast Club* that young audiences would appreciate the comic portrayal of adolescence if granted the right ratio of insight and solidarity. For another, the film would have to provide mature filmgoers with the reflexive pleasure of enjoying a familiar narrative in a new guise. *Fast Times at Ridgemont High*, with its understated allegory of the founding fathers, had shown that audiences could entertain wildly opposed yet oddly parallel storylines.[2] Once viewers recognize Cher Horowitz as a latter-day Emma Woodhouse, a matching game begins to play out across the shift from Regency Britain to 1990s Beverly Hills. The well-known cliquishness of the American high school is understood to reflect the fixed hierarchy of an English village. The devoted if conflicted daughter of a respected estate owner becomes the no-less-devoted daughter of a hard-nosed litigator. A privileged heroine remains blind to her own affections until an overlooked attachment makes them known, and *presto!*, the urgency of teenage angst collides comically with the *plus ça change* of postmodern appropriation. The result was *Clueless*, a popular success from the summer of 1995 that won director Amy Heckerling, who also directed *Fast Times*, a Best Screenplay Award from the National Society of Film Critics.

As it happens, 1995 was a year of wonders for Jane Austen adaptations, and several new productions were launched either that year or the next. That autumn saw the wide release of an art-house version of *Persuasion* with the stage actors Amanda Root and Ciaran Hinds in leading roles, and that winter Ang Lee's

Sense and Sensibility appeared in theaters with a prize-winning screenplay by Emma Thompson. The following year saw the appearance of Kate Beckinsale as Emma in an ITV made-for-television movie, *Jane Austen's Emma*, and also the wide release of Douglas McGrath's *Emma* with Gwyneth Paltrow in the title role. Meanwhile, the novel has since been reworked for a BBC miniseries directed by Jim O'Hanlon (2009). What all these versions share is the distinction of launching a lasting vogue for watching Austen onscreen, and if *Pride and Prejudice* has enjoyed a wider variety of recent adaptation,[3] *Emma* led the way.

Film has its own language, and the transfer of *Emma*'s comedy to the silver screen naturally demands new comic materials to match the arch ironies of the prose. The same film language, however, also runs the risk of missing the mark entirely. In taking up the visual-verbal humor of Austen's narrative, we might begin with Harriet Smith, who becomes a sustained object of visual and comic attention when Emma decides to paint her portrait. The comic target shifts radically in recasting the three chapters that tell the story of Harriet's portrait for the screen. As readers of Austen know, Emma's double aim in staging Harriet's portrait is to have Mr. Elton view her as a romantic object and to distract Harriet from Robert Martin. The comedy stems largely from thinking that painting an attractive likeness would cause a fellow like Mr. Elton to fall in love with the sitter when the effect is to make him enamored of the artist. The film versions tend to play down the comedy of unintended effects and substitute instead a comic treatment of the portrait itself. It's puzzling that a visual medium should fail to engage Austen's visual target in this way. In the pages that follow, I'd like to take up the way our heroine's allegiance to an outdated visual regime renders her blind to the modern romance plot in which Austen inscribes her.

Austen's novels have their own notions about how we should view them, and may even encode instructions for seeing them at their best. *Pride and Prejudice* treats the art of portraiture in a way very different from *Persuasion*. The portrait of Darcy that Elizabeth Bennet beholds at Pemberley is both a sign of continuing affection and a test of character. A speaking picture, it tells Elizabeth that Darcy has long admired her, while the commentary of the housekeeper confirms his good nature from childhood. Joe Wright's *Pride and Prejudice* (2005) transforms the picture gallery at Pemberley into a sculpture gallery and sets a bust of Darcy amid a group of classical marbles. The turn from portraiture to the plastic arts may have been a matter of convenience, since the location Chatsworth House had a sculpture gallery already in place, and all that was needed was to create a bust of Matthew Macfayden for Keira Knightley to admire. Yet the transformation is apropos because it reflects much the same period concern to assemble the iconography of classical virtue that we see in Andrew Tooke's *Pantheum Mythicum* (1698), a compilation of topoi running to dozens of editions by Austen's day. The miniature portrait of Captain Benwick from Austen's last novel, on the other hand, represents male inconstancy, because it was created as a memento for Fanny Harville and is being made over to Louisa Musgrove. It's instead the heartfelt letter that Wentworth addresses to Anne that represents abiding affection, and Austen stresses its verbal dimension by folding its written expression over the spoken utterance. When Anne is overheard telling Harville that men as well as women can be constant in their affections, Wentworth immediately scribbles down his agreement. The director Roger Michell decodes the textual moment by showing us Anne reading Wentworth's letter silently to herself before letting us hear Ciaran Hinds and Amanda Root read it aloud in voiceover. *Pride and Prejudice* is arranged for the eye, *Persuasion* is scored for the ear, and the better film adaptations recognize the difference.

Emma also includes a crucial portrait episode, again introducing the medium of painting into the differential analysis of novel and film. Austen follows the three chapters of that episode with two more involving verbal charades, we recall, and taken together they burlesque what I have called the discourse of design, the formal analogy of the sister arts of painting and poetry.[4] Emma's twice-failed efforts to attract Mr. Elton to Harriet, in other words, form a parody of the shared rhetoric of text and image.[5] William Galperin has suggested that we view the film adaptations through the differential lens of cultural change,[6] and *Emma* reflects a stark gap between the nostalgic vision of *Pride and Prejudice* and the modern iconoclasm of *Persuasion*.[7] If we take the two novels to represent the poles of a spectrum, we can place *Emma* closer to the iconoclasm of *Persuasion*. Austen likens Emma's matchmaking to the slapdash placement of a figure in painting, so that Harriet becomes disposable, what John Dryden calls a "figure to be let."[8] After Emma's reliance on a dated symbolic discourse fails her, she becomes confused until her devotion to Mr. Knightley dawns upon her as a sudden revelation. The stark difference entails a second more abstract distinction between the perfect beauty of the individual and the perfection of human benevolence shared across community. Austen meanwhile tempers the comedy with sympathy for Robert Martin, whose proposal of marriage Harriet initially rejects, and also draws a sharp contrast between the leisured amusements at Hartfield and the improvements under way at Donwell Abbey, where Martin works as a tenant farmer.

IS *EMMA* REALLY A COMEDY?

We might step back momentarily to ask what sort of comedy *Emma* is, and even with Marshall Brown, whether we should call it a comedy at all.[9] As unhappy as its heroine may become, *Emma* certainly seems a comic action when viewed from a formal perspective. The narrative arc begins with a "melancholy change" of fortune (E, 5) in the removal of a beloved girlhood companion and ends with "an exquisite flutter of happiness" (E, 473) at the prospect of Knightley's marriage proposal. The novel affirms a familiar axiom about comedy by concluding not with one wedding but three,[10] while a secret engagement runs nearly its full length. The world of Highbury is peopled with comic eccentrics. Mr. Woodhouse is a well-defined comic type, an amiable humorist,[11] and we smile at his small portions and short walks while warming to his generous spirit in finding employment for the daughter of a servant. He is joined by those great communicators of matters small, the nattering Miss Bates and the silent Mr. Perry, whose dicta Mr. Woodhouse reports secondhand. The Perry children with their stolen slices of wedding cake, Farmer Mitchell dispensing umbrellas when it rains, and others round out a whimsical host of extras.

There is also a threat of unhappiness to be accounted for, and in saying that "low spirits are epidemic in this depressed community" Brown brings convincing lexical evidence to bear against those who would see the novel closing in perfect bliss.[12] Of the two kinds of perfection in play, the Neoplatonism of the early chapters leads to misery and regret, while the ideal of social benevolence promoted in the later chapters remains a work in progress. For much of the novel, Highbury is a backward place. Mr. Woodhouse dreads change of any sort, and Emma is very much her father's daughter, unable to marry for fear of parting from him and unable to part from him even in marriage. Her boredom is from the outset unmistakable. An attentive daughter, she entertains her father's women friends during their regular rounds of "tea and quadrille" (E, 20) by serving as a fourth at cards when needed.[13] Like other forms of sociability, the occasions are described in terms of a particular instance and a typical activity, and like the alternating visits of Cummings and Gowing in *The Diary of a Nobody*,[14] they make for "long evenings" (E, 21). When the schoolmistress Mrs. Goddard brings along Harriet, a boarder whose good looks and unknown parentage intrigue Emma, the narrative is off and running, if decidedly down the wrong track. Harriet is a class cipher, a social wild card, the "natural daughter of somebody" (E, 21) later identified as an anonymous but respectable tradesman. Imagining her birth to be equal to her beauty, Emma sets out to groom her for a good match.

We know Emma as well as we do because Austen grants us wide access to her subjectivity, from its moments of high exultation to its lows of abject embarrassment. We can watch her make solid inferences and startling mistakes alike, and from several critical angles. A Freudian would see her wish to direct the romantic lives of others as repetition compulsion, a way of coping with the loss of first her mother and now her governess Miss Taylor,[15] and the ending as a way of managing unresolved paternal conflict. A Marxist might see her disdain for Robert Martin as symptomatic of a stratified society blind to the worth of its most productive members.[16] Already attuned to social nuance, Emma must learn to value honest labor. The prime target of the humor is the self-delusion of the heroine regarding her own desires, a fault that Emma actively overcomes, and feminist readers have taken her newfound agency to contest patriarchal notions of passive femininity.[17] Her belated recognition lends the narrative closure the sense of a narrow escape. Readers forgive her failure to see what is right before her eyes because her willingness to make amends is forthright and because her experience of twenty years has left her absolutely unprepared for error. Until now Emma has never faced any possibility of ever making a mistake.

The metaphor of psychological blindness approaches farce during the portrait episode and its aftermath. Harriet's portrait represents what Emma cannot see even when it is right in front of her, and even when she herself has produced the scene. When Mr. Elton is asked to help assemble an album of riddles and charades for Harriet to transcribe, the lone charade he offers is misconstrued. And when Emma is told what the reader has long known, that her actions have encouraged Mr. Elton to think of courting *her* rather than Harriet (E, 120), she remains doubtful until, overheated by wine, he proposes. Mr. Elton eventually marries Harriet but strictly in his role as vicar of Highbury and to someone else. The paired episodes form a visual-verbal set piece, a Rorschach test to be parsed against different forms of misapprehension. They shape a comedy in which perspectives as incongruous as chalk and cheese must be approximated in a shared view. The task belongs to the reader no less than to those, like Knightley, who to one degree or another must sort them out for the sake of the greater good. De Quincey reminds us that farce is never far from tragedy,[18] and the early episodes lead directly to Emma's later admission of "insufferable vanity" and "unpardonable arrogance" (E, 449) in ever playing Cupid.

THE PORTRAIT

By Austen's day, academic painting had settled on portraiture as the best way to express the grand style. Modern sitters could mediate ancient virtue by adopting an iconographic pose, gesture, or attribute from antiquity. Sir Joshua Reynolds represents Mrs. Sheridan as St. Cecilia, Mrs. Blake as Juno, and Sarah Siddons as the muse of tragedy in just this way, as Mario Praz long ago pointed out.[19] There is nothing particularly comic about the practice, far from it, but the Miramax and

Figure 5.1. Brittany Murphy as Tai Frasier, from *Clueless* (1995).

BBC films render Harriet's classical pose ludicrous. Instead of giving her a seated posture, they represent her standing and holding a classical attribute, a lyre in one instance and an amphora in the other. Although the basic pose might be traced from ancient Greece to Henri Matisse without raising a smile, the awkward discomfiture of the sitter makes it ridiculous. Where the portrait episode in *Emma* sponsors a comic confusion of means and ends, the films with the exception of *Clueless* point to the humor of taking an awkward English schoolgirl for a classical icon.

Clueless compresses the portrait episode into a group photograph that Cher takes of her close friends at school. The protégée standing in for Harriet, a transfer student named Tai Frasier, is destined by Cher for a classmate named Elton. Tai bespeaks her otherness by pronouncing Elton's name with the glottal stop of the Eastern Seaboard, and has already become interested in the counterpart of Robert Martin, Travis Birkenstock. She is nonetheless willing to undergo the rigors of a makeover in forming a new attachment. For his part, Elton misconstrues Cher's intentions much as his namesake does. The parallel moment occurs as the soundtrack plays the nineties anthem "Alright" by Supergrass, and Cher asks Elton

Figure 5.2. Toni Collette as Harriet Smith, from *Emma* (1996).

for the sake of the photo to put his arm around Tai. He complies and integrates Tai in the group portrait. Cher then creates a new frame by asking Tai to strike a pose away from the others, picking a red hibiscus for her to hold (Figure 5.1).

Elton follows them, and Cher asks him in a sequence of shots whether Tai doesn't look classic. "Yeah, this is beautiful," Elton replies vaguely. Cher refers the compliment to her friend, adding, "She looks like one of those Botticelli chicks."[20] Elton unwittingly confirms his interest by asking for a copy of the photo for his locker, a nod to the amatory confusion surrounding Mr. Elton's London errand. Much as Mr. Elton confesses his love for Emma in the uncomfortably close quarters of a carriage, Elton arranges in a funny bit about gauging the demands of traffic against the Los Angeles streetscape to give Cher a ride in his convertible, where he likewise presses a futile and embarrassing case.

The Miramax film directed by Douglas McGrath stages the portrait scene in an elaborate rustic setting (for our purposes we may set aside the ITV film, where Harriet is briefly shown reading indoors). The painting is now Mr. Elton's idea: "An idea has just dropped into my mind, surely from heaven itself,"[21] he says, when suddenly Harriet appears in soft focus in an ungainly Arcadian posture (Figure 5.2).

Cradling a Grecian lyre at her waist with her left arm, she raises her right so that the hand points back toward her shoulder. The humor is aimed scattershot at Regency neoclassicism. In addition, having Mr. Elton put forward the portrait rather than Emma obviates the comic force of his misunderstanding that she intends by it. The mise-en-scène of the Miramax version typically foregrounds

Figure 5.3. Jefferson Hall as Robert Martin, from *Emma* (2009).

the mischievous plotting of Emma by placing her in conspiratorial dialogue with others or else acting at cross-purposes with them. A case in point is when Emma and Knightley practice archery, and she discloses that Robert Martin has been refused. Punctuated by the release of arrows, their dialogue becomes increasingly heated as they struggle to maintain both their composure and their aim. Lacking textual precedent, the setting recalls a similar scene in the Greer Garson-Laurence Olivier *Pride and Prejudice* (1940) and anticipates the language of Emma's awakening when as Austen puts it, love darts through her "with the speed of an arrow" (E, 444).[22]

The 2009 BBC miniseries adapts the novel to four hour-long episodes, and the screenplay stages a crucial scene only reported in the novel. A cross-cutting sequence foregrounds the social dimension of the narrative by introducing a contrast between Martin's proposal letter and Emma's portrait of Harriet. We watch Emma encounter Harriet in the schoolyard on a visit to Miss Goddard's. On impulse she invites her to supper at Hartfield, where their friendship blossoms. The painting episode opens with Emma and Harriet standing at easels creating watercolors of the topiary gardens behind the house. An establishing long shot shows Mr. Elton riding downhill toward Hartfield. He begins to commend their handiwork with stilted and unctuous hyperbole when Emma suddenly proposes that she paint Harriet. In contrast to the amusements taking place at Hartfield, the next shot shifts to an interview that never actually takes place in the novel and that we only learn about after the fact from Knightley. That would be the conversation with Robert Martin reported in chapter 8 when Knightley lets Emma know that

Figure 5.4. Louise Dylan as Harriet Smith, from *Emma* (2009).

her friend might receive a proposal of marriage, and she answers that Martin has already been refused—the same colloquy staged during the archery contest in the Miramax film.

We watch Robert Martin striding across the countryside to consult with Mr. Knightley on a matter of some urgency. The abbey towers above him on his approach. We view it from the height of his knees, the low angle opposed to Elton's elevated view of Hartfield from horseback. The camera angle suggests Martin's trepidation as well as his relative status (indeed, he turns back momentarily; Figure 5.3).

The scene then shifts back to Hartfield in order to enforce a further contrast. We leave Martin standing before the abbey gathering his nerve and cut back to Emma and the painting scene proper. Dressed in Grecian garb, Harriet holds an amphora above her left shoulder with both hands as the camera pulls back, bringing into the frame Emma standing at her easel (Figure 5.4). Harriet finds the pose uncomfortable and picks up a bit of pencil, evidently to brace the weight of the pot. Elton is heard stiffening her resolve when the scene shifts back to the abbey.

Knightley tells Martin that if he's sure that the course of action he proposes is a prudent one, then he should certainly proceed, and that, by the way, he doesn't need permission. Martin has presumably told Knightley of his intention to take Harriet for his bride since his offer of marriage reaches Harriet in the next scene. Like the novel, the film juxtaposes the portrait to the proposal letter, each confirming the active role that Emma has played in conjuring up the one and defeating the other. Again like the novel, the film fosters a narrative contest of earnest word and fanciful image and also foregrounds the countervailing role that Martin plays in pointing the comedy.

All of these adaptations capture something amusing. In *Clueless*, Elton misreads the attentions of Cher just as his namesake misreads Emma and so must suffer the same bewildering rejection. The Miramax *Emma* places Emma at a puzzling remove from the intrigue and uses impassioned repartee to heighten the conflict between Emma and Knightley. The lengthier BBC miniseries includes Knightley's early discussion with Mrs. Weston, letting us hear his critique of Emma's willfulness. The same film also develops a minor character only belatedly made visible in order to point to Emma's error. As enjoyable as these last films are, the portrait episode that provides Austen with the occasion for a meditation on proportion becomes in both little more than a sight gag. We hear even less about whether or not Harriet's beauty and disposition promise more substantial good qualities, a prime topic of debate between Emma and Knightley.

HARRIET'S SILENCE

When sitters visited Sir Joshua Reynolds's studio to have their likeness taken, he would open a portfolio of engravings and ask them to select a pose.[23] Emma likewise asks Harriet to choose from several unfinished family portraits before fixing unilaterally on the size and medium herself. Although fond of Robert Martin, Harriet is overawed by the Hartfield set and amenable to finding another admirer. Naturally timid, she hardly consults her own preferences either in posing, selecting a charade, or anything else before prompting Emma's belated awakening by setting her sights on Knightley. Her letter rejecting Robert Martin's proposal of marriage is all but dictated to her, as Knightley suspects. Nor do we hear a word from her regarding the experience of sitting, though the word that Emma applies to the business, "irksomeness" (E, 48), is surely accurate. To lessen the tedium, Emma asks Mr. Elton to read to them, and we notice in passing an approximation of text and image.

Harriet's silence differs from the fluency of other sitters. Sarah Siddons famously takes the iconic pose of the tragic muse for her own creation, though tradition says that Reynolds borrows the composition from Michelangelo's Isaiah. As she tells the story, Sir Joshua instantaneously approved of the way she arranged herself in his chair: "He took me by the hand, saying, 'Ascend your undisputed throne, and graciously bestow upon me some grand Idea of The Tragick Muse.' I walked up the steps & seated myself instantly in the attitude in which She now appears. This idea satisfyed him so well that he, without one moments hesitation, determined not to alter it."[24] Harriet's comparative reticence forms a sharp contrast to the narrative focalization of Emma, whose least thought finds its way to utterance.[25] With such small appreciation of her friend's inner life, Emma is perhaps the last person to take Harriet's likeness. Reaction to the picture is predictably mixed, with each beholder noticing something different. Mr. Woodhouse makes what a psychologist would call an illusory correlation, seeing a risk of illness in the alfresco portrait, although it depicts a summer day and is painted indoors. Mrs. Weston notes that Emma has given Harriet's eyes a beautiful expression but brows and lashes not her own. Mr. Elton sees the picture as perfection itself, naturally, and refuses to brook even the slightest criticism (E, 50). Knightley alone hits the nail of disproportion squarely on the head: "You've made her too tall, Emma," he says (E, 49).

In showing Emma the letter from Robert Martin proposing marriage, Harriet reaffirms the concern for proportion by asking, "Is it a good letter? or is it too short?" (E, 53). Conceding that the letter is sincere and intelligent, Emma finds specious grounds for disapproval. Having the slightest equivocation about entering into a marriage, she explains, is a sure sign of its inadvisability, while the least deviation from the ideal necessarily disqualifies a prospective spouse. Besides, making the wrong choice might well banish a young bride forever from good society, including her own. Rather than worry about the moment when Robert Martin receives her letter of rejection, Harriet should try to imagine Mr. Elton's private viewing of her portrait. The passage is worth pausing over because it brings into sharp focus the ongoing *paragone* or contest between text and image, with the proposal letter tugging Harriet's sentiments in one direction and Emma's portrait of her in another. Mr. Elton has taken the picture to London for framing, and Emma imagines it as the object of an erotic reverie on his part. She envisions him gazing at it alone before offering it to the view of his nearest and dearest, and so invites Harriet to indulge a reverie of her own. Too precious to be consigned to the framer just yet, Emma says, "The picture will not be in Bond Street till just before he mounts his horse tomorrow. It is his companion all the evening, his solace, his delight. It opens his designs to his family, it diffuses through the party those pleasantest feelings of our nature, eager curiosity and warm prepossession. How cheerful, how animated, how suspicious, how busy their imaginations all are!" (E, 59). The scene is charged to the point of manipulation. Imagining a family to huddle around her portrait would carry a special emotional appeal for an orphan. Like the comparison of Wentworth's letter to Benwick's portrait miniature, the visual-verbal differential elevates the straightforward expression of Robert Martin's letter, which Emma admits is "strong and concise" (E, 53), above the deceptiveness of the painted image. Each object is emblematic of the role that Emma has played in Harriet's life to date. The portrait conjures up the false hope that she is asked to entertain of marrying one man while the proposal letter symbolizes the frustrated plans of another to take her for his bride. We should also notice how poorly Harriet's portrait predicts the ongoing course of romance. Where Martin's letter contains a promise that its author finds a way of keeping, the scene that Emma envisions evaporates into nothing.

A CHARADE OF LOVE

Nor does the visual-verbal interplay end there. As a complement to her portrait, Emma plans a collection of "really good enigmas, charades, or conundrums" (E, 74) that Harriet will copy out for Mr. Elton to admire.[26] The categories name three well-defined kinds of word puzzles. An enigma asks for a simple identification—

> A Word of one syllable, easy and short,
> Read backwards and forwards the same
> It expresses the sentiments warm from the heart
> And to beauty lays principal claim[27]

—and the answer to this one is "Eye." A subset of the enigma is the riddle, which casts the question of identity in the first person, as in these lines taken from a longer example—

> Ye who in riddles take delight,
> Attend to me, a wondrous wight;
> All forms I take that e'er were seen,
> All colours wear, red, brown, blue, green
> Sometimes all loveliness appear,
> Sometimes a monst'rous figure wear;
> Yet in all forms I pleasure give,
> And tho' I'm dead, I seem to live[28]

—where the answer is "A Picture." A conundrum is a question with a punning answer like "Why is the seeing of a Sign a manifest token of Sight? Because it is a Sign you see."[29] Mr. Weston offers a conundrum during the Box Hill episode: "What two letters of the alphabet are there, that express perfection?" (E, 404), and Mark Loveridge has suggested that the answer, M. and A. or Emma, owes to a passage in Francis Hutcheson's *Inquiry into the Original of our Ideas of Beauty and Virtue* (1728) on the need for individuals to produce the greatest public good that they are capable of producing.[30] We can recall it again later.

Austen's family enjoyed playing charades, and one of three surviving examples from Austen's hand runs so:

> You may lie on my first by the side of a stream,
> And my second compose to the nymph you adore,
> But if, when you've none of my whole, her esteem
> And affection diminish—think of her no more![31]

The first two lines describe two words to be combined in the solution "banknote." The charade is succinct in launching its two terms from a single situation. Mr. Elton leaves a charade at Hartfield to be read but not copied, claiming his own reworking of a familiar puzzle as the work of a friend:

> My first displays the wealth and pomp of kings,
> Lords of the earth! Their luxury and ease,
> Another view of man, my second brings,
> Behold him there, the monarch of the seas! (E, 76)

Emma is convinced that it's meant for Harriet. Unfamiliar with charades, Harriet obeys the deictic imperative only to descry a figure of Neptune. She also admires its length, unaware that a short charade is better than a long one, and in her innocence again raises the question of proportion.

In sorting the charade into its parts, a contemporary pamphlet draws a sharp contrast to the logical syllogism. The charade "consists of three Members—not in Imitation—but in Ridicule of the dull Syllogism of old," we read: "Yet it still resembles the antique in this Respect, that as the Conclusion is drawn from the two premises in the logical Fabrick,—so in the charade the last Member is formed of the foregoing two, and the happy Union of these *two* renders the poignancy of the third more brilliant."[32] The charade compounds two words into a third so that their meanings take on a hidden sense revealed by the imagination, a process the author opposes to syllogistic logic. If we take a major premise like "all rivers have banks" and add a minor premise like "the Itchen is a river," we can conclude that "the Itchen has banks." Where a syllogism includes a distributed middle term like "river," no such rule for the charade applies, and the process of finding a lexical solution depends upon the imagination rather than logic. Mr. Elton's charade has four parts rather than three because it includes the envoi that Emma rightly considers private—

> Thy ready wit the word will soon supply,
> May its approval beam in that soft eye! (E, 76)

8   EMBLEMATA

Seneca.   OPTIMVM AMORIS POCVLVM, VT AMERIS, AMA.

Philoftrat.   *Sume meas, fumam ipfe tuas, mea vita, fagittas;*
              Non aliter nofter conciliatur amor.

Cic.   Nihil minus hominis effe videtur, quàm non refpondere
              in amore ijs, à quibus prouocere.

_____

              A wifhed warre.
              The woundes that louers giue are willingly receaued,
              When with two dartes of loue each hits each others harte,
              Th'ones hurt the others cures and takes away the fmarte,
              So as no one of both is of his wifh bereaued.

                    Reciproco.

              Di reciproche piaghe Amor fi gode;
              Qui fi ferifcon duo leali amanti,
              Et ambo lieti godono ne i pianti,
              Scoccando tienfi l'vn', e l'altro prode.

                                                    GRA-

Figure 5.5. Cornelis Boel, engraved emblem, "A Wished Warre" (text), English trans. Richard Verstegan, from Otto van Veen, *Emblemata Amorum*, 1608, 8. Courtesy of the Huntington Library, Art Galleries, and Botanical Gardens, San Marino, CA.

—but otherwise performs according to Hoyle with the first two lines naming the first syllable of the nominal compound (*court-*) and the second two lines the second syllable (*-ship*), giving the answer *courtship*. Emma guesses it right away.

The intersection of word and image here also recalls the emblem or impresa of the two prior centuries,[33] with its symbolic interrelation of three parts, an image, a motto, and an explanation. An example from Otto van Veen's *Amorum Emblemata* depicts a pair of cupids in the happy combat of reciprocal love, the motto tells us, while the explanation turns upon the give and take of human affection (Figures 5.5 and 5.6).

The references include Seneca, who says that in order to be loved one must first show love (in the form quoted, "*ut ameris, ama,*" the commonplace actually belongs to Martial); to Philostratus the Elder, who gives us the image of two cupids shooting one another with love darts; and to Cicero, who maintains that

Figure 5.6. Cornelis Boel, engraved emblem, "A Wished Warre" (image), English trans. Richard Verstegan, from Otto van Veen, *Emblemata Amorum*, 1608, 9. Courtesy of the Huntington Library, Art Galleries, and Botanical Gardens, San Marino, CA.

nothing becomes us less as humans than an inability to respond to the challenge of affection.[34] Emma ignores these lessons of reciprocity but borrows their symbolic aspect in encouraging Harriet to read the courtship charade as a coded plea from Mr. Elton. The *impresa* or emblem tradition was from the outset chivalric, a "philosophy of the knight" that became popular by virtue of its "socially useful ambiguity and capacity for guarded revelations," according to Robert Klein.[35] In some writers the impresa represents what Klein calls the "intellectual intuition"[36] of a perfect Neoplatonic knowledge. Emma intuits a hidden request in just this way. "'Pray, Miss Smith, give me leave to pay my addresses to you,'" she translates the envoi for Harriet. "'Approve my charade and my intentions in the same glance'" (E, 76).

Emma regards the charade as a sure sign of future nuptials, going on at great length about the matter. "There is so pointed, and so particular a meaning in this compliment," she intones in the manner of an oracle, that I cannot have a moment's doubt as to Mr. Elton's intentions. You are his object—and you will soon receive the completest proof of it. I thought it must be so. I thought I could not be so deceived; but now, it is clear; the state of his mind is as clear and decided, as my wishes on the subject have been ever since I knew you. Yes, Harriet, just so long have I been wanting the very circumstance to happen which has happened. I could never tell whether an attachment between you and Mr. Elton were most desirable or most natural. Its probability and its eligibility have really so equalled each other! I am very happy. I congratulate you, my dear Harriet, with all my heart. This is an attachment which a woman may well feel pride in creating. (E, 78)

Emma believes what she says and tests it against her doubts only to find her judgment correct. The situation is ripe with comic misdirection, and Mr. Elton becomes so puffed up with pride that he provokes Emma to muffled laughter, while Harriet can only marvel at his inscrutably abstruse wit and his choice of her of all people to love. The larger puzzle is what could have possessed our heroine to place her two friends in such a false position.

Part of the answer rests in Emma's artistic or writerly temperament. The narrator goes on to characterize Emma as an "imaginist," that is, someone "on fire with speculation and foresight" (E, 362). Emma confuses speculation—and here we should grant the word its full range of meaning from vision to uncertainty to mercantile revaluation[37]—with genuine foresight. If sympathy is the imaginative transfer of another person's situation into our own, what Adam Smith calls "fellow-feeling,"[38] then Emma is an unsympathetic character for much of the narrative. In place of compassion she practices the imaginative projection of her present feelings onto what she might be expected to feel in the future. When Frank Churchill attracts her attention, she tests the limits of her affection by devising romantic scenarios that never fail to relapse into mere friendship. The practice involves a distinct visual-verbal aspect. "Pleasing as he was," she might think "as she sat drawing or working, forming a thousand amusing schemes for the progress and close of their attachment, fancying interesting dialogues, and inventing elegant letters; the conclusion of every imaginary declaration on his side was that she *refused him*" (E, 284; italics original). She declines his imaginary proposals because neither party requires of the other the self-sacrifice needed for genuine mutual affection. If the step is a positive one, her motive for promoting the attachment of Mr. Elton to Harriet seems by contrast personal, owing either to resentment of the emotional demands made by her father or a misplaced sense of duty. The same motive makes itself known in her defensiveness about social rank, whether directed at Harriet's worthy suitor or the upstart Coles, and also leads to the wild supposition of a liaison between Jane Fairfax and Mr. Dixon.

More to the point, a prior share of error owes to the elitist visual discourse Emma adopts, a point of view so dated that it necessarily envisions a counterfactual future. Well before anyone thinks of portraiture, we hear Mr. Elton praising Emma for the improvements she has made in her docile companion, commending above all Harriet's newfound "decision of character" (E, 44). Harriet displays all the decisiveness of a marionette, of course, and Mr. Elton only repeats the ill-judged phrase after Emma, the emphasis hinting at larger comic stakes. "Skilful has been the hand," he adds (E, 44), an allusion to Psalms 78:72: "So he fed them according to the integrity of his heart; and guided them by the skilfulness of his hand." Elton pays extravagant tribute to Emma's grooming of her young charge by likening it to the stewardship of King David in safeguarding Israel from its enemies. It's the sort of thing a gallant country parson might say to his intended bride[39] if he were looking forward to a time when their hands could be joined together in the spiritual and material care of a shared flock. So it's not surprising to see Mr. Elton following after Emma on an errand of charity a few chapters later. For the moment she answers simply, "Great has been the pleasure," acknowledging the compliment before adding, "I never met with a disposition more truly amiable" (E, 44). Mention of the word *disposition* leads by association to the plan of taking Harriet's likeness.

FROM DISPOSITION AND DESIGN . . .

It also rings a bell. Emma means the word to denote her friend's engaging personality or temper, but its use earlier reminds us of her own tendency to think too well of herself. In the opening sentence, the word names the blessing of a contented temperament or "happy disposition" only to denote a few sentences later what the narrator calls the evil of a slight inclination, once again a "disposition," toward conceit (E, 3).[40] The suggestion is that our personal temperament and situation in life should be viewed as a divine gift, and that a tendency toward pride should be seen as the all-too-human sin of its misuse. An unspoken corollary is that when brought to our attention, the error should be corrected. The same word has a long history in baroque painting as a synonym for the linear outline or design of a picture, meaning both the preliminary charcoal sketch and again the finished arrangement of the whole. The English word *design* substitutes for the Latin *dispositio* in naming the middle stage of a three-part part visual rhetoric: *inventio, dispositio,* and *elocutio.* Sir Joshua Reynolds instructs the aspiring painter to cultivate an idea of beauty leading to the creation of a "correct and perfect design."[41] The mannerist painter Federico Zuccaro grants disposition or *disegno* a supernatural aspect, so that it becomes a *segno di Dio in noi* or a sign of God in ourselves.[42] As an artist figure, Emma affects powers little short of godlike, assuming with her father that the universe radiates outward from Hartfield. She tells Harriet that by accepting Mr. Elton she will move toward "the centre of all your real friends, close to Hartfield and to me, and confirm our intimacy for ever" (E, 79). Inevitably, her plans go awry. The larger design never reflects the initial sketch, or as the narrator puts it when Emma brings out her family portraits, the least finished are often the best (E, 46). Eventually, Emma's friendship with Harriet runs its course.

Emma stages the comic release of an individual awakening[43] as a movement away from the covert symbolism of a closed caste toward a more open social order. Even as the novel mocks the matchmaker-as-painter metaphor, it recognizes the just proportion necessary to human arrangements. The decentering of authority at the close offers a compromise proportional to the wishes of the principals, preferences reflected in the new arrangements. Knightley's move to Hartfield answers the motives of Mr. Woodhouse for security, of Emma for her father's well-being, and of Knightley for Emma's happiness and his own. Francis Hutcheson calls the power to enable the larger good "moral Beauty" and describes social virtue as "a compound Ratio of the Quantity of Good, and the Number of Enjoyers."[44] According to Hutcheson, Emma could never be the solitary model of perfection that Mr. Weston claims because benevolence is a social virtue. If Emma's generosity is subject to individual limits, her ability to promote the general good is redoubled by her marriage to Knightley. The same holds true for the union of Harriet Smith and Robert Martin, and also of Jane Fairfax and Frank Churchill, allowing for their limitations of rank and temperament. In theory Hutcheson's system is not conducive to privilege. In practice the boundaries of social rank prove neither firm enough to preclude Emma from inviting Robert Martin and his bride to Hartfield nor porous enough to allow Emma to continue to socialize with Harriet as an intimate. The prime social model for the exercise of benevolence is the family. Its finest instance is probably the fraternal love of John and George Knightley, a "real attachment which would have led either . . . to do everything for the good of the other" (E, 107), as Austen puts it.

Hutcheson was among the first to argue that comedy derives not from superiority, as Hobbes had thought, but rather from incongruity. Something happens that confirms our expectation of a character or event, he explains, and that at the same differs surprisingly from it.[45] When the comic target remains ignorant of the surprise, the humor only intensifies. Harriet's unexpected confidence that Mr. Knightley returns her affection is a case in point, and so is Knightley's doleful commiseration with Emma over the loss of Frank Churchill. Comic errors like these not only prove harmless, a comedic constraint dating to Aristotle, but actually lead to the good. If Harriet hadn't disclosed her newfound ambition, then Emma might never have known love, and if Emma hadn't revealed her tepid feelings toward Churchill, then Knightley might never have declared his own. Emma keeps the new emotion and its subjective revelations resolutely to herself, hiding them from Harriet and even from Knightley. The reader knows all too well her secret history of self-abnegation, of course, and the knowledge renders the proposal of Knightley lambent with what the novel calls the "glow of attendant happiness" (E, 469), a light gradually if unequally diffused over the others. A wider view of agency might see Knightley and Harriet quietly conspiring to bring Martin back into the picture. Emma discerns a certain tone of "resentment" (E, 492) in her correspondence with Harriet, understandably enough, and Knightley may well have done more matchmaking in London than he admits since he clearly expects Emma to disapprove. Reading against the narrative grain in this way heightens the realism without lessening the comedy.

Harriet by contrast lacks the newfound psychological awareness of Emma. In chapter 40 she opens the reliquary labeled "*most precious treasures*" (E, 366) to show Emma two objects associated with Mr. Elton before consigning them to the flames to seal the end of infatuation. Sacrifice is an act of propitiation as well as banishment, and Harriet seeks Emma's help in attracting another suitor, someone she declines to name. Emma thinks she may have her sights set on Frank Churchill, but of course Harriet has Knightley in mind. The pair of relics are a "court plaister" (E, 368), or decorative bandage, and a pencil stub. Surprised to find that her friend has kept them, Emma inspects the objects for their usefulness and notes that while the pencil lacks its lead, the bandage might still prove handy. Fetishes of imagined affection, the objects also symbolize the empty union of image and text, and they align the discourse of design with superstitious imposture. The episode is reflected in the BBC *Emma* when Harriet appropriates the pencil stub during the portrait episode, as we've seen, and in *Clueless* when Tai consigns a towel used by Elton to the fireplace, but neither film registers the visual-verbal turn from mystery to utility as a marked thematic shift.

. . . TO THE EMPIRICAL IMAGE

Most readers will think of the visual field of *Emma* in terms of the detailed view that Emma beholds from the window of Ford's shop as she waits for Harriet to finish a purchase midway through volume two. There may be a hint that Harriet dallies in hopes of again running into the Martins, but if so, Emma is oblivious. The passage represents Highbury as a broad canvas with its inhabitants so many figures moving in dynamic social relation to one another, and it has attracted commentary enough to preclude quotation.[46] Emma is literally at a crossroads. She will be joined by Mrs. Weston and Frank Churchill and will accompany them to Mrs. Bates's rather than go directly back to Hartfield. Austen sketches in Highbury with a few well-chosen gerundive clauses describing the townsfolk in motion. Emma observes them in her mind's eye as they have always appeared to her, and then again as they appear now before her as sense impressions, until she finally finds the difference negligible. The dogs she observes growling over a scrap from the butcher are strays, not the hounds of Diana. Where the academic discourse of painting typically avoids the representation of commerce, Emma beholds the mercantile scene with pleasure and so arrives at another kind of crossroads, taking an aesthetic turn toward empirical realism.

It's not difficult to imagine a verbal discourse to complement Emma's new vision. All we need do is to turn over the coin of secrecy. The novel looks forward to social improvement. Like crops ready for harvest, meaning in language should be gleaned from the surface of utterance, as when the brothers Knightley discuss the rotation of "wheat, turnips, or spring corn" (E, 107) by way of increasing the yield per acre on the family farm. Practical discourse should reach its end by the most direct route, avoiding divagation into the realm of fancy, as when the brothers decide to reroute the "path to Langham" across the fields (E, 114; and just one of a surprising number of roads, pathways, and walkways mentioned in *Emma*). As a guide to the future, the narrative provides readers with Robert Martin, who does much more to improve the general well-being than would be expected from someone of his background, being obliging to Harriet, indispensable to Knightley, and polite to Emma. He manages his acreage well enough to marry young, and like Hardy's Jude is a great reader. According to Harriet, among the books he enjoys reading aloud is *Elegant Extracts*, a compilation of uplifting texts aimed at the young. Austen's family owned an annotated copy, and under the heading "Benevolence and Humanity," we find an excerpt from Hugh Blair marked for special attention:

> Let a sense of justice be the foundation of all your social qualities. In your most early intercourse with the world, and even in your youthful amusements, let no unfairness be found. Engrave on your mind that sacred rule, of 'doing in all things to others, according as you wish that they should do unto you.' For this end, impress yourselves with a deep sense of the original natural equality of men. Whatever advantages of birth or fortune you possess, never display them with an ostentatious superiority.[47]

These axioms affirm the Golden Rule, the universal principle of treating one's neighbor as oneself despite accidental differences,[48] of course. They shine a light into the dark corners of exclusion and secrecy, and the Austen family copy brackets them with emphatic X's.[49] On meeting the Martin family, Emma likes them well enough to wish that they held a higher rank (E, 201). In the same vein, Knightley tells Emma that if he could change Martin's rank, he would (E, 516). Treating others with the fairness of a considered reciprocity is vital in a world where even a respected family like the Westons requires "two or three generations" to rise into "gentility and property" (E, 13). It lessens the burden of condescension, promotes civility in competition, and through cooperation renders individual excellence or advantage a blessing to society at large. Emma becomes the comic target of the narrative so long as she seeks to "arrange everybody's destiny" (E, 449) while neglecting her own. She awakens from the dream of one visual culture to the reality of another, learning along the way to substitute plain speech for symbolic codes. Meanwhile, the still-silent but no-longer-invisible Robert Martin is able to add Harriet to his family circle, making him the unlikely wit pointing the social moral.[50]

NOTES

1. L, 350.
2. In several interviews, Robert J. Thompson has suggested that *Fast Times at Ridgemont High* sets the free-spirited Jeffersonianism of Jeff Spicoli against the centralized federalism of Brad Hamilton. See Amy M. Braverman, "Culture Jock," *University of Chicago Magazine* 98, no. 2 (2005), http://magazine.uchicago.edu/0512/features/thompson.shtml (accessed May 18, 2018).
3. A selective list would extend from the BBC television series (1995) through the Bollywood musical *Bride and Prejudice* (2004), and the Joe Wright adaptation the following year to the Bridget Jones films (2001, 2004, and 2016); and *Pride and Prejudice and Zombies* (2016).
4. In Timothy Erwin, *Textual Vision: Augustan Design and the Invention of Eighteenth-Century British Culture* (Lewisburg, PA: Bucknell University Press, 2015), 6–11 passim. The discourse of design looks back to the formal metaphor linking the temporal unfolding of narrative to the spatial arrangement of painting. Its prime text is C. A. DuFresnoy, *De arte graphica* (1668), a verse tribute to the practice of the Carracci academy treating the art of painting under the rhetorical headings of invention, design, and coloring.
   The basic resource for studying design in art history is Rensselaer W. Lee, *Ut Pictura Poesis: The Humanistic Theory of Painting* (New York: W. W. Norton 1967), esp. Appendix 2, "*Inventio, Dispositio, Elocutio,*" 264–65; and in literary study, Jean H. Hagstrum, *The Sister Arts: the Tradition of Literary Pictorialism and English Poetry from Dryden to Gray* (Chicago: University of Chicago Press, 1958). See also my "*Ut Rhetorica Artes*: The Rhetorical Theory of the Sister Arts," in *Haydn and the Performance of Rhetoric*, ed. Tom Beghin and Sander M. Goldberg (Chicago: University of Chicago Press, 2007), 61–79.
5. Or "scopic regime," as Martin Jay calls the visual equivalent of verbal discourse; see his "Scopic Regimes of Modernity," in *Vision and Visuality*, ed. Hal Foster (Seattle: Bay Press, 1988), 3–23; and also Martin Jay, "Scopic Regimes of Modernity Revisited," in *Essays from the Edge: Parerga and Paralipomena* (Charlottesville: University of Virginia Press, 2011), 51–63.
6. William Galperin, "Adapting Jane Austen: the Surprising Fidelity of *Clueless,*" *Wordsworth Circle* 42, no. 3 (Summer 2011): 187–93.

7. The discourse of the image is the response of British empiricism to the discourse of design. It replaces the formal analogy of perspective and arrangement to plot with a linguistic analogy of vivid description or striking figuration to visual coloring. Among its prime values is the novelty of Addison: "Every thing that is *new* or *uncommon* raises a Pleasure in the Imagination, because it fills the Soul with an agreeable Surprise, gratifies its Curiosity, and gives it an Idea of which it was not before possest. We are, indeed, so often conversant with one Sett of Objects, and tired out with so many repeated Shows of the same Things, that . . . it serves us for a kind of Refreshment, and takes off from that Satiety we are apt to complain of in our usual and ordinary Entertainments" (Joseph Addison, *The Spectator*, ed. Donald F. Bond [Oxford: Clarendon Press, 1965], no. 412, 3: 541).

8. Or as John Dryden renders the Latin of the *De arte graphica*: "Nothing deadens so much the Composition of a Picture, as Figures which are not appertaining to the Subject: We may call them pleasantly enough, *Figures to be let*" (*Prose 1691–1698*, ed. George R. Guffey et al. in *The Works of John Dryden*, gen. ed. H. T. Swedenberg, Jr., assoc. gen. ed. George R. Guffey, text ed. Vinton A. Dearing (Berkeley and Los Angeles: University of California Press, 1989), 133–34.

9. Marshall Brown raises the question in "Emma's Depression," *Studies in Romanticism* 53, no. 1 (2014): 3–29. Brown attributes the psychology of depression in part to the economic isolation of Highbury. He surveys a variety of critical opinion, including Tony Tanner, *Jane Austen* (Cambridge, MA: Harvard University Press, 1986), in support of the view that *Emma* is a dark comedy.

10. See, for example, Lord George Gordon Byron, *Don Juan*, in *The Complete Poetical Works*, ed. Jerome McGann (Oxford: Clarendon Press, 1986), vol. 5, canto 3, stanza 9, lines 65–66: "All tragedies are finished by a death, / All comedies are ended by a marriage."

11. Stuart M. Tave, *The Amiable Humorist: A Study in the Comic Theory and Criticism of the Eighteenth and Early Nineteenth Centuries* (Chicago: University of Chicago Press, 1960). Tave borrows the term "amiable humorist" from Lord Kames to show how risible rather than ridiculous character types like Fielding's Parson Adams and Goldsmith's vicar of Wakefield replace the comic foils of the Restoration (see passim, esp. 96–105).

12. Brown, "Emma's Depression," 11.

13. Quadrille was a trick-taking game based on ombre, the card game played in Pope's *Rape of the Lock*, and by Austen's time had become old-fashioned. In *Pride and Prejudice*, Lady Catherine de Bourgh plays quadrille with Mr. and Mrs. Collins and Sir William Lucas, while her daughter's younger set plays the fishing game casino. See further "Q. Quanti," *The Game of Quadrille* (Cheltenham: G. A. Williams, 1822).

14. George and Weedon Grossmith, *The Diary of a Nobody* (London: J. W. Arrowsmith, 1892). Penned by the two brothers who founded the humor magazine *Punch*, and ostensibly the daily record of one Charles Pooter, the narrative makes high comedy of the lowly social visit.

15. In *Character and Conflict in Jane Austen's Novels* (Detroit: Wayne State University Press, 1978), Bernard J. Paris describes Emma's personality type as egotistical: "*Emma* is the story of a young woman with both narcissistic and perfectionistic trends . . . induced by her early environment" (73). On this view her narcissism leads her to avoid marriage, her perfectionism owes to a sense of guilt about falling short in the support of her dependent father, and her insulting of Miss Bates betrays unconscious resentment of her father.

Alan Richardson explores the psychological play of gaze, gesture, and expression in *Emma* by using a cognitive neuroscience called Theory of Mind to trace the implicit emotional interaction among the various characters. See *The Neural Sublime: Cognitive Theories and Romantic Texts* (Baltimore: Johns Hopkins University Press, 2010), 79–96.

16. In a succinct history of the realist novel as represented by Austen, James Thompson, in *Models of Value: Eighteenth-Century Political Economy and the Novel* (Durham, NC and Lon-

don: Duke University Press, 1996), describes a basic "dialectic between the self and the world" that is "the consequence of alienation, the objectification of social relations under capital" (193). The passage where Emma explains never having noticed Robert Martin makes the point: "A young farmer, whether on horseback or on foot, is the very last sort of person to raise my curiosity. The yeomanry are precisely the order of people with whom I feel I can have nothing to do. . . . A farmer can need none of my help, and is therefore in one sense as much above my notice as in every other he is below it" (E, 29). See also Elsie Michie, "Austen's Powers: Engaging with Adam Smith in Debates about Wealth and Virtue," *Novel* 34, no. 1 (2000): 5–27.

17. In *Jane Austen: Women, Politics, and the Novel* (Chicago: University of Chicago Press, 1988), Claudia L. Johnson writes that what "makes Emma unusual . . . is that she is a woman who possesses and enjoys power, without bothering to demur about it" (125). See also *Jane Austen and Discourses of Feminism*, ed. Devoney Looser (New York: St. Martin's, 1995), esp. Laura Mooneyham White, "Jane Austen and the Marriage Plot: Questions of Persistence," 71–86.

18. *The Collected Writings of Thomas De Quincey*, ed. David Masson (London: A. & C. Black, 1896–1897), vol. 6, 251.

19. Mario Praz, *Mnemosyne: The Parallel Between Literature and the Visual Arts* (London: Oxford University Press, 1970), 7.

20. *Clueless*, directed by Amy Heckerling (1995; Hollywood, CA: Paramount Home Entertainment, 2005), DVD. Cher mentions painters on two occasions, the second time as she and Tai spot their friend Amber at a party dancing with Elton. She looks like a "full-on Monet," Cher remarks. "It's like the painting, see," she explains, "from faraway it's ok but up close it's a big old mess." Horace uses the metaphor of viewing distance in the *Ars Poetica* in connection with the well-known phrase *ut pictura poesis*: "A poem is like a picture: one strikes your fancy more, the nearer you stand; another, the farther away," quoted from the Loeb Classical Library, *Satires, Epistles and Ars Poetica*, trans. H. Rushton Fairclough (Cambridge, MA: Harvard University Press, 1966), 481.

21. *Emma*, by Jane Austen, directed by Douglas McGrath (1996; Santa Monica, CA: Miramax Home Entertainment, 1999), DVD.

22. Emma realizes her secure place in Knightley's affection in what Austen describes as a "velocity of thought" (E, 469). For Roland Barthes velocity always figures in the discourse of the lover: "The lover . . . cannot keep his mind from racing, taking new measures and plotting against himself. His discourse exists only in outbursts of language, which occur at the whim of trivial, of aleatory circumstances" (*A Lover's Discourse: Fragments*, trans. Richard Howard, with a foreword by Wayne Koestenbaum [New York: Farrar, Strauss, Giroux, 1978], 3).

23. James Northcote, *The Life of Sir Joshua Reynolds* (London: Henry Colburn, 1818), vol. 1, 83.

24. Sarah Siddons, *Reminiscences of Sarah Kemble Siddons*, ed. with a foreword by William Van Lennep (Cambridge, MA: Widener Library, 1942), 17. C. Fanshawe repeats the claim: "She talked of the portraits that had been made of her, and the painful fatigue several painters gave her by trying a variety of attitudes; while Sir Joshua Reynolds, with whose portrait of her as the Tragic Muse she was alone satisfied, had led her to the chair, and desired her to choose her own position. She immediately placed herself in that which he has so happily adapted" (Appendix to Robert Charles Leslie and Tom Taylor, *Life and Times of Sir Joshua Reynolds* [London: John Murray, 1865], vol. 2, 646). For an acute reading of the performative dimension of the portrait, see Richard Wendorf, *Sir Joshua Reynolds: The Painter in Society* (Cambridge, MA: Harvard University Press, 1996), 153–58.

For a contemporary account of sitting for a portrait, see Martin Gayford, *Man with a Blue Scarf: On Sitting for a Portrait by Lucian Freud* (London: Thames and Hudson, 2010). Gayford sat for Lucien Freud during seven months in 2003–2004: "The tension of working can make LF seem very agitated at times. He gestures . . . like an Italian taxi driver encountering a perplexing configuration of traffic. He steps forward and back, and on occasion darts forward and springs away from the canvas, bringing his mouth down in a one-sided grimace" (69). Austen transfers the painter's agitation in the throes of creation, which must be nearly universal, to Mr. Elton.

25. We can hear her thinking aloud across three narrative modes. Austen uses two versions of free indirect discourse, one quoting the thoughts of Emma indirectly ("Yes, good man! thought Emma . . ."; 45), and the other directly ("'This man is almost too gallant to be in love,' thought Emma"; 51), both referring to Mr. Elton. A third narrative mode, what narratology calls psycho-narration, is heard in her grudging appreciation of Robert Martin's letter writing skills ("The style was much above her expectations"; 53).

26. The charades episode is absent from *Clueless* and serves mainly as the occasion for a quip in the Miramax film. When Knightley complains to Emma that he hasn't been asked to contribute to the collection, the screenplay turns him into a comic foil. "Your entire personality is a riddle," replies Emma. "I thought you overqualified." The BBC *Emma* includes the charades episode without developing it at any length.

27. Quoted from *A New Collection of Enigmas, Charades, Transpositions, Etc.* (London: Hurst, Rees et al., 1810), 2, and cited again in the text.

28. Quoted *New Collection of Enigmas*, 109,

29. Quoted from "Christopher Conundrum," *A Pretty Riddle Book* (London: R. Bassam, 1785?), 58–59.

30. Mark Loveridge, "Francis Hutcheson and Mr. Weston's Conundrum in *Emma*," *Notes & Queries* 30, no. 3 (1983): 214–15. The reference is to the Hutcheson's *Inquiry into the Original of our Ideas of Beauty and Virtue*, 3rd ed. (London: J. and P. Knapton 1729). Hutcheson uses a mathematical theorem to suggest that moral perfection involves a one-to-one ratio where M represents the good to be produced and A represents the ability of the individual to produce it. Assuming these to be equal, M=A represents the moment "when the Being acts to the utmost of his Power for the publick Good," and M/A represents unity or "the Perfection of *Virtue*" (190).

On acrostic play see further Jillian Heydt-Stevenson, "Games, Riddles and Charades" in *The Cambridge Companion to Emma*, ed. Peter Sabor (Cambridge: Cambridge University Press, 2015), 150–65; and Linda Bree, "*Emma*: Word Games and Secret Histories," in *A Companion to Jane Austen*, ed. in Claudia L. Johnson and Clara Tuite (Oxford: Wiley-Blackwell, 2009), 133–42.

31. Jane Austen, *Charades Etc. Written a Hundred Years Ago by Jane Austen and Her Family* (London: Spottiswoode, 1895), 28.

32. "Rondeaulet, Sieur," in *A Treatise on the Charade*, trans. Tobias Rigmerole (London: T. Davies, 1777), 7. A mild satire on modernism, the treatise is useful in describing the way charades were thought to work. The author and translator alike are pseudonymous.

33. "An impresa or device is nothing else than a symbolical representation of a purpose, a wish, a line of conduct (*impresa* is what one intends to *imprendere* (that is, to undertake) by means of a motto and a picture that reciprocally interpret each other," writes Mario Praz in *Studies in Seventeenth-Century Imagery* (Rome: Edizioni di Storia e Letteratura, 1975), 58. The basic difference between an impresa and an emblem is that one reflects the aims of an individual or family while the other speaks to a symbolic truth, Peter M. Daly explains in *Literature in the Light of the Emblem: Structural Parallels between the Emblem*

and Literature in the Sixteenth and Seventeenth Centuries (Toronto: University of Toronto Press, 1979), 23.

34. Otto van Veen, *Amorum Emblemata* (Antwerp: H. Swingenij, 1608), 8; Seneca, *Ad Lucilium Epistulae Morales*, trans. Richard M. Gummere, Loeb Classical Library (Cambridge, MA: Harvard University Press, 1925), vol. 1, 44–45; Martial, *Epigrams*, trans. D. R. Shackleton Bailey, Loeb Classical Library (Cambridge, MA: Harvard University Press, 1993), vol. 2, 8–9; Philostratus, *Imagines*, trans. Arthur Fairbanks, Loeb Classical Library (Cambridge, MA: Harvard University Press, 1936), 22–23; and Cicero, *Letters to Quintus and Brutus*, trans. D. R. Shackleton Bailey, Loeb Classical Library (Cambridge, MA: Harvard University Press, 1972), 244–45. Select emblems from van Veen were translated and reissued by Philip Ayres (1638–1712) as *Cupid's Addresse to the Ladies* (London: R. Bentley, [1683]); and at least twice as *Emblems of Love, in Four Languages*, once by printer Henry Overton (London, 1701?); and again by John Wren (London, 1750?).

35. Robert Klein, *Form and Meaning: Writings on the Renaissance and Modern Art*, trans. Madeline Jay and Leon Wieseltier, foreword Henri Zerner (New York: Viking Press, 1979), 3.

36. Klein, *Form and Meaning*, 22.

37. Johnson's *Dictionary* doesn't give the third sense of mercantile revaluation, but the *Oxford English Dictionary* (*OED*) dates the sense to 1785, citing a letter by Thomas Jefferson, s.v. "speculate."

38. Adam Smith, *Theory of Moral Sentiments*, ed. D. D. Raphael and A. L. MacFie. *The Glasgow Edition of the Works and Correspondence of Adam Smith*, gen. ed. A. S. Skinner (Oxford: Clarendon Press, 1976–1983), vol. 1, 10.

39. Harriet says of Mr. Elton that Miss Nash has "all the texts he has ever preached from" (E, 80), and Psalms 78:72 may well be among them, as readily as it comes to mind. The text was taken for an important midcentury sermon by the Whig bishop John Conybeare commending the good government of George II, and its use here may carry a Whig overtone. In *A Sermon Preach'd before the House of Lords* (Oxford: James Fletcher, 1751), George II is seen in the wake of the Jacobite rebellion of 1745 to deserve the obedience, reverence, and affection of his subjects. Conybeare collapses civic and spiritual obedience so that royalty and divinity enforce a uniform authority. Speaking of the similar roles of prince and pastor, Conybeare says "there is a great Analogy between the Offices belonging to each of these Characters" (6). John Gordon Spaulding lists just two other published sermons taking Psalms 78:72 for their text (*Pulpit Publications 1660–1782*, 6 vols. [New York: Norman Ross, 1996], 3: 77).

40. The words *disposition*, *dispose*, and *disposed* are found a combined thirty times during the course of the novel. *Disposition* is most often used in the general sense of personality or temper and less frequently to mean personal inclination.

41. Sir Joshua Reynolds, *Discourses on Art*, ed. Robert R. Wark (New Haven, CT and London: Yale University Press, 1975), quoted from Discourse three, 49.

42. Quoted in Anthony Blunt, *Artistic Theory in Italy, 1450–1600* (Oxford: Clarendon Press, 1940), 142n1, from Zuccaro, *Idea de' Pittori, Scultori, e Architetti* (Turin, Italy: A. Disserolio, 1607).

43. C. S. Lewis calls the textual feature "undeception" in "A Note on Jane Austen," *Selected Literary Essays*, ed. Walter Hooper (Cambridge: Cambridge University Press, 1969), 177.

44. See Hutcheson, *Inquiry*, 179–80.

45. Francis Hutcheson, *Reflections upon Laughter, and Remarks upon the Fable of the Bees* (Glasgow: Urie, 1750). "That then which seems generally the cause of laughter," Hutcheson says, "is the bringing together of images which have contrary additional ideas, as well as some resemblance in the principal idea: this contrast between ideas of grandeur, dignity, sanctity, perfection, and ideas of meanness, baseness, profanity, seems to be the very spirit

of burlesque; and the greatest part of our raillery and jest is founded upon it" (19). See further Elisabeth Telfer, "Hutcheson's Reflections upon Laughter," *Journal of Aesthetics and Art Criticism 53*, no. 4 (1995): 359–69.

46. Many fine critics have commented on the passage. For Michael Irwin, *Picturing: Description and Illusion in the Nineteenth-Century Novel* (London: Allen & Unwin, 1979), the scene is essentially social: "The enclosed life of the village is seen to involve an elaborate pattern of small reciprocities" (147); for Penny Gay, "*Emma* and *Persuasion*," in *The Cambridge Companion to Jane Austen*, ed. Edward Copeland and Juliet McMaster, 2nd ed. (Cambridge: Cambridge University Press, 2011), the scene is ironic: "Emma is apparently content with her little world—but is she really?" (56); and in *The Cambridge Introduction to Jane Austen*, 2nd ed.; Cambridge: Cambridge University Press, 2015) Janet Todd answers the question in the negative: "The lack of story is in part the subject of *Emma* . . . : life's tedium and how to make it bearable" (102).

47. Vicesimus Knox, *Elegant Extracts: or Useful and Entertaining Passages in Prose Selected for the Improvement of Scholars* (London: Charles Dilly, 1790?), bk.1, 41–42. On Martin's reading and Knox's *Extracts*, see further Susan Allen Ford, "Reading *Elegant Extracts* in *Emma*: Very Entertaining!" *Persuasions Online* 28, no. 1 (Winter 2007), http://www.jasna.org/persuasions/on-line/vol28no1/ford.htm (accessed May 18, 2018). The excerpt is taken from Hugh Blair, *A Sermon on the Duties of the Young* (London and Edinburgh: T. Cadell, Jr., W. Davies, and W. Creech, 1799), qtd. 24–25.

48. In *The Golden Rule* (Oxford and New York: Oxford University Press, 1996), Jeffrey Wattles explores the contexts of the golden rule in the teachings of Confucius, Rabbi Hillel, the New Testament, Augustine, Aquinas, and Luther, among others.

49. Correspondence from Marilyn Francus. I would like to thank Professor Francus for kindly checking the Austen copy of *Elegant Extracts* in the Jane Austen House Museum for the emphasis (the annotation cannot be ascribed to Austen herself).

50. John Mullan points out in *What Matters in Jane Austen: Twenty Crucial Puzzles Solved* (New York: Bloomsbury Press, 2013), that Robert Martin is never actually heard to speak (139–41).

Part Three

COMEDIC FORM, COMEDIC EFFECT

6

ON AUSTEN, COMEDY, AND FUTURE POSSIBILITY

Erin M. Goss

My question eagerly did I renew,
"How is it that you live, and what is it you do?"
—William Wordsworth, "Resolution and Independence"[1]

Baby, the fact that you know that's funny is going to save your whole life.
—Carrie Fisher, *Wishful Drinking*[2]

I N AN ABBREVIATED EXPLORATION OF comedic form called "The Visit: A Comedy in 2 Acts," a very young Jane Austen puts into motion eight characters: four of each sex, and three of each of these unmarried. During the unfolding of the titular visit, these eight characters dine, drink, and engage in nearly content-less conversation, often returning to a recurring joke about a grandmother whose various eccentricities have, for example, left the family with not enough chairs to go around. The drama's odd humor is accentuated by stilted dialogue, and the whole thing concludes at a rather arbitrarily determined moment when it becomes evident that the three unwed couples should, of course, marry one another: "And now my amiable Sophia," says Lord Fitzgerald at a moment no less clearly appropriate than any other in the play, "condescend to marry me" (J, 68). Sophia, of course, says yes; Stanly then asks Cloe, who also says yes. Finally, Miss Fitzgerald, the last remaining unpromised female, says to the last remaining male ("brazenly," according to the *Jane Austen Encyclopedia*[3]), "Since you, Willoughby, are the only one left, I cannot refuse your earnest solicitations—There is my Hand" (J, 68). The stage directions mark the characters' advance to the front of the stage; Lady Hampton, the play's matron, wishes that they may "all be Happy!" and *Finis*.

This brief theatrical exercise, which Penny Gay calls "a deadpan parody of society drama," shows Austen's keen sense of humor in its deployment not only to highlight the absurdity of certain comic situations but also to accentuate the action of comedic form itself.[4] The primary joke of the play appears in its titular status as a comedy that does precisely the thing it is supposed to do and neither any more nor any less. After a brief interlude of hilarity and uproar, in which men sit in women's laps, punnish food is eaten, and absurd grandmothers are revealed to continue to govern everyday life, everyone is married off and the play can end. Written when Austen was barely more than a child, this short, charming, and remarkably odd playlet foreshadows her more mature work by demonstrating her precocious interest in formal expectations and her willingness to engage with and exploit those expectations to produce a good laugh.[5] In that laugh, I will argue, Austen offers a serious contribution to thinking about both comedy's formal expectations and the marriages that are the very core of its plot. "The Visit," that is, anticipates Austen's lifelong interest in both the form and content of comedy.

This essay reads Austen's novels as building on "The Visit" to develop a form of thinking about comedy that crystallizes into a joke continuing throughout her writing career. Readers of this juvenile experiment rightly recognize it as a send-up of the formulaic nature of its contemporary stage productions.[6] However, it also offers a celebration of the rigidity of those productions and an embrace of the laughter that they can produce in their adherence to the arbitrary expectations of formalized plot. Not only do the later novels continue the focus on form that this delightfully absurd theatrical endeavor began, but they, too, I will claim, delight in their exploration of what that form has to offer: a future.

While the rushed and mechanical nature of the early theatrical's insistently matrimonial resolution can be explained by its brevity, Austen's novels also refuse to satisfy a reader's desire for developed portraits of their courtships' consummations. Again and again the novels lead their readers to the moment at which their marriage plots are to culminate, and then, almost as quickly, they leave us trailing beyond them. Often that beyond is quite literally a new place, ever so slightly different from where we started. It is the distance between Barton and Delaford as opposed to a settled site in Sussex, a new and expansive establishment in Derbyshire rather than one filled to capacity in Hertford. Invited into this new space, the reader leaves behind the tantalizing promise of a lavishly illuminated wedding or even an aptly described engagement. Austen's novels disappoint, and though they do end with an appropriate number of marriages—sometimes more but never fewer than one—those marriages are merely announced as facts rather than detailed as part of the narrative.

Noted by many, and featuring prominently in the classroom, where students often lament not getting to "hear what they say" or "at least see them kiss!" the fact of Austen's unrepresented endings forms a crucial aspect of both her style and her inscrutability. Refusing to provide narration of the moments to which the plot has most insistently carried their readers, Austen's texts demand self-awareness when readers want transport; repeatedly, longing for an escape into sympathetic transference, we are instead reminded that we are reading a book. For Lloyd W. Brown, Austen's conclusions are "basically parodic in structure and theme," calling attention as they do to the mechanisms of sentimental plot structure as they report on the book's progress through the plot rather than continue to immerse the reader within it.[7] For readers like Brown, with these emphatically conscious endings, Austen thwarts an understanding of her work as simplistically sentimental; by conforming only in word to the conventions that her plots invoke, Austen asks her readers to think beyond such conventions and to recognize them for the impositions that they are. Similarly, Janis P. Stout reads Austen's reticence to provide culminating visions of romantic bliss as part of her critique of the sentimental conventions that permeate not only the genre of the novel but also acts of everyday language. Rather than an expression of the psychological insecurities and fears of inadequacy cited by critics like Marvin Mudrick, for Stout, Austen's undepicted proposal scenes constitute a "deliberate aesthetic choice" and a "theory of language" that seeks to maintain the sanctity of strong feelings threatened to achieve expression only through sentimental cant.[8] One does not, after all, simply forget to write a love scene.

One can, however, refuse to narrate one. And this, again and again, Austen does. From her early refusal to describe how Edward Ferrars gets from his "errand at Barton" to "the proper resolution" in which he might complete that errand to the opening question of *Persuasion*'s final chapter ("Who can be in doubt of what follows?"), Austen is consistent in her holding back (S&S, 409; P, 270). The primary exception—the engagement of Emma and Knightley—is noteworthy not only for its inarticulate effusiveness ("I cannot make speeches," Knightley proclaims) but for its notable untimeliness (E, 469). What kind of romantic resolution, after all, occurs in the forty-ninth of fifty-five chapters? *Emma* becomes remarkable in the sheer percentage of its pages given up to what should be dénouement. It is not, of course, that Austen's characters don't get paired off, and it is not that those pairings are not announced. Rather, at the moment of their pairing, the moment to which the plot has inexorably led us, the narrator diverges in a tonal shift that reminds us that caring too much about these characters may, after all, be a trifle silly. In *Northanger Abbey*, readers should be unsurprised by the narrator's intervention, given its omnipresence in the narrative that has come before, and yet they might also be startled by the curtness of the narrative dismissal of matrimonial expectation: "Henry and Catherine were married, the bells rang, and everybody smiled" (NA, 261). The wedding was, in short, and as it is in *Emma*, "very much like other weddings" (E, 528).

Though Austen truncates and elides the standard fare of the sentimental novel, she maintains its allegiance with the matrimonial plot on which it depends. To some readers, she maintains that allegiance to her work's detriment. Tony Tanner, for example, laments the "devitalised symmetry" of *Sense and Sensibility* that transforms Marianne into an "automaton which submits to the plans of its relations and joins the social game" as convention overtakes character in the rush to conclusion and resolution; while John Halperin bemoans her "obvious and over-hasty desire, near the ends of her novels, to wrap up loose ends and get the thing over with" as the "mistake Jane Austen makes in all of her books."[9] For other readers, the allegiance to strictly formal necessity is the very point. Pam Perkins, in response to Tanner's critique, claims that Austen's "adherence to conventions is a joke at the expense of both the conventions themselves and the readers who insist that they be observed."[10] The usual oscillation of critical opinion remains: Is Austen too conventional, too governed by standard issue plot devices and readerly expectation? Or, is she a voice of parody, a critic and ironist of the very conventions that she embodies and dances with in her own prose?

In eliding the culminating plot point that determines the plot in its conclusion to have always been headed precisely where it arrives, Austen's novels crystallize the expectations of their form. While it is certainly the case that one looks to Austen for the "enlargement of the courtship and marriage plot into a variable pattern for detailing the growth of successive heroines," that enlargement is possible only because her novels lay out their expectations so very clearly.[11] Austen writes courtship narratives, and courtship narratives that, first and foremost, take the form of comedy, understood not only as part of that "heterogeneous set of loosely-related works whose only common denominator is their use of laughter-eliciting devices," but rather as partaking in a history of the form that places Austen within a particular literary tradition.[12] Within that history, comedy is marked by a temporary uncertainty rectified by the union of those who most deserve to be united; it is a form that revels in mischance and misdirection but settles down finally in the celebration of stable continuity that is announced in the binding of a heterosexual pair who will, assumedly, produce the heirs to the new version of the present. In eliding the courtship's culmination from her comedies, Austen leaves us focused on this form itself. The novels end with marriage not because marriage is itself necessarily the greatest good but because that is what their form dictates, and each novel in its own way reminds its reader of the formal rather than moral necessity of its matrimonial resolution.

In turning to the form of comedy to discuss Austen's novels, I embark upon the somewhat old-fashioned critical endeavor of genre criticism in the hopes of reminding us of something we might have forgotten about Austen's own formalism.[13] I take for my precedents the likes of Joann Ryan Morse,[14] who turns to Shakespeare's comic form in an effort to articulate the specificity of Austen's; or Robert Polhemus, who not only pronounced Austen the writer of comedy but insisted that fact to be the most crucial thing to know about her: "Jane Austen was the first woman to write great comic fiction in the English language. Nothing about her is more important or more original than the comic vision and the sense of humor that *Emma* shows, and no word signifies more in the novel than the last one, 'union.'"[15] Polhemus goes on to clarify this union as the specificity of marriage, which, as he puts it, "has often been to comedy what death is to tragedy."[16] The union so crucial to Austen's vision is not only the one that combines handsomeness, cleverness, and richness into the single body of Emma Woodhouse; it is more crucially the union that unites that single body to another, allegedly in perpetuity. Pairing her characters off in appropriately designated heteronormative marital units, Austen's novels do the very thing that one expects them to do, and the very thing that designates them comedies.

Ian Watt claimed Austen turned to comedy when she found herself with no "established narrative tradition that would serve her turn."[17] By this, rather clearly, Watt does not suggest that Austen only made jokes because no one had written novels quite like hers before, but rather that the generic shape of comedy provided a form within which she could work. Though the fact of Austen's wit has led her to be associated with the comedy of manners, especially as it appears on the Restoration stage with which she was familiar, her novels rarely indulge in the kind of mordant satire and precise typology that one finds in Sheridan, Goldsmith, or even Behn—not to mention the novels' rather more determinedly PG rating. No one who has spent much time with Austen would claim that her characters adhere as strictly to type as they must to populate a universe characterized primarily by manner and mannerism; despite Tanner's critique of Marianne's emergent marriageability, hers are not automata, operating by rule, but individuals, operating by the many minutiae of idiosyncrasy that render them occupants of a moral universe. Though her novels share with the comedy of manners the union that resolves their action, the implications of that resolution vary significantly.

Perhaps the likeliest precedent for Austen, at least as far after the fact as we now are—seeking precedence from the long view of the distant future—is that of Shakespeare himself. Recent work has sought to show the degree to which Austen's reputation and legacy vie only with that of Avon's Bard, and her own fictions remind her reader persistently of his presence within the lives of her characters.[18] Not only in the presence of the "banal Shakespeare" identified by Kate Rumbold and further explored by Megan Taylor, Jane Austen infuses her fictional world with allusions to a Shakespearean universe, and perhaps this is most true in the very nature of her plot structure.[19] For, if his most ardent critics are to be believed, Shakespeare invented the very idea of marital love so key to Austen's moral universe and plot structure alike. "It was Shakespeare," asserts Edward Berry, "who developed the myth of romantic marriage," and he did so as an assertion of form on the formless.[20] Shakespeare's comic plots offer, according to Berry, "a nerve-wracking, potentially dangerous, chaotic, but ultimately re-creative time out of which may emerge the form and meaning of marriage."[21] Though Austen may replace the inchoate danger of chaos with the querulousness of a heroine seeking a moral education, certainly that querulousness—its own form of personal chaos—ends with the insistent affirmation that is each novel's final marriage.

Indeed, in Austen's comedy as in Shakespeare's, we find the "integration of society" that Northrop Frye insists constitutes comedy's "theme."[22] Even more than laughter, for Frye comedy depends on the movement from one society to another, and on the "act[s] of communion with the audience"[23] that make it possible for the new society to be "crystallized on the stage around the hero and his bride."[24] For Frye, as for so many classical notions of comedy, it is masculine desire that propels the plot and masculine prerogative that blocks it. A good hero, driven by good desires, is thwarted in his satisfaction by embodiments of arbitrary law or unexamined lust until eventually the hero succeeds. Comedy moves from the habit and arbitrary law of *pistis* to the pragmatic freedom of *gnosis*, a state of awareness in which desire comes to be governed by self-knowledge and therefore does not have to be given up. Such is the plot, Frye will tell us, of Menander's plays, of most of Shakespeare's comedies, and of the films of Charlie Chaplin. And such, with some significant substitutions, is the plot of Jane Austen's novels, the product of what Peter Knox-Shaw calls "her commitment to an almost uniquely realistic mode of classical comedy" that pits her potentially thwarted heroines against an impersonal social world offering only vaguely dire threats of irrelevance and solitude.[25] The law of this world brings its female characters into being as marriageable women by prodding them not only to come to know themselves but to realize, as Elizabeth Bennet does, that they never have before. If "Reader, I married him" can be imagined as the culminating cry of the marriage plot, "Till this moment, I never knew myself" is the cry of Austen's version of it (P&P, 230).[26]

As comedies, the peak moment of Austen's novels should be the marriages defining their ends both by marking their conclusions and constituting the goal of their plots' trajectories. Austen builds upon the skeleton of the comedic form that she inherits from Shakespeare (or Terence, or Plautus, or Menander) an expansive diegesis that leaves very little undescribed and leads her reader inexorably to the marriages we anticipate from each novel's beginning. Through that diegesis, a reader knows Austen's characters in ways one simply cannot know characters on a stage, or in a novel less invested in their exposure. Yet, those moments of resolution that are most constitutive of Austen's novels as comedies remain unrepresented, as Austen refuses to depict the moments when the union the novel has promised is most assured, either in its moment of being promised (an engagement) or its moment of being consecrated (a wedding). Repeatedly we are led to the culmination and, as Halperin says dismayingly of the conclusion of *Emma*, "the writer avoids the direct depiction of strong feelings; again an ending disappoints."[27] I agree with Lloyd Brown's assessment that these inconclusive conclusions are fundamentally parodic, but I also find in them another aim—perhaps fitting for a comic and ironic mode that asks a reader to understand multiple, perhaps contradictory, things at the same time. Austen's endings ask us to laugh at our own expectations for such endings and invite readers to recognize the sentimental delusions they have come to accept as reality. These undescribed resolutions also offer another simple but crucial result. Denied the pleasure of description, and in fact reminded of that denial, the reader focuses on form. In that form emerges a simple promise: a promise that there is and will be life after the conclusion of this particular story. Insisting on their conclusiveness even as they frustrate the desire to witness their conclusions, Austen's comedies end not by offering a picture of marriage as conclusion but rather by insisting that life carries on after plot complications are resolved.[28] In drawing attention to their status as comedies, they remind a reader of the formulaic nature of the story that a comedy can tell, and they suggest that comedy's conclusions are arbitrary and impermanent. Ultimately, Austen's novels end by insisting on future possibility.

The future toward which Austen directs us is unknown. One thing we can know about it, though, is that in it there will be laughter. And we know that because as each of her novels ends, it asks its readers to laugh. Sometimes it offers a mirror for that laughter in the characters themselves. Such becomes a way to read Elizabeth Bennet's insistence on her own laughter at the end of her novel: "I am happier even than Jane," Elizabeth attests, "she only smiles, I laugh" (P&P, 424). At times such laughter occurs at the expense of characters, as in *Emma*'s concluding jibe at Mrs. Elton's scoff about Emma and Knightley's "extremely shabby" wedding party (to which she herself was not invited) or Lady Catherine's condescension to visit Elizabeth and Darcy at Pemberley, even "in spite of that pollution which its woods had received" through association with the Bennets and Gardiners (E, 528; P&P 430). At other times, laughter emerges at the absurdity of the novel's events. Along these lines, Margie Burns offers a series of tantalizing reminders of the hilariously awkward nature of the future into which many of Austen's characters will enter by imagining Catherine Morland's future holiday dinners with Frederick Tilney, for example, or Elinor and Edward Ferrars' Christmases with their new sister-in-law.[29] While the events themselves inspire laughter, we are also invited to laugh at the likelihood that we have not made the proper sense of them; that is, we are invited to laugh at the absurdity of our own quest for signification. The quippy narrator of *Northanger Abbey*, in concluding the novel by refusing to describe the marriage of the heroine-who-is-not-a-heroine, also makes a joke on the Gothic convention that transmutes plot into meaning. In leaving "it to be settled by whomsoever it may concern, whether the tendency of this work be altogether to recommend parental tyranny, or reward filial disobedience," *Northanger Abbey*'s narrator asks us to laugh at the very idea that there could have been a lesson in this novel, or that we might have even known for whom such a lesson could have been intended (NA, 261).[30] The reader is invited to find herself like Marianne, another object of laughter on account of her "extraordinary fate" of coming to "discover the falsehood of her own opinions" (S&S, 429). And just as our laughter at Marianne is tempered by the affection the narrator has developed for her, we are invited to treat our own misunderstandings similarly kindly.

The apparent exceptions to the rule of laughing endings are those novels that form the exceptions to so many rules about Austen's novels. First, *Mansfield Park*, with its apparently rather straight-faced conclusion, and second, *Persuasion*, the only of Austen's novels to leave her readers suspended in the possibility of future threat, seem to resist a claim about concluding laughter. These two seem singularly uninvested, at least at first glance, in embarking upon a future marked by mirth. After all, the primary laughing character in *Mansfield Park* is the ever-suspect and ultimately unrepentant Mary Crawford, whose laughter is rather transparently often aimed at an effort to "laugh off her feelings"—that most Austenian crime of inauthenticity and self-delusion (MP, 264). And who remembers anyone laughing in *Persuasion*? One of the few mentions of the phenomenon comes from the sickly Mary, who complains to Anne that her neighbors the Misses Musgrove "talk and laugh a great deal too much for me"—hardly a ringing endorsement of either party (P, 41).

Both *Mansfield Park* and *Persuasion*, though, include the same acceleration of plot found in the other four completed novels. The entirety of *Mansfield Park*'s culminating romance is contained in a single paragraph, in which the narrator "purposely abstain[s] from dates on this occasion, that every one may be at liberty to fix their own, aware that the cure of unconquerable passions, and the transfer of unchanging attachments, must vary much as to time in different people.—I only intreat every body to believe that exactly at the time when it was quite natural that it should be so, and not a week earlier, Edmund did cease to care about Miss Crawford, and became as anxious to marry Fanny, as Fanny herself could desire" (MP, 544). While it may not be a laugh-out-loud sort of funny, this conclusion offers the same joke that has been made in *Sense and Sensibility*, in *Northanger Abbey*, in *Pride and Prejudice*, and in "The Visit," and that will go on to be made in *Emma* and indeed in *Persuasion*. The joke is both on and for the reader, pointing out a desire for consummation and culmination that cannot be satisfied and that thus will only be whetted. Along with all the invitations to laughter listed above, each novel asks its reader to indulge in a laugh at the pretense that they could be surprised by the conclusion they should have expected all along.

Despite more difficulty locating its humor, of Austen's novels none falls more directly in line with a theory of comedy like Northrop Frye's than *Mansfield Park*. Fundamentally a novel of geography, *Mansfield Park* demonstrates, as does *Sense and Sensibility*, comedy's formal dependence on being able to mark its beginnings and ends not only through marriage but also through a difference between an initial stable situation that begins the plot and a final stable situation that concludes it.[31] Whereas the earlier novel, however, traces the movement from one location (Sussex) to another (the road from Barton to Delaford), the latter begins and ends in (or near) Mansfield Park, as the estate acquires first one mistress and then another. Nothing in Austen's novels more directly embodies Frye's comic theme of "the integration of society"[32] than the beginning and ending at Mansfield Park that allows oversight of the estate to transfer from a manor house governed by a mistress brought there through happenstance to a parsonage governed by a mistress who arrives there as if through the machinations of nature itself. Lady Bertram, laughably indolent and endearingly vapid, becomes the lady of Mansfield Park only because she possessed, as the opening sentence tells us, "the good luck to captivate Sir Thomas Bertram" by means of which captivation she was elevated in fortune (MP, 3). Through the movement of its plot, *Mansfield Park* concludes with a marriage offered up as fulfilling a logic that goes beyond the circumstantiality of the luck of Miss Maria Ward of Huntingdon. Edward, after all, turned to Fanny "exactly at the time that it was natural that it should be so," and the home they are to occupy together "complete[s] the picture of good" with which the novel concludes (MP, 547). And yet, even within this picture of integration remains the residue of the novel's opening chance. After all, Edmund and Fanny would have no Parsonage at which to reintegrate and establish a better society were it not for the perhaps too timely death of Dr. Grant, who shuffles off this mortal coil "just after" and by no means *before* Fanny and Edmund "had been married long enough to begin to want an increase of income, and feel their distance from the paternal abode an inconvenience" (MP, 547). One of the subtle jokes of Austen's darkest novel is thus that the second society that offers the concluding moral vision of Mansfield Park remains dependent on the arbitrary luck that determines its opening. While not the sort of humor that characterizes the jubilant ends of the

Dashwoods' or the Bennets' tales, its dark wryness nevertheless leads a reader to a kind of laughter, even if only in recognition of the absurdity of luck's perfection.

Persuasion, too, ends with a joke on the reader who persists in desiring to see its romance plot come to a conclusion. "Who can be in doubt of what followed?" the narrator asks to open the novel's final chapter (P, 270). Who indeed could doubt that what would follow would be the very thing the form had promised: the twice-denied culmination of the love of Anne Elliot and Captain Wentworth—denied first to them and then to the reader. And yet, it is within the unconcluded storylines of *Persuasion* that one finds some of Austen's most ridiculous futures. It is the imagined future of *Persuasion* that provides Margie Burns with her key example of Austen's "loose ends": "one can but imagine the future family gathering that brings Mrs. William Elliot, formerly Mrs. Clay, and her husband together with Mrs. Frederick Wentworth and Miss Elliot" (P, 238). There is a joke here, even if it is embedded only in an imagined future that readers must carry on themselves.

If Austen's novels end by insisting on their comedic form, they thus do so twice over. They draw attention to the fact of a form that promises a future insofar as comedy's culminating marriages insist on a world to come, and they provide an opening into that future that is characterized first and foremost by laughter. The future Austen gives us is a future in which we may, and perhaps even must, laugh. The connection between these two observations about Austen's comedy is not incidental. In reflecting on form to generate a reminder of the future, Austen invites an acknowledgment of future uncertainty even as the end of her comedy seems to insist on final knowledge. (Though one might ask what could be more certain than marriage, after all, one would likely have to ask it with a wink.) Though *Persuasion*'s conclusion with its suggested tax of quick alarm seems to leave the future open in ways that Austen's other novels do not, an attention to Austen's interest in the form of comedy reminds us that all of her novels end with an investment in the future. Indeed, in their refusal to provide conclusive knowledge of the last present the novel could describe they suggest that our attention might be best directed to that future itself. It is not only in *Persuasion* that the future remains uncertain, at least insofar as the minute details of a life to come cannot be known. It is in those minute details, after all, that a life is lived.

Ultimately, even as they direct our attention to an unknown future, each of the six completed novels also ends with a call for laughter, as each produces a joke at which a reader is invited to laugh. While never clear on whom or what exactly this joke might be, it is always clear for whom the joke is told. It is for us, for any who are willing to laugh at it and to allow that laughter to carry them into a future. As Austen invites us to imagine an unknowable future, she thus also adjures us to laugh—itself an invitation to embody and inhabit what may be an unchartable psychosocial landscape. For while we may all be able to recognize the moments when we do laugh, a dip into an effort to describe and define laughter can quickly disabuse us of any notion that we know what we're doing when we do it.

Generally understood via three main explanatory strains of thought, laughter ultimately thwarts efforts to categorize and explain it with any real neatness, even despite the promise that the existence of three distinct strains seems to offer. In the first line of thinking and perhaps the most commonly accepted one, laughter is an act of aggression and malice. For Plato, for example, laughter stems from the specific pleasure taken in the misfortunes of others, especially those with less power than the laugher.[33] For Aristotle, whose treatise on comedy was of course lost (to be discovered briefly as a key element of Umberto Eco's *Name of the Rose* before being lost even there in fire), a joke is "a kind of abuse" and is to be avoided by the "sophisticated gentleman . . . as a sort of law unto himself."[34] Both Plato and Aristotle provide a prehistory for the sense of laughter bequeathed to the Western world by Thomas Hobbes, for whom laughter emerges as the "sudden glory" of experiencing superiority over another; the "triumph" of feeling one's own situation rise at the expense of another's derogation or diminishment produces a state that Hobbes, in his way, calls "joy," and this "joy" subsequently causes laughter.[35] Hobbesian laughter is aggressive and violent, the natural explosion of a species as nasty and brutish as humanity.

Aggression and violence are, of course, not the only ways to understand a propensity to laugh, and thinkers like Immanuel Kant offer a second way in to thinking about laughter. Laughter, for Kant, emerges as a result of absurdity, or the thwarting of expectation. Rather like the experience of the sublime for Kant, laughter provides an intellectual and even bodily experience that trains the subject to rely less on his or her expectations, and thus expands the subject's capacity to experience the world. Laughter emerges when "a tense expectation" is caused to "suddenly vanish, transformed to nothing," when the perceiving subject realizes she has been deceived by a supposed understanding of the world as she had found it.[36] Such may be the result, suggests Kant, of seeking to lift something assumed to be very heavy and finding it featherlight; such may also be the case, we might note, of expecting to find elaborate wedding scenes or emotionally charged celebrations of love and finding instead a sardonic narrator reminding us of our own presumptions.

Laughter, finally, is often understood through its production of certain forms of release, or relief. For some, that release is psychological, a circumventing of the Freudian superego, for example; for others, like Herbert Spencer, laughter provides a physiological reprieve intrinsically tied to physical health. Laughter releases energy; it lets off proverbial steam.

I include these three possible explanations of laughter largely out of duty, for including the three strains of explanation is simply what one does when discussing laughter. Nevertheless, I agree with Mary Beard that laughter remains "much messier" than the existence of three more or less persistently consistent strains would have any of us believe.[37] Also like Mary Beard, I seek to "preserve some of this disorder," insisting that laughter is "a messier rather than a tidier subject" than predecessors may have claimed.[38] This messiness is as true of Austen's laughter as it is of any.

Just as there have been few critics taking up the relationship of Austen to her chosen form of comedy, there have also been surprisingly few who have directly addressed her representation or production of laughter. When they have taken it up, more often than not they have aligned Austen with the aggressive drive for superiority that emerges in a Hobbesian notion of laughter. The variant seems to be whether they find that aggressivity to contain "a flavor of humour which robs [it] of ill-nature," as does William James Dawson in 1905, or to find it evidence of the "streak of heartlessness in her" that renders her almost but maybe not quite the "bitch-monster" that Halperin names her (but doesn't) in an almost deft act of apophasis.[39] Ultimately, Austen's laughter remains as difficult to categorize as does laughter more broadly.

Patricia Meyer Spacks offers a series of things and ways that Austen's laughter can mean, though ultimately, Spacks, like the present essay and indeed the present collection, arrives at questions that Austen's laughter raises rather than at a straightforward answer about what it might be, do, or mean. Spacks's catalog is nevertheless illustrative, and she demonstrates that it is often clear why the characters in Austen's novels laugh, or don't—even if those explanations do not cohere into a unified statement about what laughter is or does more broadly. In *Pride and Prejudice* alone, Spacks writes, "Laughter allows useful defensive transformations of pain into pleasure; it records the freedom and power of a kind of wit closely allied with intelligence."[40] "Its dangers are equally clear," she goes on to detail.[41] Laughter can demonstrate vision as well as self-delusion, cruel mockery as well as gentle love. Too much can make one a Lydia Bennet or a John Thorpe, too little an Elizabeth Elliot or a William Collins.

A few other critics are similarly helpful in their catalogs of Austen's characters' laughter. Just as Spacks provides a helpful compendium of the times that Austen's characters laugh, John Lauber focuses on those who incite laughter by becoming the butts of jokes for the pleasures of both characters and readers. Identifying the "fools" at which discerning characters and readers alike can laugh with minimal cruelty, Lauber imagines only one thing such laughter might mean. "The delight that we take in literary fools no doubt can largely be accounted for by

Hobbes's principle that we laugh when we feel a 'sudden glory' or sense of our own enormous superiority," he avers.[42] Such "delight" renders the laugher always an egoist, a self asserting itself at the expense of the weakness of others. Though Lauber also turns to Henri Bergson's understanding of laughter as occurring in response to the startling intrusions of mechanical behavior into human actions, even there he imagines that a Hobbesian sense of one's own superiority governs one's laugh: "We laugh because we feel ourselves to be living and therefore superior," he explains.[43] Lauber thus imagines Austen as someone who invites her reader in to her own superiority, and the ability to identify and respond appropriately to the fools of one's world becomes the greater lesson that her books may have to teach. Kathy Justice Gentile identifies a similar comedic intent in Austen's depiction of absurd male figures who repeatedly fail to meet the expectations they establish for themselves. Turning to Plato's earlier and more specified version of a kind of Hobbesian superiority, Gentile describes the ways that Austen invites both her female characters and her female readers to laugh at the foibles of men deluded by their own masculine privilege to believe that they are endowed with attributes that make their privilege well deserved. The joke, for Gentile's version of Austen, is on the men.[44] Accepting this version of Austen's laughter, though reading it to very different effect, Sarah Emsley wonders if Jane Austen's tendency to laugh at her neighbors might make her "cruel and unfeeling" and at least floats the possibility that those accusations against Austen of "intolerance, insensitivity, and a general lack of charity" might have the ring of justice.[45] To laugh at one's neighbors, Emsley suggests, is a cruelty unworthy of anyone eligible to be deemed truly good. Emsley, rather unlike Lauber in this, suggests that the key to understanding Austen is to see her laughter as something that characters, author, and readers alike must overcome in the spirit of a Christian charity that emphasizes acceptance over ridicule and sympathy over criticism.

Certainly it is sometimes clear why Austen's characters laugh. When the narrator announces that Mary Crawford, for example, makes a joke as she "tried to laugh off her feelings," or that Mrs. Elton repeatedly laughs "affectedly" or, that Emma, like Miss Crawford, laughs to keep feelings at bay, we can understand laughter as a defense mechanism, or even as an assertion of the kind of superiority manifested in a phrase like "the last laugh," which only one participant in any given conversation can have (MP, 264; E, 319, 330). When Mr. Bennet laughs at Mr. Collins, we understand that he does so both because he is a little too invested in his own intellectual superiority, as well as because Mr. Collins is eminently laughable. Sometimes it is, however, less clear why characters laugh. Elizabeth Bennet's laughter, for example, can be mockery, but it can also be an outpouring of joy that in its explosive purity exceeds any feeling we are led to expect from any of her sisters. Finally, the fact that Austen's novels conclude in repeated jokes invites great care in any blanket assertion about what Austen's laughter means. The novels depict numerous characters laughing—often for dubious moral and ethical reasons; they show various results of those various acts of laughter. They, then, to a one, conclude by inviting their readers to leave the book laughing themselves.

As has been noted by many who have attempted to explain it, laughter marks a site of personal and social coincidence as few phenomena do. Norbert Elias' recently published essay on laughter details the ways that philosophers and critics have sought after laughter's causality—focusing at times on physiological explanations for laughter's specific motions, and, more frequently, on an imagined final cause for laughter's existence. What good does it do an individual to laugh? And what good does it do a society for there to be laughter? These questions underscore laughter's theorization as much as do the three theoretical branches outlined above. For either we are to understand that laughter serves a personal, psychological function as it does for, say, Sigmund Freud, or Herbert Spencer, or even Immanuel Kant, all of whom imagine that laughter releases certain tensions, the excessive pressure of which is harmful to some version of the self, understood variously. Or, we can understand that laughter serves some social function, as it does for someone like Bergson, who imagines that laughter might help to keep everyone more or less in line.[46] Ultimately, in outlining this dichotomy Elias, like so many others, arrives at an impasse: "What, then," he asks, "are we to believe? Is laughter an expression of our revolt and a relief from social constraint? Or is it a social corrective, punishing us if we do not conform?"[47] Much as in the discussion of comedy that opened this volume, laughter ultimately falls on neither side of this question with any ease or consistency.

Comedy's emphasis on self-improvement and education, especially in Austen's version of it, can accommodate certain understandings of laughter easily, particularly those that are associated with what Jillian Heydt-Stevenson calls Austen's "knowingness."[48] Understood as a satirist, Austen's goal becomes the correction or redemption of those for whom and at whom she invites laughter; such correction might yield space within the socially just world imagined to be encompassed by her conclusions. Within the frame of satire, laughter is thus a means of improvement and an invitation to the "critical thinking" that makes cognitive self-awareness possible. Laughter acquires use-value as merely another avenue for the critique that makes liberal self-improvement possible, and it becomes weaponized as part of what Mark Canuel calls "Austen's abiding interest in blame."[49] Such laughter is rarely, if ever, funny.

In the preponderance and sheer variety of efforts to explain what it means when a person laughs, it seems that the only thing we can know is that we don't quite know what is happening. When another person laughs in front of us, it is entirely possible that they could be doing nearly anything at all. As Elias somewhat ostentatiously elaborates, "Laughter may be the laughter of exultation or triumph or that of derision and gloating, the laughter of irony or romping and teasing; it may be the side-splitting laughter of merriment, the hilarious laughter of rejoicing and good cheer; the spontaneous and uproarious laughter of children or the near restraint of polite adults; the controlled and thoughtful laughter of the sophisticated or gay and soft, the laughter of young lovers."[50] What we do know, it seems, is that laughter is "usually an immediate, unpremeditated reaction" that is "wholly bound up with the present moment."[51] Whatever it is that laughter is and does, it is and does those things now. Always happening in its own moment, laughter produces a relationship to time that does not allow for the space of critique or reflection. Laughter, as Diane Davis describes, "shatters," remaining ultimately unavailable either to forms of social meaning-making or to the constant negation of dialectic and critique.[52] Laughter is always of its own present moment. It also, however, promises a future. Remaining unsubsumed into critique and unavailable for signification, laughter ultimately displays little more than one's current ability to laugh, though that is no small thing. Laughter attests to one's indisputable current survival.

Austen's emphasis on a rigid formalism that calls attention to its own structures relies on the expectations of a certain comic tradition. Fundamental to that tradition is not only the laughter caused by the mishaps and upheaval that constitute the plot but also the assumption that whatever upheaval may happen will be corrected by the resolution that concludes it, usually with the marriages that promise to maintain the resolution at which the plot has arrived. In their movement from a social state that requires some rectifying (even if only because of their inclusion of a number of unmarried women) to a newly and better organized social world that promises a just future, Austen's novels further emphasize their structural dependence on formal comedy, even calling attention to that dependence in their final jokes. Austen's novels' heroines render themselves ready for the state of marriage to which their plot trajectories have inexorably tended by coming to know themselves. However, they also reap as the reward for having achieved a knowable self the act of dissolving it into the marriage that has been so hard-won.[53]

Austen's refusal to narrate her plots' conclusions in marriage, however, leave a reader somewhere other than in the simple promise of marriage required by the comedic plot she adopts. Though her novels may well be, as Eric C. Walker puts it, "systemically epithalamic," they also refuse to narrate or describe the very thing on which they depend for their coherence, producing, as Walker calls it, "a representational crisis as wide as writing itself."[54] By attending to the laughter that

Austen's novels elicit in the place of a culminating vision of matrimonial resolution, we see that Austen takes the marriage plot of comedic tradition and makes it distinctly her own, focusing on the laughter that comedy produces rather than the marriages that put an end to it. After all, the laughter induced by traditional comedy comes in response to its upheaval and absurdity, both of which are exiled by conclusive and just marriages. For Austen, however, the laughter continues and, even if subtly, overshadows the marriage that ends the plot by formal necessity.

E. M. Dadlez notes that "Austen uses some of the same material as the tragedian," especially that which reveals a flawed sense of human character and that shows tendencies to bad moral judgment;[55] Willoughby, for example, could be a character in a tragedy, as, perhaps, could Wickham. However, Dadlez concludes, Austen parts from tragedy in the way she "lingers on the everyday absurdity of these things rather than showing them to be intolerable. She presents them as funny, and not as tragic."[56] Like Dadlez, I am invested in Austen's distance from tragedy and the way that Austen's decidedly nontragic depiction of human weakness generates a particular value of comedy. Comedic value emerges not simply because it is pleasurable to laugh and momentarily empowering to laugh at bad guys, but because of a more powerful and precise sense of comedy's link to the possibility of time and the future. The difference between comedy and tragedy—if one may still assert such a thing—emerges in their relationship to time, though the dichotomous relation between the two is more often described as relating to affect or importance. Tragedy is serious, important, heavy; comedy is light and frivolous. Most important for the present discussion, though, is the fact of what follows the resolution of each. In tragedy, there can be no future; the entire trajectory of the plot is the eradication of the possibility that anything might come after it ends, even if there remains a messenger or two to narrate what has befallen. Comedy, on the other hand, insists on its own persistence. There will be a new state of affairs and a new social order. Traditionally such a promise of futurity comes from the implicit continuity of social order made possible by the future generation that is implied in the heterosexual pairing that is comedy's culmination. As such, comedy's future promise is denied to the women who achieve and celebrate their autonomy over the course of comedy's plot; in a comedic future they will be subsumed in marriage, their names changed and their importance given over to the children they will produce. In deemphasizing the marriages that conclude her narratives, however, Austen refuses to privilege a vision of marriage that promises a future in which women disappear, assimilated into the "smallest unit" of patriarchal order.[57] Instead, she depicts and produces a future in which women laugh. Comedy is a form of survival, a form that emphasizes the mundane and every day because it assumes that there will always be yet another day. And in Austen's version, it is a day in which we might all be laughing.

NOTES

1. William Wordsworth, "Resolution and Independence," in *Selected Poems and Prefaces*, ed. Jack Stillinger (Boston: Houghton Mifflin, 1965), 169, lines 118–19.
2. Carrie Fisher, *Wishful Drinking* (New York: Simon & Schuster, 2008), 148.
3. Paul Poplawski, *A Jane Austen Encyclopedia* (Westport, CT: Greenwood Press, 1998), 305.
4. Penny Gay, *Jane Austen and the Theatre* (Cambridge: Cambridge University Press, 2002), 1.
5. As Peter Sabor's introduction to the Cambridge edition of the *Juvenilia* attests, "The Visit" was likely composed in early 1789, when Austen was thirteen years old.
6. Misty G. Anderson, for example, claims that its final joke "clarifies the absurdity of the marriage ending as comic closure," in *Female Playwrights and Eighteenth-Century Comedy: Negotiating Marriage on the London Stage* (Basingstoke: Palgrave Macmillan, 2002), 45.
7. Lloyd W. Brown, "The Comic Conclusion in Jane Austen's Novels," *PMLA* 84, no. 6 (1969): 582.
8. Janis P. Stout, "Jane Austen's Proposal Scenes and the Limitations of Language," *Studies in the Novel* 14, no. 4 (1982): 320. I am thinking here of Marvin Mudrick's assertion, cited in the introduction to this volume, of Austen's coldness and personal defensiveness. See *Jane Austen: Irony as Defense and Discovery* (Berkeley: University of California Press, 1974), esp. 1–6.
9. Tony Tanner, *Jane Austen* (Cambridge, MA: Harvard University Press, 1986), 101; John Halperin, *The Life of Jane Austen* (Baltimore: Johns Hopkins University Press, 1984), 78.
10. Pam Perkins, "A Subdued Gaiety: The Comedy of Mansfield Park," *Nineteenth-Century Literature* 48, no. 1 (1993): 23.
11. William H. Magee, "Instrument of Growth: The Courtship and Marriage Plot in Jane Austen's Novels," *Journal of Narrative Technique* 17, no. 2 (1987): 198. He calls the dual plots of *Sense and Sensibility* "conventional rather than innovative, and at their closing disappointing" (199).
12. Eli Rozik, *Comedy: A Critical Introduction* (Brighton, UK: Sussex Academic Press, 2011), 1.
13. The turn here is similar to Emily Rohrbach's when she suggests "the fruits of an investigation at the level of the 'abstract art'—that is, the discovery of a self-reflexivity in Austen's representations" ("Austen's Later Subjects," SEL 44, no. 4 [2004]: 738).
14. Joann Ryan Morse, "The Course of True Love Never Did Run Smooth: Shakespearian Comedy in *Emma*," *Persuasions On-Line* 26, no. 1 (2005): n.p.
15. Robert Polhemus, *Comic Faith: The Great Tradition from Austen to Joyce* (Chicago: University of Chicago Press, 1982), 24.
16. Polhemus, *Comic Faith*, 58.
17. Ian Watt, "Jane Austen and the Traditions of Comic Aggression: Sense and Sensibility," *Persuasions* 3 (1981): 14.
18. I mean here to indicate work like that of Janine Barchas and Kristina Straub, whose recent exhibit at the Folger Shakespeare Library brought together the afterlives of these two renowned figures in the delightful (and at least at times, quite comic) "Will & Jane: Shakespeare, Austen and the Cult of Celebrity" (August 6, 2016-November 6, 2016). For their discussion of the exhibit and the thinking behind marrying these two literary icons of the English-speaking world, see "Curating *Will & Jane*," in *Eighteenth-Century Life* 40, no. 2 (April 2016): 1–36.

19. Kate Rumbold, "'So Common-Hackneyed in the Eyes of Men': Banal Shakespeare and the Eighteenth-Century Novel," *Literature Compass* 4, no. 3 (2007): 610–21; and Megan Taylor, "Jane Austen and 'Banal Shakespeare,'" *Eighteenth-Century Fiction* 27, no. 1 (2014): 105–25.

20. Edward Berry, *Shakespeare's Comic Rites* (Cambridge: Cambridge University Press, 1984), 31.

21. Berry, *Shakespeare's Comic Rites*, 32.

22. Northrop Frye, *Anatomy of Criticism: Four Essays* (Princeton: Princeton University Press, 1957), 43.

23. Frye, *Anatomy of Criticism*, 164.

24. Frye, *Anatomy of Criticism*, 44.

25. Peter Knox-Shaw, *Jane Austen and the Enlightenment* (Cambridge: Cambridge University Press, 2004), 139.

26. Charlotte Brontë, *Jane Eyre,* ed. Richard Nemesvari (Peterborough, ON: Broadview Press, 1999), 552.

27. Halperin, *Life of Jane Austen*, 278.

28. Michael Kramp in this volume cites Kate Fullbrook's reminder that Austen's chosen form of comedy provides assurances that "life will and can go on" even as it also threatens to undermine the grounds that make such life recognizable, Kate Fullbrook, "Jane Austen and the Comic Negative," in *Women's Reading Women's Writing*, ed. Sue Roe (New York: Harvester Publishing, 1987), 41.

29. Margie Burns, "Comic Resolution, Humorous Loose Ends in Austen's Novels," *Persuasions* 33 (2011): 238–43.

30. Lloyd Brown makes a similar point about Austen's conclusions and her refusal to satisfy a reader's desire for moral certitude. His main example is the villainy of Willoughby, which is left more or less unpunished in the expectations of his characteristically normal life ("Comic Conclusion," 585).

31. Edward Said, of course, draws attention to *Mansfield Park* as operating in a fundamentally "spatial" mode ("Jane Austen and Empire," in *Culture and Imperialism* [New York: Knopf, 1993], 81).

32. Frye, *Anatomy of Criticism*, 43.

33. See *Philebus*, 48–50, in which Socrates aligns the comic with a pleasure taken in the misfortunes of others, and thereby with an evil (*Plato's Examination of Pleasure: a Translation of the Philebus*, trans. R. Hackworth [Cambridge: Cambridge University Press, 1958], 95–98). In the *Republic*, offering another perspective on laughter's threat, Plato acknowledges, "Abandonment to violent laughter, generally speaking, is a violent agent for change" (*The Republic*, trans. Tom Griffith, Cambridge Texts in the History of Political Thought [Cambridge: Cambridge University Press, 2000], 75, bk. 3, 388e).

34. Aristotle, *Nicomachean Ethics*, ed. and trans. Roger Crisp, Cambridge Texts in the History of Philosophy (Cambridge: Cambridge University Press, 2014), 77, bk. 4, 30.

35. Thomas Hobbes, *Human Nature, The Elements of Law, Natural and Politic*, ed. J. C. A. Gaskin (Cambridge: Oxford University Press, 1999), chap. 9, at 54–55. It should certainly be noted, as Mary Beard also points out, that a more nuanced reading of Hobbes may reveal a less necessarily interpersonal violence, if still a competitive and nasty sort of situation. That is, Hobbesian laughter is often self-directed, even when it may not at first glance appear to be so.

36. Immanuel Kant, *Critique of Judgment*, trans. Werner S. Pluhar (Indianapolis: Hackett, 1987), pt. 1, 204.

37. Mary Beard, *Laughter in Ancient Rome: On Joking, Tickling, and Cracking Up* (Berkeley: University of California Press, 2014), 40. This book, though well outside the scholarly purview of Austen studies, offers a delightful approach to the study of humor, and I

recommend it highly for a model on how to escape the false rigors of the tripartite schema of humor discussion. See also Beard's quippily concise precis of the book's main points about humor: "What's So Funny?" *Chronicle of Higher Education*, July 14, 2014.

38. Beard, *Laughter in Ancient Rome*, 42.

39. William James Dawson, *The Makers of English Fiction* (New York: Fleming H. Revell, 1905), 50; Halperin, *Life of Jane Austen*, 79.

40. Patricia Meyer Spacks, "Austen's Laughter," *Women's Studies* 15, nos. 1–3 (1988): 74.

41. Spacks, "Austen's Laughter," 74.

42. John Lauber, "Jane Austen's Fools," *Studies in English Literature, 1500–1900* 14, no. 4 (1974): 511.

43. Lauber, "Jane Austen's Fools," 511.

44. Kathy Justice Gentile, "'A forward, bragging, scheming race': Comic Masculinity in *Northanger Abbey*," *Persuasions* 32 (2010): 78–89. Here we might think again of Margaret Atwood's assertion that men fear nothing more than women's laughter at their foibles and impediments; Austen becomes not only a woman who laughs but a woman who invites other women to do so as well. However, the second part of Atwood's formula asserts that while men fear women might laugh at them, women fear that men might kill them. And Austen, we might note, does little about that.

45. Sarah Emsley, "Laughing at Our Neighbors: Jane Austen and the Problem of Charity," *Persuasions On-Line* 26, no. 1 (Winter 2005), n.p., http://jasna.org/persuasions/on-line /vol26no1/emsley.htm (accessed May 20, 2018).

46. See, for example, Henri Bergson's *Laughter: An Essay on the Meaning of the Comic* (1911), in which he calls laughter a "social gesture" that "restrains eccentricity" and ultimately "pursues a utilitarian aim of general improvement" (trans. Cloudesley Brereton [New York: Macmillan, 1914], 20).

47. Norbert Elias, "Essay on Laughter," ed. Anca Parvulescu, *Critical Inquiry* 43, no. 2 (2017): 299.

48. For Jillian Heydt-Stevenson, Austen's bawdy humor and use of double entendre "announce her 'knowingness'" (*Austen's Unbecoming Conjunctions: Subversive Laughter, Embodied History* [New York: Palgrave Macmillan, 2005], 5).

49. Mark Canuel, "The Importance of Being Wrong," *Studies in Romanticism* 44, no. 2 (Summer 2005): 147.

50. Elias, "Essay on Laughter," 282.

51. Elias, "Essay on Laughter," 283.

52. D. Diane Davis, *Breaking Up (at) Totality: A Rhetoric of Laughter* (Carbondale: Southern Illinois University Press, 2000), 2.

53. Emily Rohrbach's reading of *Persuasion* undercuts the notion that Austen's conclusions always provide a closed self, claiming that Anne Elliot's "provisional relation to the future" ultimately leads a reader to see "'self' and 'world' as ongoing revisionary constructions" rather than completed products (*Modernity's Mist: British Romanticism and the Poetics of Anticipation* [New York: Fordham University Press, 2016], 25).

54. Eric C. Walker, *Marriage, Writing, and Romanticism: Wordsworth and Austen After War* (Stanford: Stanford University Press, 2009), 1, 4.

55. E. M. Dadlez, "Form Affects Content: Reading Jane Austen," *Philosophy and Literature* 32, no. 2 (2008): 315–29.

56. Dadlez, "Form Affects Content," 328.

57. Mary Poovey, *The Proper Lady and the Woman Writer: Ideology as Style in the Works of Mary Wollstonecraft, Mary Shelley, and Jane Austen* (Chicago: University of Chicago Press, 1985), 203.

7

LOST IN THE COMEDY

Austen's Paternalistic Men and
the Problem of Accountability

Michael Kramp

Liberal permissiveness is of the order of *videlicet*—it is permitted to *see*,
but the very fascination with the obscenity we are allowed to observe
prevents us from *knowing what it is that we see.*
—Zizek, *First as Tragedy*[1]

Equally important is the way in which benevolent paternalism may reduce
women's resistance to patriarchy. Benevolent sexism is disarming. Not only
is it subjectively favorable in its characterization of women, but it promises
that men's power will be used to women's advantage.
—Glick and Fiske, "An Ambivalent Alliance"[2]

I N *THE EIGHTEENTH BRUMAIRE OF LOUIS NAPOLEON (1852)*,
while considering Napoleon I and the subsequent rise of his nephew, Napoleon
III, Marx alludes to Hegel's belief that "all great events and characters of world
history occur, so to speak, twice." Marx immediately amends: "He forgot to add:
the first time as tragedy, the second time as farce."[3] Slavoj Zizek references Marx's
language in his unsettling manifesto, *First as Tragedy, Then as Farce* (2009), adopting his ideas to theorize how commentators have strangely used farcical conventions and explanations to rationalize tragic events of the early twentieth
century; he claims we have been "permitted to *see*, but the very fascination with the
obscenity we are allowed to observe prevents us from *knowing what it is that we see.*"[4]
Zizek identifies one of the immense powers of farcical experiences and expressions:
they can obscure the workings and ramifications of the very obscenities—including
dangerous obscenities—they present. As Michael R. Booth points out, as a genre,
the farce is not amenable to critical investigations because its participants "[come]
under increasingly unbearable pressure to conceal the truth." Booth specifically

notes how the actors in a farce seek to "once again inhabit the state of domestic quietude."[5] Farce hinders careful inquiry and prompts viewers to accept the unlikelihood of its plot, the amusement of its simple humor, and the inevitable resolution of any crisis—particularly any crisis associated with the home or family. In effect, we embrace, enjoy, and laugh at the work of the farce and prefer not to unpack its intricacies or implications. As with farce, we usually accept the activities and ends of paternalism because it often appears benevolent, at times amusing, and even natural. Paternalism is deeply interwoven into the structures of patriarchy and hegemonic masculinity, preventing scholars from clearly identifying its damaging results. And when paternalism is masked by farce, its effects are especially difficult to appreciate. Zizek emphasizes that this inability to *know what it is that we see* is the great danger, because we become witnesses without skills to analyze or explain, and instead view farcical episodes as if they were inevitable, scripted, and determined à la a highly stylized comic structure. When we fail to understand the real effects of farcical experiences and paternalism, we accept them and the tragedies they can obscure as given and inherent to our lives—that is, *videlicet.*

Farce can, in effect, entice us to understand traumatic events and oppressive ideological structures as inescapable or appropriate. Feminist critics over the past half century have worked diligently to identify the causes, agents, and damages of such events and structures, including institutional sexism, homophobia, and hegemonic masculinity. During this time, Austen scholars have drawn particular attention to her engagement with the patriarchal structures of her historical moment. Paternalism is an integral component of patriarchy, but as Peter Glick and Susan T. Fiske have famously argued, its repressive functions can be challenging to identify because "it [is] subjectively favorable in its characterization of women" and "promises that men's power will be used to women's advantage."[6] It is difficult to evaluate the effects of paternalism because its agents understand their actions as harmless or even magnanimous, cast their privileges as integral to normal everyday life, and present the outcomes of their behavior as expected and obvious. In addition, paternalism consistently employs humor and laughter to obscure its tactics; and like farce, it offers to resolve problems quickly and tidily, restoring domestic felicity. As a comic writer, Austen also famously promises to provide neat and orderly conclusions, and her comedic structure both exposes and envelops the activity of paternalism. She often shows us paternalistic men who ostensibly treat women with politeness, kindness, sensitivity, or wit but who use these strategies to maintain control, manage relationships, and inflict serious, even tragic, damages. With her depictions of General Tilney and Mr. Bennet, two patronizing men who are frequently viewed as humorous, ironic, or even farcical figures, Austen's narratives mask their consistent paternalism in comedy. Tilney and Bennet's activities and aims are obscured from readers even as their harmful behavior is put on display. Though the two men represent different types of masculinity—General Tilney a bourgeois man of chivalry and Mr. Bennet a degenerate man of feeling—their patronizing conduct functions similarly in the world of Austen's comedy. In this essay, I focus on the painful impacts of benevolent paternalism as Austen represents it and draw attention to the role of farcical comedy in protecting these men and the patriarchal system from which they benefit.

HEGEMONIC MASCULINITY, PATRONIZING BEHAVIOR, AND THE CHALLENGE OF AUSTEN'S COMIC METHOD

General Tilney and Mr. Bennet are representative members of the gentry and enjoy the privileges of what R. W. Connell discusses as hegemonic masculinity. According to Connell, hegemonic masculinity "is not a fixed character type," but "the configuration of gender practice which embodies the corrected accepted answer to the problem of the legitimacy of patriarchy which guarantees (or is taken to guarantee) the dominant position of men and the subordination of women."[7] General Tilney and Mr. Bennet speak, act, and function with the assumption of both male power and female submission, but they rarely speak, act, or function in an explicitly sexist or dominating manner. Instead, they specifically employ patronizing techniques to interact with women, such as witticisms, condescending niceties, and exaggerated compliments. Glick and Fiske note that paternalistic men use these methods, in part, because they often "possess genuine affection for those whom they exploit."[8] They practice what Glick and Fiske term "*Benevolent sexism*," which "relies on kinder and gentler justifications of male dominance and prescribed gender roles" as well as "a romanticized view of sexual relationships with women."[9] General Tilney and Mr. Bennet can be somewhat charming at times; their performances of benevolent sexism are frequently polite, occasionally funny, and enable them to exercise and retain power over women without perpetual violence— and often without others recognizing their performances or power. Glick and Fiske argue that "ideologies of benevolent paternalism allow members of dominant groups to characterize their privileges as well-deserved, even as a heavy responsibility that they must bear."[10] They conclude: "If men's power is popularly viewed as a burden gallantly assumed, as legitimated by their greater responsibility and self-sacrifice, then their privileged role seems justified."[11] The single greatest difficulty in writing or talking about paternalism is that it appears natural, "legitimated," or "well-deserved." And like farce, it obscures its roots, casts its injuries as fleeting, and presents its resolutions as inevitable. If we consistently identify the abusive behavior of paternalism—including the behavior masked by farce—we can begin to analyze critically its origins, actions, and effects.

But it is inevitably difficult to expose patronizing men because they usually appear to compliment, comfort, or simply joke with others, especially disempowered young women. This struggle is especially notable in Austen's novels in which her comic structure often functions to maintain patriarchal order through concluding marriages that seemingly restore domestic stability, even as she provides humorous and ironic portrayals of selective characters. Our critical understanding of her comedic technique is still strongly influenced by the midcentury work of D. W. Harding and Marvin Mudrick. Harding describes Austen as a satirist whose "first necessity was to keep on reasonably good terms with the associates of her everyday life." He writes: "She had a deep need for their affection and a genuine respect for the ordered, decent civilization they upheld."[12] He insists that her comedy, and indeed her hatred, is "regulated;" so while she mocks and even "hates" certain figures of this gentry society, according to Harding, she wants—even needs—to maintain proper relations with its representatives. Mudrick modifies Harding's approach but makes a similar argument about Austen's comedic effect. He announces that her "compulsion, and genius, is to look only for incongruity," and adds that she treats such incongruities "with a detached discrimination."[13] Mudrick asserts that her comedy creatively uses the distance of irony; she reveals the humorous incongruities in a social incident, a character, or a larger cultural trend that show us "failures of wholeness which in life have consequences and must be judged but in comedy—and for Jane Austen—are relieved of guilt and responsibility at the moment of perception."[14] Harding and Mudrick develop theories of Austen's comedy that highlight her apparent commitment to the preservation of social order rather than the denunciation or revelation of patriarchal systems of power; they accentuate her wit as a comic writer and suggest how she manages her narratives to avoid angering her audience or disrupting dominant structures.

The critical legacy of Harding and Mudrick is specifically important to my attempt to identify and analyze the activities of patronizing men because these scholars established Austen's supposed investment in sustaining the hegemonic privileges of the gentry. If Austen's comedy repairs and retains the social system from which such men benefit, it is challenging to uncover the complexity and effects of their condescending behavior; likewise, if Austen's comedy is not concerned with guilt or responsibility, it is difficult to hold these men accountable for behavior that often appears benevolent but is actually quite oppressive—even obscene. Numerous scholars have, of course, challenged and complicated the thinking of Harding and Mudrick.[15] Kate Fullbrook, for example, claims that Austen "speaks with the pure voice of comic negation" and explains how her fiction "undermines everything that feels itself secure . . . while it insists that life will and can go on." For Fullbrook, Austen does critique authority, including hegemonic masculinity and patriarchy, and then reverts to the comic structure to restore some semblance of order; but as Fullbrook concludes, Austen "doesn't leave out pain; comedy is as impossible as tragedy without suffering . . . it subverts from within life itself, it is the literary mode of endless struggle."[16] Austen's novels most assuredly do not erase pain or discomfort, and while her comic form insists that "life will and can go on," problems and pain do not dissolve. Her depictions of General Tilney and Mr. Bennet are no doubt comic, and the farcical repetition of their paternalistic behavior distracts us from seeing the pain they engender. These patronizing men, nonetheless, create difficult situations for women that not even an unlikely farcical event or the closing weddings of a comic narrative can resolve completely. Austen repeatedly showcases their paternalistic behavior, and it is easy to dismiss them, laugh at their odd actions, or simply accept their conduct as natural. Men like General Tilney and Mr. Bennet, however, produce serious consequences—pain, suffering, and even trauma—and to study the complexity of their paternalism, we must critically examine and *see* their benevolent words and actions as well as the comic techniques that mask or obscure their effects.

GENERAL TILNEY AND THE MANIPULATIVE
METHODS OF BOURGEOIS CHIVALRY

Austen depicts General Tilney as a degenerate man of chivalry who employs gallantry to control Catherine Morland. He rehearses a modernized form of chivalric masculinity, adapting the precepts that Edmund Burke famously identified in his *Reflections on the Revolution in France* (1790) to a gentry lifestyle.[17] Tim Fulford helpfully explains that despite Burke's memorable eulogy, "Chivalric manhood did not die; it was relocated in the middle classes."[18] The general embodies this bourgeois chivalry; he rehearses excessive gallantry and knows how to behave with ceremonial politeness, but he also displays a fondness for material possessions, an obsession with promptness, and an incessant middle-class ambition—or anxiety. He uses excessive courtesy to manipulate social situations and manage others, but this patronizing technique ultimately reveals his vanity and insecurity, anticipating Austen's depiction of men like Sir Walter Elliot. As an older military man, his conduct also reminds us of Mary Wollstonecraft's memorable critiques of soldiers: "Like the *fair* sex, the business of their lives is gallantry.—They were taught to please, and they only live to please."[19] His mechanical

commitment to formality lacks sincerity, as he patronizes and belittles the heroine in a desperate attempt to impress her. Austen's portrayal alludes to the painful
effects of his paternalistic behavior, but her comic narrative also inhibits our ability to see the motivations and impacts of his actions.

In *Northanger Abbey*, we first meet the general while Henry and Catherine
dance at Bath. The heroine realizes she is being "earnestly regarded by a gentleman who stood among the lookers-on;" she identifies him as "a very handsome
man, of a commanding aspect, past the bloom, but not past the vigour of life; and
with his eye still directed towards her" (NA, 77–78). Catherine acknowledges the
general's genteel appearance and demeanor, but she is also at once puzzled and
frightened by his attention. The narrator explains: "Confused by his notice, and
blushing from the fear of its being excited by something wrong in her appearance,
she turned away her head" (NA, 78). Austen's introduction of the general accen-
tuates his discomforting effect on the heroine, and Kenneth W. Graham even
identifies what he terms "a slight sexual threat" in his admiration of Catherine's
dancing.[20] His surveillance may appear complimentary, but like much patronizing behavior, it is unsettling, especially for a young woman who is unused to such
attention from unknown men. When Catherine visits the Tilneys, immediately
prior to their departure for Northanger, she notes his "great civilities to her," but
also relates "it had been a release to get away from him. It puzzled her to account
for all this. It could not be General Tilney's fault. That he was perfectly agreeable
and good-natured, and altogether a very charming man, did not admit of a doubt,
for he was tall and handsome, and Henry's father" (NA, 131). Catherine's reflection
is at once comic and revelatory; like a viewer of farce, she does not question the
unlikelihood of his behavior or its effects, and her acceptance exposes the power
of the older man's paternalism. The naive young heroine is unable to imagine how
the general might be responsible for her distress because he possesses all the features of a stereotypical gentleman: he is polite, good-looking, tall, and so on.
She naturalizes his behavior as benevolent, yet his paternalistic treatment of her
is, no doubt, overbearing and disturbing. As they ready to depart for Northanger,
Austen remarks extensively on the general's "incessant attention," and the heroine's
uneasiness. The narrator elaborates: "Perverse as it seemed, she doubted whether she
might not have felt less, had she been less attended to. His anxiety for her
comfort—his continual solicitations that she would eat, and his often-expressed
fears of her seeing nothing to her taste . . . made it impossible for her to forget for
a moment that she was a visitor. She felt utterly unworthy of such respect, and
knew not how to reply to it" (NA, 157–58).

The general's tireless devotion to Catherine's comfort is exhausting, serves
to subordinate her, and secures his control of the situation. Austen depicts him as

an ostensibly genteel man who knows how to rehearse forms of decorum in order to maintain his hegemonic power, but she also references the painful effects of his patronizing behavior on the heroine.

When they arrive at Northanger, the general continues to aggressively court Catherine's favor. He tours the heroine around the Abbey, and takes special care to show her the modernized servants' quarters. Austen relates how Catherine "would willingly have been spared the mortification of a walk through scenes so fallen, had the general allowed it; but if he had a vanity, it was in the arrangements of his offices" (NA, 189). The general, determined to impress Catherine with a display of improvements and materiality, foolishly believes she wants to see his stock of servants and their updated facilities, but his ongoing attempts to affect the heroine with his patronizing gallantry and architectural renovations exhausts her and suggests both his insecurity and his selfish, strategic aims. Catherine does, of course, grow suspicious of the general's behavior, famously suspecting him of involvement with his late wife's death. She muses: "How many were the examples to justify even the blackest suspicions!—And, when she saw him in the evenings, while she worked with her friend, slowly pacing the drawing-room for an hour together in silent thoughtfulness, with downcast eyes and contracted brow, she felt secure from all possibility of wronging him. It was the air and attitude of a Montoni!" (NA, 192). The heroine's thought process reflects her deep investment in gothic romances, and the comic narrative mocks her logic and persistence. She employs an explanation for the general's behavior that is as unlikely as the plot elements of a farce. Austen's humorous depiction of Catherine, who views the general as a horrific gothic villain, also masks his ongoing belittling treatment of the young heroine; she can only fathom his damaging demeanor and actions within a ridiculous narrative feature that resolves humorously.

Soon after she compares him to Montoni, he tells her: "I have many pamphlets to finish . . . before I can close my eyes; and perhaps may be poring over the affairs of the nation for hours after you are asleep. Can either of us be more meetly employed? *My* eyes will be blinding for good of others; and *yours* preparing by rest for future mischief" (NA, 193; emphasis in the original). He patronizes Catherine and Eleanor by juxtaposing their supposed "mischief" to his perusal of pamphlets of purported national importance.[21] Catherine interestingly dismisses his paternalistic language and returns to her gothic interpretation of his behavior: "To be kept up for hours, after the family were in bed, by stupid pamphlets, was not very likely. There must be some deeper cause: something was to be done which could be done only while the household slept" (NA, 193). Austen again humorously portrays the heroine and her seemingly ridiculous conclusions, but as Graham notes, the general's pamphlet reading "may be part of a government campaign to detect opinions that might be regarded as treasonable."[22] His late-night activity is a classic example of the work of hegemonic masculinity, as he reviews documents looking for potential dissenters before they become disruptive, but the heroine's rather farcical explanation of gothic villainy distracts us from his patronizing comments and obsession with domestic control. As a polite, paternalistic man, he gently belittles the heroine while he carefully maintains such order, inhibiting Catherine from detecting how his patronizing behavior and hegemonic masculinity are mutually supportive.

When the family discusses an outing to Woodston to see Henry's parsonage, General Tilney again directs the arrangements and patronizes Catherine, telling her that he must delay their visit because of obligations to his extensive social relations. He explains how he "cannot in decency fail attending the club," and continues: "I really could not face my acquaintance if I staid away now; for, as I am known to be in the country, it would be taken exceedingly amiss; and it is a rule with me, Miss Morland, never to give offence to any of my neighbours" (NA, 216). He uses his devotion to homosocial relations as an excuse to suspend the trip to Woodston, and expresses his obligation to fulfill such commitments as a form of modern decorum. As he tries to dictate and direct social situations, including the opinions of the heroine, he reveals his obsession with control as well as his anxiety; and like many paternalistic men, when he loses control, he reverts to violent, vindictive action. Soon after their visit to Woodston, the general announces that he must travel to London. He bemoans how "any necessity should rob him even for an hour of Miss Morland's company, and anxiously recommend[s] the study of her comfort and amusement to his children as their chief object in his absence." While he offers a gallant expression of concern for the heroine during his time away from Northanger, the narrator reports that "his departure gave Catherine the first experimental conviction that a loss may be sometimes a gain" (NA, 227). His excessively polite, yet oppressive treatment throughout the novel has left her confused and tired, and the general's removal offers the heroine some relief, but he performs his cruelest action following this absence, shamelessly sending the heroine home.

He cowardly directs Eleanor to deliver the news, and his daughter reluctantly complies. She uncomfortably relates: "Tomorrow morning is fixed for your leaving us, and not even the hour is left to your choice; the very carriage is ordered, and will be here at seven o'clock, and no servant will be offered you" (NA, 232). The news is devastating, even traumatic; Catherine is to complete "a journey of seventy miles . . . alone, unattended" (NA, 233). The general's action reveals how his insecurity has become spiteful, and likewise shows his willingness—perhaps even need—to involve Eleanor in his stratagems. Once he learns the truth of the

Morland family's finances, he loses interest in associating with the heroine; he has no further motivation to court her graces or treat her with pointed chivalric politeness, dismissing Catherine from the Abbey in a way that legitimately endangers her. Claudia L. Johnson identifies the general's ungentlemanly manner at this moment in the novel, arguing that his decision to exile the heroine exposes him as a man who does not care "benevolently and responsibly [for] inferiors, but who on the contrary behaves as though his social superiority absolved him from responsibility to inferiors."[23] Austen presents him as a degenerate gentleman who abuses his power, and the heroine now recognizes the impact of his actions. She reflects: "The manner in which it was done so grossly uncivil; hurrying her away without any reference to her own convenience, or allowing her even the appearance of choice as to the time or mode of her traveling" (NA, 234). Catherine enunciates the pain and discomfort of her situation; she understands not only that she has been treated poorly, but that this mistreatment could potentially compromise her safety.

And yet, Austen's comic novel prevents us from fully appreciating the ramifications of the general's patronizing behavior that has devolved into a harsh and resentful reaction; like a farce, the narrative obscures the discomforting truth that it portrays and seemingly protects the paternalism that it dramatizes. B. C. Southam memorably argues that the general "is an anti-Montoni, no stage villain, but an urbane man-of-property and man-about-town." He adds that "Jane Austen's joke, within this, is of course that the General really is a scheming, ruthless, villain, and that Catherine Morland really is his victim."[24] Numerous critics have followed Southam's lead and identified the *real*—as opposed to gothic—terror engendered by General Tilney; he is a manipulative, controlling man, and his dismissal of the heroine is not simply impolite but alarming.[25] Still, as Austen resolves her comedic marriage plot and alludes to the distressing effects of his words and actions that linger with the heroine, the narrator both highlights his conniving techniques and paternalistic tendencies and obfuscates their effects with farcical devices that mask the general's agency. For example, upon her return to Fullerton, Catherine reminisces about the outing to Woodston that she enjoyed with the general. She muses: "It was there, it was on that day that the General had made use of such expressions with regard to Henry and herself, had so spoken and so looked as to give her the most positive conviction of his actually wishing their marriage." As she returns to this memory, she remembers that it was "only ten days ago [that] he elated her by his pointed regard." She has no ability to understand the severe shift in his conduct and questions: "What had she done, or what had she omitted to do, to merit such a change?" (NA, 238). Catherine is despondent and again confused; rather than holding the general accountable for his cruel actions, she blames herself and only remembers his affected politeness. While her self-effacing reflections are pathetic and even amusing, they also remind us of the pain he has inflicted, even as they point to her inability to understand the reality of his uncivil and vengeful actions.

Henry's visit to Fullerton at the close of the novel finally provides explanations for General Tilney's incessant courting of Catherine as well as his abrupt decision to exile her from the Abbey. Henry explains how John Thorpe's misinformation led the general to "[court] her acquaintance in Bath, [solicit] her company at Northanger, and [design] her for his daughter in law." Henry concludes that his father, "on discovering his error, to turn her from the house seemed the best, though to his feelings an inadequate proof of his resentment towards herself, and his contempt of her family" (NA, 253–54). Henry's words reveal the spitefulness of the general; his insecurity prompts him to act out of "resentment" and "contempt," and with disregard for the safety or care of the young heroine. Catherine listens to Henry's story, and Austen then provides her heroine with an opportunity to reflect on the general and his behavior. In a self-conscious moment, Catherine concludes she had "heard enough to feel, that in suspecting General Tilney of either murdering or shutting up his wife, she had scarcely sinned against his character, or magnified his cruelty" (NA, 256). Despite Henry's revelatory account of his father's real motivations and petty response, she reverts to the discourse of gothic romance to analyze his conduct, and while the comparison helps us to consider the terror induced by his recent actions, her analogy also impedes our ability to appreciate the general's lingering paternalistic behavior, its privileges, and its actual effects. She does not address the immediate and true impacts of his patronizing abuse, which still appear hidden beneath the rather farcical apparatus of a gothic romance.

In the story's final pages, Eleanor once more participates in the maintenance of her father's patriarchal masculinity, and Austen uses farcical components to ensure his hegemonic identity. We learn of Eleanor's marriage to "a man of fortune and consequence," which "threw [the General] into a fit of good-humour, from which he did not recover till after Eleanor had obtained his forgiveness of Henry." Austen's farce-like device of Eleanor's offstage marriage to an ex machina character facilitates the resolving wedding of Catherine and Henry, and it also reaffirms the general as an affected man of ceremony. Eleanor's union to a wealthy man overwhelms his reason, and he permits Henry to marry Catherine—or, to use his patronizing language: "To be a fool if he liked it!" (NA, 259–60). Despite his cruel treatment of the heroine, and Henry's account of his rationale, Austen continues to present him as a privileged yet insecure figure who, despite his attempts to control situations, is susceptible himself to manipulation. The narrator even offers one final reminder of his arrogance when she notes how "never had the General loved his daughter so well in all her hours of companionship, utility, and patient endurance, as when he first hailed her, 'Your Ladyship!'" (NA, 260). His daughter's ascension to a title fulfills his clear need for social status—a status he sought through his excessive politeness toward Catherine—and resolves the tensions surrounding the romance of Catherine and Henry. To remain functional, both farce and paternalism must ensure that the truth of their workings, structures, and effects are hidden or obtuse; while we can uncover the general's conniving behavior throughout the story, analyze his demeaning words, and begin to reflect on the damage caused by his belittling and spiteful acts, Austen's comic novel preserves his privileged status by making it difficult to see and assess the full impact of his paternalism.

MR. BENNET AND AUSTEN'S FARCE OF FEELING

In *Pride and Prejudice*, Austen offers a second example of a patronizing male figure who at times becomes farcical yet also retains his privileges as a hegemonic man. Mr. Bennet does not employ chivalry, however; instead, Austen portrays him as a comedic version of a familiar eighteenth-century fictional character: the sentimental, fatherly adviser. These men, popular in the novels of Jane West and Ann Radcliffe, provide sage advice to young men and women alike and demonstrate delicacy of feeling, recalling the tradition of the sentimental male hero in novels such as Samuel Richardson's *Sir Charles Grandison* (1753–1754), Laurence Sterne's *A Sentimental Journey* (1768), and Henry MacKenzie's *The Man of Feeling* (1771).[26] But as Mary Burgan points out, "Mr. Bennet is shown as a man whose indifference causes him to lose his capacity to feel." Burgan explains how "by the end of the novel his fatherhood and his feelings have become debased in such a way that neither his most sympathetic daughter nor the reader can take him seriously." As Burgan indicates, Mr. Bennet is an apathetic man, and his apathy impairs his sensitivity, his ability to feel properly, and perhaps most important, his ability to express his feelings with sincerity. Austen highlights his numerous shortcomings as a parent, including his negligence, reticence, and patronizing conduct toward his daughters; and yet as Burgan concludes, "The reader can be temporarily lured into sympathy with Mr. Bennet."[27] He is, no doubt, an amusing character who pokes fun at his ridiculous companions, especially his wife, casting serious situations rather farcically—a technique that, no doubt, disguises his paternalism. We enjoy his witty tongue and sharp retorts, and Austen's humorous depiction often occludes his patronizing language, imprudent parenting, and impaired sensibility.

Mr. Bennet repeatedly demonstrates his emotional awareness as well as his knowledge of paternal duties, yet Austen depicts him as an ineffective father who often reverts to farcical language and behavior rather than acting as a sensitive man to resolve potential crises. Midway through the narrative, Elizabeth reflects that early in his life, he was "captivated by youth and beauty, and that appearance of good humour, which youth and beauty generally give." The heroine's comment helps us to understand Mr. Bennet as a man of sensation—or at least a former man of sensation. He was once deeply affected by beauty and good feeling, but after years of marriage to the insipid Mrs. Bennet, "all his views of domestic happiness were overthrown" (P&P, 262). Despite his early predisposition toward feeling and sensitivity, he has become rather crass, and the narrator introduces him early as "so odd a mixture of quick parts, sarcastic humour, reserve, and caprice" (P&P, 5). Austen highlights the peculiarity of Mr. Bennet's character: he is intelligent, witty, and yet rather passive, even distant; he is happy to offer his assessment of others, or his advice on a situation, much like a traditional father figure from eighteenth-century literature, but his comments are often laced with cynicism rather than kindness or wisdom. He understands his role as a patriarch and rehearses his conventional responsibilities, but he paternalistically performs these duties, and Austen's comic treatment inhibits our ability to appreciate the dangerous effects of his inept parenting.

Mr. Bennet's most pressing responsibility as a father is the care of his five daughters, and yet he does not always demonstrate the fondest affection for his children. Indeed, in one of his first commentaries on them, he refers to Lydia and Kitty as "two of the silliest girls in the country," and adds: "I have suspected it some time, but I am now convinced." When his wife challenges him, he simply responds: "If my children are silly I must hope to be always sensible of it" (P&P, 32). His reaction reminds us how viewers of farce simply accept characters and events; he makes no attempt to temper or question his evaluation and acts with the belief that his daughters' lives are predetermined, presuming that any fatherly advice or assistance from him would be pointless. Even at this early moment in the novel, he draws attention to his skewed sensibility that does nothing to facilitate his judgment of emotional dilemmas or aid the discernment of his children's problems; rather, it allows him to exploit the foibles of others, including his own daughters. He provides sharp rebukes of their improper behavior, jokes about their romantic activities, and offers harsh appraisals of their financial predicaments. For example, he fully understands the entailment of his family's home to Mr. Collins, is in theory sensitive to his daughters' situation, but offers little in terms of fatherly guidance. Rather, he responds with paternalistic wit and derision. When Elizabeth asks if Mr. Collins might be a sensible man, he humorously responds: "I have great hopes of finding him quite the reverse. There is a mixture of servility and self-importance in his letter, which promises well" (P&P, 71). When Mr. Collins does arrive, the narrator explains how "Mr. Bennet's expectations were fully answered. His cousin was as absurd as he had hoped, and he listened to him with the keenest enjoyment" (P&P, 76). Mr. Bennet is, of course, accurate in his evaluation of Mr. Collins, but his sarcastic comments and "enjoyment" of the suitor's silliness serve to amuse himself and do nothing to quell the anxieties of his wife and daughters. He humorously dismisses the danger posed by Mr. Collins to his children, and later, when he grows tired of his cousin, he "was most anxious to get rid of him, and have his library to himself" (P&P, 79). Susan Fraiman describes Mr. Bennet as "a reclusive man and seemingly ineffectual."[28] His secluded library refuge may mark him as an educated and presumably wise man, but it also serves to remove him from the affairs of his family and his responsibilities as a father. When the domestic realm becomes hectic or confusing, he retreats to his library to laugh, regain his serenity, and preserve his control.

His refuge in the library allows him to escape the chaotic events of his home and treat them farcically, offering quick and humorous solutions to real domestic problems. Mrs. Bennet interrupts his solitude with news of Elizabeth's refusal to accept Mr. Collins's proposal, but he shows little interest; when Mrs. Bennet presses him to act on Elizabeth's obstinacy, he calmly responds: "Let her be called down. She shall hear my opinion" (P&P, 124). He appears to speak as a learned father with balanced emotions and a sensible approach to difficult questions, yet when Elizabeth arrives, he offers a paternalistic resolution to his daughter's difficult situation that draws on the logic of farce. He explains: "An unhappy alternative is before you, Elizabeth. From this day you must be a stranger to one of your parents.—Your mother will never see you again if you do *not* marry Mr. Collins, and I will never see you again if you do." His language is clearly humorous, but it is also patronizing and controlling. He knows how to rehearse the part of a wise patriarch, and he employs this discourse to appear as a responsible parent, but he ultimately makes a joke out of his wife's anxiety as well as Elizabeth's enduring financial insecurity. He dismisses their concerns and expresses a desire for "the free use of my understanding on the present occasion; and secondly, of my room. I shall be glad to have the library to myself as soon as may be" (P&P, 125). Fraiman indicates that Mr. Bennet "controls his family by being not tight-fisted but tight-lipped." She notes that he exercises a "right to have the last word."[29] Mr. Bennet, like the plot of a farce, seeks to resolve crises promptly. His goal is to regain the privacy of his library, and his condescending rhetorical strategies allow him to manage the conversation and return the domestic sphere to a semblance of peace, all while appearing charming and amusing rather than rude or negligent.

His paternalistic behavior becomes more notable when he uses his wit and sarcasm to patronize and ridicule his children, placing them in uncomfortable and even dangerous social scenarios. When Mr. Bingley quits Netherfield, he rather cynically addresses Jane's romantic difficulties. He tells Elizabeth: "Your sister is crossed in love I find. I congratulate her. Next to being married, a girl likes to be crossed in love a little now and then. It . . . gives her a sort of distinction among her companions." Mr. Bennet is conscious of Jane's anxiety following Mr. Bingley's sudden departure, but he displays no true sensitivity; instead, he uses the situation as an opportunity to patronize his elder daughters and make a joke of their melancholy. He asks Elizabeth: "When is your turn to come?" and insists, "You will hardly bear to be long outdone by Jane. Now is your time. Here are officers enough at Meryton to disappoint all the young ladies in the country" (P&P, 156). Mr. Bennet recognizes the workings of young romance; he knows the lure of attractive men and the pangs of disappointed lovers, but he presents the experiences as components of a highly stylized comic plot and jokes suitable for a father's benign amusement rather than concerns that merit his attention. In addition, his droll remarks suggest his carelessness as a parent and foreshadow the negligence that will endanger his daughters.

Mr. Bennet's fatherly disregard is most apparent with Lydia. His lack of concern for her youthful social exuberance is especially disconcerting, and when she approaches him about traveling with Mrs. Forster to Brighton, he shows little resistance, again adopting the rhetoric of a mock patriarchal adviser who offers only comic words of wisdom much like a farcical figure. He tells Elizabeth that "Lydia will never be easy till she has exposed herself in some public place or other, and we can never expect her to do it with so little expense or inconvenience to her family as under the present circumstances" (P&P, 256). He attempts to manage Lydia as if she were an uncontrollable phenomenon like the weather rather than a child in need of guidance, and he again demonstrates a condescending investment in his daughters' romantic activities, but his affected interest exposes his insensitivity to the actual dangers awaiting Lydia. When the heroine challenges her father, claiming that her sister will soon be "beyond the reach of amendment," her father paternalistically attempts to calm her: "Do not make yourself uneasy, my love. . . . We shall have no peace at Longbourn if Lydia does not go to Brighton. Let her go then. Colonel Forster is a sensible man, and will keep her out of any real mischief; and she is luckily too poor to be an object of prey to any body." Mr. Bennet presents his daughter's proposed trip as if it were a plot element in a farce, viewing her future life as part of a conventional narrative. And such a perspective, of course, is strikingly paternalistic. He understands that young women can be threatened in environments such as Brighton; he is not ignorant, but he patronizingly dismisses the heroine's objections because he believes Lydia's future is predetermined. He trusts she must be too poor to become the target of men's attentions, and his logic also suggests his belief that the young woman's situation will resolve itself without his fatherly intervention. He concludes: "At Brighton she will be of less importance even as a common flirt than she has been here. The officers will find women better worth their notice" (P&P, 256–57). In his final assessment, he denigrates and belittles his youngest daughter, rendering her relatively worthless, suggesting that the officers must see more value in other women, and abandoning his responsibility to help guide Lydia.

Mr. Bennet patronizes Elizabeth and demeans Lydia; he treats both with a lack of sincere regard, but he uses humor to soften or at least confuse the effects of his condescending language. He claims to be doing what is in the best interest of Lydia *and* his family, even as he endangers his youngest daughter and mockingly dismisses the intelligent heroine. When news breaks of Lydia's elopement, Mr. Bennet departs for London with Colonel Forster in an attempt to find her, but Elizabeth expresses little confidence in his ability to fulfill traditional paternal obligations. She notes "His indolence and the little attention he has ever seemed to give to what was going forward in his family," and claims "that *he* would do as little, and think as little about it, as any father could do" (P&P, 312; emphasis in the original). Elizabeth exposes him as an inept father, and her harsh words denote how his lack of concern has led to Lydia's scandalous elopement. She does not trust her father to resolve the familial crisis, and even the nonsensical Mrs. Bennet can only imagine her husband going to London to "fight Wickham, wherever he meets him." She concludes: "Then he will be killed, and what is to become of us all?" (P&P, 317). Elizabeth and her mother present Mr. Bennet as a ridiculous, even farcical figure; he is apathetic, ineffectual, and lampooned as a helpless father. When he returns from his "ill-success" in London, the narrator relates that "he had all the appearance of his usual philosophic composure. He said as little as he had ever been in the habit of saying: made no mention of the business that had taken him away" (P&P, 328–29). He initially adopts a familiar pose as a reflective man, even reporting to Elizabeth: "Let me once in my life feel how much I have been to blame." His language again reminds us of his ability to rehearse the discourses of a patriarchal figure of sentiment, but he quickly reverts to paternalistic humor to make a joke of his emotional response. He tells the heroine that he holds "no ill-will for [her] being justified in [her] advice" regarding Lydia, but he immediately adds: "This is a parade which does one good; it gives such elegance to misfortune! Another day I will do the same; I will sit in my library, in my night cap and powdering gown, and give as much trouble as I can,—or, perhaps, I may defer it, till Kitty runs away" (P&P, 330). He presents himself as a comically pathetic father who reverts to the language and conventions of farce, including a "parade," elopements, stylized costumes, and crass humor. He now awaits the flight of Kitty, and he promises to maintain a ridiculously strict disciplinary code with his second-youngest daughter, announcing: "No, Kitty, I have at last learnt to be cautious, and you will feel the effects of it." He outlines how "no officer is ever to enter my house again, nor even pass through the village. Balls will be absolutely prohibited, unless you stand up with one of your sisters. And you are never to stir out of doors, till you can prove that you have spent ten minutes of every day in a rational manner" (P&P, 330–31). His newfound enthusiasm for parenting is, of course, outlandish, ridiculous, and farcical, illustrating both his absurdity as a father and his continued reliance on patronizing modes of relating to others and resolving crises.

Following the aftermath of Lydia's elopement, Mr. Bennet wants little to do with his youngest daughter. The narrator reports, "When the first transports of rage which had produced his activity in seeking her were over, he naturally returned to all his former indolence" (P&P, 341). He resumes his role as a lethargic, apathetic patriarchal figure, holes up in his library, and initially refuses to welcome the newlyweds or purchase clothes for Lydia. He, likewise, resumes his patronizing treatment of Jane and Elizabeth, even deriding the former as he attempts to celebrate her engagement with Bingley. He paternalistically congratulates her: "You are a good girl . . . . I have not a doubt of your doing very well together. Your tempers are by no means unlike. You are each of you so complying, that nothing will ever be resolved on so easy, that every servant will cheat you; and so generous, that you will always exceed your income" (P&P, 386). He mocks Jane's kindness, citing her liberality and easy manner as he humorously predicts her future economic troubles. Mr. Bennet, likewise, unintentionally discomforts Elizabeth when he receives word of Mr. Darcy's supposed plan to propose to the heroine. He is unable to fathom Darcy's sincere interest in Elizabeth and amusedly relates: "Could [Mr. Collins], or the Lucases, have pitched on any man, within the circle of our acquaintance, whose name would have given the lie more effectually to what they related?" He treats the rumor as an absurd joke and asks his unsettled daughter: "Are you not diverted?" (P&P, 402). Mr. Bennet, retaining his humorous language even at this critical moment, expects the heroine to enjoy his remarks, but Austen again highlights how he employs a paternalistic rhetoric masked by ostensibly amusing words. In this unintended act, he blatantly reveals his lack of sensitivity to the heroine and her development throughout the narrative, even as he preserves his paternalistic privilege.

As he continues his unsettling conversation with Elizabeth, he quizzes the heroine: "But, Lizzy, you look as if you did not enjoy it. You are not going to be *missish,* I hope, and pretend to be affronted at an idle report. For what do we live, but to make sport of our neighbours, and laugh at them in our turn?" (P&P, 403). He dismisses the pain or compunction of his derisive humor and reminds his daughter that mocking others is essential to his character and indeed his life. He is a cynical figure who exploits his community and exaggerates everyday events for comedic effect, even when his family and friends explicitly turn to him for help. When Elizabeth finally explains her sincere affection for Mr. Darcy, he momentarily relents and admits he "could not have parted with you . . . to any one less worthy." But when the heroine comments that Darcy was responsible for settling Wickham's debts and arranging his future position, Mr. Bennet again turns to condescending jest. He announces: "This is an evening of wonders, indeed! And so, Darcy did everything; made up the match, gave the money, paid the fellow's debts, and got him his commission!" He claims he would have paid Mr. Gardiner, "but these violent young lovers carry every thing their own way. I shall offer to pay him to-morrow; he will rant and storm about his love for you, and there will be an end of the matter." Mr. Bennet can only understand the kindness of Mr. Darcy as a part of a farce, replete with the actions of a "violent young lover," implausible events, and a rather forced conclusion. He transforms the situation into a comedic play, and he finishes his conversation with the heroine by pronouncing, "If any young men come for Mary or Kitty, send them in, for I am quite at leisure" (P&P, 418–19). In his final line of dialogue in the novel, he sarcastically presents himself as a willing romantic coordinator for his two unmatched daughters. Austen returns to her depiction of Mr. Bennet as a degenerate patriarchal adviser who passively waits in his library. As readers, we identify his persistent failures as a father, but the narrative does little to hold him accountable for his ineptitude or curtail his paternalism. Instead, he returns to the solitude of his library to await his next patronizing performance.

And like General Tilney, he retains the privileges of hegemonic masculinity. In the closing pages, the narrator informs us that "Mr. Bennet missed his second daughter exceedingly," and "delighted in going to Pemberley, especially when he was least expected" (P&P, 427). Austen's comment reminds us of his fondness for the heroine, and perhaps suggests their enduring convivial relationship, but it also points to his sustained privilege. His attendance at Pemberley is apparently not by invitation; rather, he arrives at his discretion, indicating his freedom and license as a paternalistic man. Mr. Bennet and General Tilney preserve their power by patronizing others, especially young women, and Austen obscures the damaging effects of their behavior by depicting their language, actions, and even situations as farcical. They use condescending words and action to maintain control while masking their intentions with comedy, excessive politeness, or wit. They manipulate situations and people to achieve their desired ends, aided by farcical events. Austen does not indict them as vicious figures; instead, General Tilney and Mr. Bennet often perform as benevolent men, though their paternalistic behavior repeatedly demeans women. Glick and Fiske theorize how "benevolent sexism . . . serves as a crucial complement to hostile sexism that helps to pacify women's resistance to societal gender inequality."[30] General Tilney and Mr. Bennet may primarily operate as excessively courteous, humorous, detached, even farcical figures, but their condescending words and actions function to naturalize the oppression of women. Their deployment of comedic actions and language, and Austen's use of farcical solutions to resolve their relationships and conflicts, can thwart critical attempts to evaluate their paternalism. Austen's comic structures may even invite us to accept this naturalization of women's oppression, but the pain and trauma that these men engender is real and must not be lost in the comedy. *Pride and Prejudice* and *Northanger Abbey* document the damages caused by patronizing men, and as Zizek reminds us, we must *know what it is that we see.*

NOTES

1. Slavoj Zizek, *First as Tragedy, Then as Farce* (London: Verso, 2009), 7–8; emphasis in the original.
2. Peter Glick and Susan T. Fiske, "An Ambivalent Alliance: Hostile and Benevolent Sexism as Complimentary Justifications for Gender Inequality." *American Psychologist* 56 (2001): 111.
3. Karl Marx, "The Eighteenth Brumaire of Louis Bonaparte," in *Surveys from Exile*, trans. and ed. David Fernbach (Harmondsworth: Penguin, 1973), 146.
4. Zizek, *First as Tragedy*, 8; emphasis in the original.
5. Michael R. Booth, "Comedy and Farce," in *The Cambridge Companion to Victorian and Edwardian Theatre*, ed. Kerry Powell (Cambridge: Cambridge University Press, 2004), 140–41.
6. Glick and Fiske, "Ambivalent Alliance," 111.
7. R. W. Connell, *Masculinities*, 2nd ed. (Berkeley: University of California Press, 2005), 76–77.
8. Peter Glick and Susan T. Fiske, "Hostile and Benevolent Sexism: Measuring Ambivalent Sexist Attitudes Toward Women," *Psychology of Women Quarterly* 21, no. 1 (1998): 120.
9. Glick and Fiske, "Hostile and Benevolent Sexism," 121; emphasis in the original.
10. Glick and Fiske, "Ambivalent Alliance," 110.
11. Glick and Fiske, "Ambivalent Alliance," 111.
12. D. W. Harding, *Regulated Hatred and Other Essays on Jane Austen* (1940), ed. Monica Lawlor (London: Athlone Press, 1998), 11.
13. Marvin Mudrick, *Jane Austen: Irony as Defense and Discovery* (Princeton: Princeton University Press, 1952), 1, 3.
14. Mudrick, *Jane Austen*, 3.
15. See, for example, Jillian Heydt-Stevenson's *Austen's Unbecoming Conjunctions: Subversive Laughter, Embodied History* (New York: Palgrave Macmillan, 2005), which offers "the first comprehensive investigation of the formative role that dissident comedy plays in Austen's writing" (1–2).
16. Kate Fullbrook, "Jane Austen and the Comic Negative," in *Women's Reading Women's Writing*, ed. Sue Roe (New York: Harvester Publishing, 1987), 41.

17. For a detailed account of Burke's despair over the decay of chivalric masculinity in the wake of the French Revolution, see Claudia L. Johnson's *Equivocal Beings: Politics, Gender, and Sentimentality in the 1790s: Wollstonecraft, Radcliffe, Burney, Austen* (Chicago: University of Chicago Press, 1995) and Michael Kramp's *Disciplining Love: Austen and the Modern Man* (Columbus: Ohio State University Press, 2007).

18. Tim Fulford, *Romanticism and Masculinity: Gender, Politics and Poetics in the Writings of Burke, Coleridge, Cobbett, Wordsworth, DeQuincey and Hazlitt* (New York: St. Martin's Press, 1999), 9.

19. Mary Wollstonecraft, *The Vindications: The Rights of Men and the Rights of Woman*. Ed. D. L. Macdonald and Kathleen Scherf (Peterborough, ON: Broadview Press, 1997), 132; emphasis in the original.

20. Kenneth W. Graham, "The Case of the Petulant Patriarch," *Persuasions: Journal of the Jane Austen Society of North America* 20 (1998): 127.

21. For an extensive discussion of this scene, see Robert Hopkins, "General Tilney and Affairs of the State: The Political Gothic of *Northanger Abbey*," *Philological Quarterly* 57 (1978): 213–24.

22. Graham, "Case of the Petulant Patriarch," 129.

23. Claudia L. Johnson, *Jane Austen: Women, Politics, and the Novel* (Chicago: University of Chicago Press, 1987), 46.

24. B. C. Southam, "General Tilney's Hot-houses," *Ariel* 3, no. 1 (1971): 59.

25. See, for example, C. L. Johnson, *Jane Austen*; Kenneth L. Moler, "Some Verbal Tactics of General Tilney," *Persuasions: Journal of the Jane Austen Society of North America* 6 (1984): 10–12; and Shinobu Minma, "General Tilney and Tyranny: *Northanger Abbey*," *Eighteenth-Century Fiction* 8, no. 4 (1995): 503–18.

26. For an extensive discussion of this tradition and its importance to the development of British masculinity, see Markman Ellis, *The Politics of Sensibility: Race, Gender and Commerce in the Sentimental Novel* (Cambridge: Cambridge University Press, 1999); Jason D. Solinger, *Becoming the Gentlemen: British Literature and the Invention of Modern Masculinity, 1660–1815* (New York: Palgrave, 2012); and Kramp, *Disciplining Love*.

27. Mary Burgan, "Mr. Bennet and the Failures of Fatherhood in Jane Austen's Novels." *Journal of English and Germanic Philology* 74 (1975): 539.

28. Susan Fraiman, "The Humiliation of Elizabeth Bennet," in *Unbecoming Women: British Women Writers and the Novel of Development* (New York: Columbia University Press, 1993), 169.

29. Fraiman, "Humiliation of Elizabeth Bennet," 170.

30. Glick and Fiske, "Ambivalent Alliance," 109.

8

SENSE, SENSIBILITY, SEA MONSTERS, AND CARNIVALESQUE CARICATURE

Misty Krueger

J ANE AUSTEN HAS BEEN RESURRECTED from the dead; for almost two hundred years after her untimely death, she has coauthored at least five monster mashups that merge parts of her novels with new plots focused on horror and humor. The Austen monster mashup derives its inspiration in part from Austen's novels, but largely from pop-culture films and television shows featuring zombies, sea creatures, vampires, mummies, and dragons. The most recognizable Austen monster mashup is from Quirk Classics: the wildly successful *Pride and Prejudice and Zombies* (2009); however, quick on the heels of *Zombies*, the publisher released another "cross-period 'collaboration,'" this one blending *Sense and Sensibility* with sea monsters.[1] *Sea Monsters* begins with a plot alteration called, appropriately enough, "the Alteration," an event that occurred "when the waters of the world grew cold and hateful to the sons of man, and darkness moved on the face of the deep."[2] Sea creatures morphed into enormous man-killing monsters, including giant lobsters and octopi, a Fang Beast, and a leviathan. Sea witches cursed by turning them into half-human, half-sea creature hybrids. In this "dystopian world," Linda Troost observes, "all the creatures of the sea have declared war on mankind."[3] Yet, *Sea Monsters* is not a tale that portrays gruesome human destruction for the sake of spectacle alone.

Contributing to the "remaking, rewriting, 'adaptation', reworking, 'appropriation', conversion, mimicking" that John Wiltshire names as crucial parts of the "current landscape" of Austen studies, the monster mashup appeals most to Austen fans looking for a laugh, and perhaps to contemporary readers who need some coaxing to see the humor in a Regency-era novel.[4] In this respect, the monster mashup helps shape a contemporary Austen mediascape by ostensibly showing readers some things implicitly funny in Austen's day through ridiculous images and ridicule. To do this, as *Sea Monsters* coauthor Ben H. Winters explains, the "parody of the Regency classic" allegorizes mankind's flaws by mocking Austen's characters.[5] *Sea Monsters* is a carnival funhouse full of mirrors that reflects and distorts the source text with the purpose of bringing to the surface the "horrors lurking in the margins of Austen's novels": suppressed desires, sexual shame, and hypersensibility.[6] In large part, Winters's conversion of Austen's esteemed Colonel Brandon into a laughable human-monster-hybrid brings these "horrors" to the surface. Brandon's grotesque body exposes and magnifies *Sense and Sensibility*'s "comic irreverence," "bawdy humor," and criticism of overwrought sensibility— traits that may be too historically distant to be recognizable to twenty-first-century readers, but that are necessary to our full understanding of Austen's novel.[7] Ultimately, the monster mashup literalizes conceptual problems embedded in *Sense and Sensibility* in order to "reveal and criticize ideological frameworks of the original."[8] *Sea Monsters* invites a "knowing audience"—readers intimately familiar with *Sense and Sensibility*—first to have fun with *Sea Monsters*' incongruous, carnivalesque doppelgangers and then to revisit *Sense and Sensibility*.[9] After having a good laugh, readers can critically reexamine Austen's depiction of Colonel Brandon and turn-of-the nineteenth-century notions of sensibility and desire.

WRITING THE AUSTEN MONSTER MASHUP
AND PLEASING AUSTEN FANS

Although fans love Austen's novels in all of their Regency-era glory, contemporary adaptations reveal that Austen devotees also appreciate when writers inject new life into the author's classic works. Often, this update materializes in rom-com films and videos. In *Bride and Prejudice*, for instance, the film trades England for India and country-dances for scenes straight out of Bollywood; in *The Lizzie Bennet Diaries*, via two-to-eight-minute vlogs, viewers can enter Lizzie's twenty-first-century bedroom on a weekly basis to hear her gab about her career and social life. While these lighthearted contemporary updates are clearly attractive to fans, in some cases, Austen fans would rather stay closer to Austen's world, but with added mayhem and even death. Such is the appeal of the monster mashup, which keeps Austen's temporal and spatial setting while weaving this world with that of monster cult classics. Indeed, sometimes fans prefer the added material of this new world to Austen's. According to Winters, "The readers who gobbled up *Zombies* reported back to Quirk that as much as they loved the Jane Austen stuff, they wanted a little less of it."[10] Thus, editorial director, Jason Rekulak, encouraged Winters to give readers what they wanted: a little bit of Austen and a lot of a new monster-verse. Winters's "mandate on *Sea Monsters* was to deliver a book that was

60 percent Austen and 40 percent [Winters]," as compared to *Zombies'* 85/15 percent ratio of old and new material.[11] Winters's "job was to introduce a B-movie action/ adventure plot while preserving Austen's original story and most of her text. [He] was allowed to add new words, sentences, and paragraphs and to delete Austen's words where necessary, for logic and length."[12] As a result, the parodic pastiche combines Austen's words with new language emulating her style.[13]

Winters also explains what is at the heart of the Austen monster mashup: "Readers want to meet familiar characters in new situations," but the new "versions should act and sound recognizably like the originals."[14] In these terms, the writer must satisfy fans by giving them something new that *sounds* like something old. Characters should behave and speak similarly to Austen's; the mashup doppelgangers should not drastically depart from their predecessors, but instead draw out something preexisting in them. Winters explains how he accomplished this: "I used the monsters and other interpolations not to replace but to accentuate what was already there in Austen's novel. She made Col. Brandon a bit too old for Marianne so she would have to struggle to see his goodness; all I did by giving him an octopus face was make her struggle a little harder. Whenever possible, I coordinated monster attacks with the moments of high emotional peril that Austen had already created."[15] Although it might seem as if *Sea Monsters* portrays radically different characters, their added monstrosities embellish and bring out embedded characteristics in Austen's characters. As Winters sees himself responding to Austen's writing, *Sea Monsters* becomes a study in Austen.

Winters gives good reasons for writing a humorous monster mashup, "not least of which being that a good satire (or sequel, or adaptation, or homage, or whatever) reminds us of the enduring power of the original."[16] Unfortunately, not all readers share this vision. In summoning up a dead author, writers must "beware of the hordes of the living . . . who cry foul" at any intrusion into the Austen world.[17] Some Austen purists, critics, and scholars perceive the monster mashup as a commercial pillaging of Austen and "an anti-academic intervention into Austen," as Juliette Wells puts it.[18] Marie Mulvey-Roberts, for example, claims that the "mash-up has enabled the modern text to vampirise the original with new textual blood."[19] Likewise, Amy Leal treats *Zombies* as a part of "the recent vampiric additions to Janeism" that "not only feed on the Austen craze but also provide a metaphor for the wider parasitic trend itself" (the monster mashup).[20] On the other hand, Troost frames it this way: "Of course, the mash-up does incredible violence to Austen's subtle touch—that's the point of satire. The joke mostly lies in playing against that famous subtlety, as well as trashing the shallow elegance."[21] Troost sees monster mashups as "acts of interpretation": they "may seem like nonsense, but they do manage to reanimate bits and pieces of Austen's novels that a modern reader might not notice in the original."[22] If we share critics' unenthusiastic mind-sets toward monster mashups, we will miss "important opportunities" to explore Austen's comedy with fresh eyes.[23] As Wells argues, we should take "Austen-inspired works," in this case, monster mashups, "on their own terms" because "we have a lot to learn from" them.[24] They show twenty-first-century readers new ways to approach aspects of Austen's novels, such as sensibility; and especially for Austen fans, monster mashups reveal understated aspects of characters—such as Colonel Brandon—that deserve further attention.

"UGLY COUPLINGS," CARNIVALESQUE, AND CARICATURE

What we have to learn from a mashup is not always pretty. Mary Ann O'Farrell argues that the "rhetorical invocation of Jane Austen" has the potential to evoke a "juxtaposition" that "turns towards ugly couplings."[25] *Sea Monsters* represents such an unpleasant union as early as the book cover, which shows a gray-haired, tentacle-faced man (Colonel Brandon) embracing a beautiful woman.[26] The cover shows that the line between monster and man is not absolute; neither is the division between Austen's source text and Winters's adaptation. Brandon becomes the image of the Austen monster mashup: a little bit of that proper Austen and a lot of that perverse monster add-on. He retains elements from the source text, such as his age ("wrong side of five and thirty"), devotion to Marianne, and hatred of Willoughby; however, the adaptation adds to these plot points oozing tentacles and awkwardly erotic behavior. This is truly an "ugly coupling" with Austen's refined Brandon, but one that makes explicit his emotional turmoil not as easily *seen* in the source text.

To illustrate this change, *Sea Monsters* inserts drawings of the human-monster Brandon and repeatedly mocks his horrific ailment. In the novel, readers first see a drawing of Brandon bearing the sign of a sea witch's curse: "The seminal misfortune written, quite literally, all over his face."[27] The narrator describes Brandon's face as "writhing this way and that, like hideous living facial hair of slime green."[28] When John Dashwood first meets Brandon, he does not recognize him as a "human being" and grabs a knife to protect himself. John shouts what others think when they first meet Brandon: "What in the name of the Father and the Son is wrong with his face?"[29] Contrary to his literary predecessor, Brandon's face is what Sigmund Freud would label "stupid and nonsensical."[30] We know that Austen's Brandon is old, but never is he described as ugly or bearing a facial defect. Rather, in *Sea Monsters*, Brandon's face bears the mark of "comic physiognomy."[31] As Henri Bergson argues, comic physiognomy "intensif[ies] ugliness to the point of deformity" and mirrors the "transition from the deformed to the ridiculous."[32] Winters's revision of Brandon generates ridiculous behaviors from his comic physiognomy. Besides Brandon's outrageous visage, his "lunatic's nightmare of a face" makes a constant "low gurgling noise."[33] It seems that "he breathe[s] wetly through the slimy hanging forest of his face."[34] Sometimes when Brandon becomes upset, he can barely utter a sentence. For instance, when Brandon confronts Elinor about Willoughby, Brandon states, "My object—my wish—glurb—hurble—is to be a means of giving comfort and gurble." He has to stop speaking to wipe away a "greenish mixture of spittle and mucus that had accumulated on his chin."[35] The addition of mucus-generating tentacles exemplifies Winters's use of comic physiognomy to parody Austen's Brandon's difficulty in communicating his feelings. Near the end of the novel, Winters directly approaches the purpose of Brandon's "bizarre appearance." As the narrator notes, from Edward Ferrars's point of view, it signifies "an outward affliction analogous to . . . inward affliction"; "some are marked within . . . and some without."[36] The effect is a Bakhtinian "world inside out," a space in which what is usually (in Austen's novel) retained inside is made manifest and even grotesque.[37]

In *Sea Monsters*, we find a horrid and humorous version of Austen's novel, a combination that signals *carnivalistic mésalliance*: a mashup of two incongruous, unsuitable things and the kind of juxtaposition that Mikhail Bakhtin claims "brings together, unifies, weds, and combines the sacred with the profane, the lofty with the low, the great with the insignificant, the wise with the stupid."[38] No doubt, Austen and *Sense and Sensibility* denote for many readers the first set of signifiers: sacred, lofty, great, wise. It is the reader's goal to decipher how the alternate universe becomes a "carnival square"—a literary space in which Winters translates the aforementioned ideals into profanity, burlesque, and absurdity.[39] As in other carnival literature, in *Sea Monsters*, Austen's "traditional plot situations radically change their meaning," and "there develops a dynamic, carnivalistic play of sharp contrasts, unexpected shifts and changes."[40] In Brandon's characterization, we see this sense of play explicitly, as well as the ritual carnivalistic "decrowning" of an archetypal noble figure. Essentially, Winters knocks Brandon off his pedestal to humanize him, ironically by turning him into a human-monster hybrid. He highlights Brandon's frailties, human as well as fishy, and shows the "dependence of [his] mental functions on bodily needs."[41] As Freud puts it, unmasking these faults shows that Austen's Brandon, positioned by the narrator and Elinor as a kind of "demigod," "is after all only human like you and me."[42] In the adaptation, the decrowned version of Brandon points to what Freud christens "one of the most frequent sources of humorous pleasure": an "economy of pity."[43] In witnessing a debunking of Austen's lofty character, readers confront a sympathetic victim of a sea witch's curse who had to become a monster in order to become vulnerable and thus mortal like the rest of us.

What makes carnivalization so useful to a study of *Sea Monsters*' Brandon is that it points to the mashup's "artistic visualization" as a kind of "heuristic" for showing readers "unseen things" in Austen's work.[44] Through dialogic "carnival freedom," the adaptation brings together elements that may seem "disunified and distant," but actually work in tandem to reveal the characters' weaknesses, some of which are physical and many of which are social.[45] A carnivalesque reading of *Sea Monsters* becomes a kind of archaeological dig that unearths the pleasure of absurdity and playful humor, predominantly by making fun of Austen's venerated hero. Winters turns Brandon into a joke in order to visually embody something socially absurd lurking in the source text—something definitely recognized by Austen's Marianne: an awkward gentleman over thirty-five years old who pines over a girl seventeen years of age who reminds him of someone he once loved in his youth. As Winters expresses in a response to why he wrote the novel, he wanted to give Marianne a concrete reason for disliking Brandon that contemporary readers can understand—Brandon is, from a certain perspective, downright creepy. After all, beyond grossing people out, Brandon's "perverse appendages" cause those who look at him "to catch a terrifying glimpse of all the terrors that lie, unknowable and unimaginable, beyond the world that we can see and feel."[46] Brandon's face and behavior remind readers visually and spiritually of a kind of Lovecraftian Cthulhu aspiring to colonize the planet, even though Winters only draws on that mythos as another way of Othering Brandon. Winters does not make Brandon "ugly" merely to scare people; he does it to make him funnier-looking and more socially awkward than the Austen prototype. One problem with Austen's Brandon is that twenty-first-century readers might not comprehend why Marianne is so repelled by him, or why this is amusing. While Austen's Brandon lacks "a comic trait," except for his age and flair for flannel, Winters's caricature provides a means to "unhesitatingly create it."[47] This exaggeration paves the way for characters and readers to laugh at Brandon.

LAUGHING AT "OLE FISHY FACE," NONSENSE, AND HYPERSENSIBILITY

As various humor theories reveal, people often laugh at others due to feelings of superiority, recognition of incongruity, and a need for comic relief. *Sea Monsters* best displays these theories through characters' reactions to Brandon. The narrator, Willoughby, Sir John Middleton, Mrs. Jennings, Mrs. Palmer, Marianne, and even Elinor laugh at Brandon's expense. As expected, Willoughby's laughter is the cruelest, for he labels Brandon "Ole Fishy Face" and makes numerous jokes in order to set Brandon apart from humans. Many of these jokes evoke comic physiognomy in order to condemn Brandon's visage. For instance, in a "tribute" to Brandon, "Willoughby execute[s] a mocking gesture with his hands, holding the flat of his palm below his nose and wiggling his fingers in comical imitation of Brandon's deformity."[48] Here the narrator's description begins with a pantomime of ugliness and ends with a confirmation of "deformity" that is "comical." Other signs of comic physiognomy occur when Willoughby animalizes and sexualizes Brandon. To Marianne, Willoughby remarks that Brandon leaves the group intending to scout out a shipwreck so that he will not be "mistaken for a mating partner by a she-squid."[49] Such jokes set out to deprive Brandon of his humanity, the part of himself he struggles to keep in check.

To address this conflict, *Sea Monsters'* jokes often draw a parallel between Brandon's face and his mind, only to eradicate the Cartesian split. Time and again, Brandon has trouble separating his thoughts from his involuntary bodily senses. Here the novel's parody of the body/mind split leaves Brandon ridiculously vulnerable to the community's laughter. In one example, Willoughby tells Marianne that he stands "a few feet away" from Brandon "so [Brandon's] animation on topics of interest does not cause his tentacles to accidentally brush against [Willoughby]."[50] In another, Willoughby claims that while Brandon has "a thinking mind," his "fish's face" might "be more comfortable out of his gentleman's coats and submerged in the tank in [Willoughby's] parlour."[51] Facetiously, Willoughby indicates that a fishy face precludes cogitation. Willoughby's "tendentious jokes" aggressively criticize a wise, thoughtful person whom the community has placed in an "exalted position."[52] These hostile jokes represent an attempt to belittle, scorn, and ridicule Brandon, as well as to gain superiority over him. Indeed, Willoughby seems to defeat his enemy and knock Brandon off his pedestal every time members of the community laugh with him. Willoughby's joking appears successful, for other characters join in the lampoon against Brandon by making their own jokes.

The community's laughter is key to Brandon's "monster treatment."[53] No other character receives this treatment, and no other character is laughed at as Brandon is. As the following examples demonstrate, the aggregate of *Sea Monsters'* jokes points to incongruity and "ritual laughter"—laughter that reproduces Brandon's physical oddities—and comic relief.[54] Marianne describes how "his voice makes that low gurgling noise that really turns one's stomach," and even Elinor cannot help but concede in the moment: "The tone of his voice . . . is indeed quite unsettlingly aqueous."[55] Sir John joins in the fun by saying to Brandon, "I can tell your resolution even now, by the way your appendages point towards the door."[56] At another point in the novel, Mrs. Jennings says to Brandon, "I am monstrous glad to see you" and, out of his presence, refers to him as "poor, fished-faced Colonel Brandon."[57] As an example of comic relief, she laughs at the thought of Brandon's elation in discovering that Willoughby will not marry Marianne and cackles, "He will have her within the reach of those tentacles that so unpleasantly decorate his maw. . . . How he'll chuckle a gurgling, unsettling chuckle over this news!"[58] Like her mother, Mrs. Palmer describes Brandon as a "pitiable creature" who "sort of gibber[s] and moan[s], as he does sometimes helplessly."[59] Charlotte concedes that Brandon at one time would have married her, but "the very thought of becoming his wife fills [her] with nausea, and a sort of queer nameless dread."[60] In some respect, the community displaces its fear of death by laughing at Brandon. He becomes a comic scapegoat for all sea monsters—while the community has little recourse against the volume and size of the sea creatures, at the very least it can get the upper hand on Brandon by mocking him. In insulting him, members of this close-knit community do not have to face their own fears or their flaws. In this alternate universe, Brandon-jokes are integral to society's social process of comic relief and serve as a sign of its privileged laughter.

The same is true for twenty-first-century readers who also are implicated in this privileged laughter. As we laugh at Brandon, we distance ourselves from his character, even think ourselves better than he is. We experience the Freudian notion of "pleasure in nonsense," particularly "comical nonsense," every time we laugh at Brandon's ridiculous facial feelers and feelings.[61] Perhaps we gain pleasure in laughing at Austen, too, for in some way *Sea Monsters'* Brandon represents her. Some readers might find themselves engaging in carnival laughter, which "deals with the very process of change, with *crisis* itself" as they question the appropriateness of enjoying the monster mashup.[62] Is it acceptable to like Austen's characters and then laugh at a parody of them? For Austen purists, the monster mashup's "mocking" or "deriding" of Colonel Brandon might engender a crisis of fidelity, but, as Gabriela Castellanos reminds us, carnival laughter can be "triumphantly regenerative."[63] *Sea Monsters* could signify an Austen renaissance, one that reinvigorates the author's work as well as the titular subjects of *Sense and Sensibility*.

While readers familiar with Austen's work tend to read the title of the novel as a series of opposites, and to see the sisters as representing those opposites, Winters offers up Brandon as another version of sensibility—a monstrous one. Rather than only reading sensibility in Marianne, Winters's caricature continually *shows* us that Brandon's hypersensibility is a problem, as his body repeatedly betrays him: his tentacles cannot help but exhibit his emotions and desires. From sadness and jealousy to excitement, the caricature depicts a weepy Brandon literally and metaphorically caught up in emotion. Literally, Brandon's senses are aroused, as shown by his face. This in itself is a parody of the self-control that is associated with Austen's metaphorical representation of Brandon. At one point in *Sea Monsters*, Brandon's "facial appendages appeared to tie themselves into knots of emotion"; at another time, "tears rolled down his cheeks and mingled freely with the effluvia of his tentacles."[64] When Brandon worries about Marianne, we read of the "woeful and melancholy hang of his tentacles" and "how his face-feelers stand at grim attention" or "[grow] rigid with concern."[65] In a somber conversation with Elinor, Brandon's "fleshy face fingers [twist] themselves into knots of awkwardness," and he "nod[s] sadly so as to cause his tentacle-mass to shake limply."[66] When Elinor shares her fears with Brandon about her sister's health, "he listen[s] to them in silent despondence, sternly stroking his appendages."[67] All of these examples reveal how the monster mashup's "increased focus on the body . . . takes the form of a reification of characters' social and mental anxieties."[68] In *Sea Monsters*, Brandon's comic physiognomy allows readers to see something about Austen's Brandon's mental state that is not glaringly apparent: he struggles, too, with hypersensitive feelings. In Austen's novel, Brandon has no physical means of betraying himself, but in Winters's tale, sensibility materializes a hybrid emotional-bodily problem.

Characters' fears of Brandon further relate this criticism of hypersensibility. Marianne wonders who will protect them from "the chance of [Brandon] strangling his accuser with his rage-stiffened face-appendages?"[69] When Sir John cautions Marianne about choosing Willoughby over Brandon, he fears Brandon's jealousy "may cause the evil spirits that inhabit his bile ducts to erupt."[70] The emotions that Austen's Brandon suppresses, Winters exposes, thus causing Brandon to appear "more fish than man" when he cannot regulate his emotions.[71] Brandon's inability to control his feelings points back to Austen's novel, to a Brandon who works to quash his longing to please Marianne, as well as his desire to spend his life with her. Yet, this caricature of Brandon also reminds readers of Marianne and any person who falls victim to hypersensibility: sensibility is mortifying and terrifying, and most often represents a threat to person and society.

Sometimes, however, sensibility can be a strength and even help the community. While in most instances the adaptation's mockery reveals that Brandon is too sensitive to control his mind and body, near the end of the novel "his fishier qualities" save the Dashwoods from imminent danger: Marianne's suffering malaria (rather than the source text's mere cold) and a pirate attack upon the houseboat where she slumbers. As Marianne lies on her deathbed, Brandon "spen[ds] hours each morning catching sardines out of the shallows with his own face, so Marianne might have sustenance readily available."[72] As the narrator explains, Elinor "knew what emotional exertion Brandon required to so embrace the fishy part of his nature." Brandon becomes a hero, in our contemporary sense of the term, when he uses his monstrosity to help save the Dashwoods—when he turns his bodily and emotional hypersensibility into an asset. For instance, Brandon "[swam] so nobly to Marianne's rescue"[73] by retrieving Mrs. Dashwood, bringing her to Marianne aboard his back, and violently killing the pirate Dreadbeard. Clearly characters dread Brandon's beard, but not as much as the pirate Dreadbeard. In giving Brandon a foil besides Willoughby, Winters shrewdly draws attention to Brandon's beard and the personal obstacles he must overcome. As the product of his hypersensibility, Brandon "hack[s] the corpse of Dreadbeard to bits with an axe seized from the deck of the ship, and [throws] bits of his body, one by one, overboard."[74] Remarkably, a visual image accompanies the text so that readers can *see* Brandon besting this bearded nemesis and vindicating himself. While this scene could read as one of terror, however, it evokes quite the opposite image. From Mrs. Dashwood's riding a saddle on Brandon's back to his slaughter of Dreadbeard, this spectacle situates Brandon as "one of the worthiest of men" in Mrs. Dashwood's eyes and causes her to see the "beauty of his heart" despite the "unbeauty of his face!"[75] Perhaps *because* Brandon is willing to murder brutally on behalf of her daughter, Mrs. Dashwood concedes that Marianne could be "most happy with him . . . if she can bring herself to forget, or tolerate, the mass of writing tentacles upon his face."[76] Finally, Brandon becomes the hero many twenty-first-century readers want him to be in Austen's novel. He overcomes his weaknesses, fights for his love, and saves the day.

SEX AND SENSIBILITY

Nevertheless, turning Brandon into an action hero is not Winters's final task for adapting the character. His ultimate goal is to make him a suitable husband for Marianne—to help twenty-first-century readers want Marianne to marry Brandon. While some readers of *Sense and Sensibility* are concerned about Marianne marrying an old thirty-five-year-old, the end of *Sea Monsters* sets this right by indicating that Brandon's monstrous features can sexually satisfy his wife, perhaps in a way no other partner could. In accepting *Sea Monsters* as a topsy-turvy version of *Sense and Sensibility*, readers have to face a subject ostensibly absent from Austen's novels: sex. This should not come as a surprise, for throughout the novel Winters laid the groundwork for Brandon's sexual vigor. In many examples, Brandon's tentacles reveal sublimated sexual passion. When Brandon sees Marianne, "his tentacles performed a sort of gentle, romantic sway as he gaze[s] upon her."[77] In moments of excitement, Brandon's "fishy fingers [grow] rigid, as they sometimes did when he became animated."[78] Brandon cannot stop his tentacles from "dancing with animation" when he speaks of Marianne.[79] Sir John explains to Marianne that when her name is mentioned, Brandon starts "gibbering and moaning and tugging at his feelers"—the physical signs of sexual arousal. The most awkward example of Brandon's sexual expression comes when Elinor notices that Brandon's "appendages at times seemed to stiffen a bit when he chanced to glance upon Marianne, as if excess blood were flowing into them."[80] If *Sea Monsters* readers share Elinor's point of view, as readers tend to do in the source text, they probably feel as uncomfortable as she does in this moment. We know that it "discomfited her to see the aforementioned tentacle-stiffness."[81]

In *Sea Monsters*, the source text Brandon's repressed sexual energy manifests itself through what Bakhtin calls a "funny monster" that represents the *id* "uncrowned and transformed."[82] It is not proper for a man to physically display his sexual arousal, but apparently a monster that cannot help but reveal it is funny. Again, this carnivalized version of Brandon brings him down to our level; the monstrous is what makes him more human to twenty-first-century readers. *Sea Monsters* is laced with this kind of sympathetic sexual humor, and the culminating example provides Brandon with a reward for his deformity. Although Marianne still has "a fast-fading horror of his nauseating appearance," at the end of the novel, readers learn that Brandon's "face was not the only region of his physiognomy that could be described as multi-appendaged, and [Marianne] found that fact to carry with it certain marital satisfactions."[83] For once, the euphemism breaks the novel's pattern of ridiculing Brandon's "feelers." Here the novel sexualizes Brandon and Marianne, again making a joke at his expense, but one that implies particular recompense for the woman who enjoys sexual activity. Perhaps twenty-first-century readers might connect better with this version of Marianne, too, for this "appropriation . . . comments perceptively on the original as well as on our culture."[84] Lo and behold, women may have enjoyed sex in Austen's time and may continue to do so in ours. Although in Austen's novel, Marianne represents Brandon's (and the community's) reward, in Winters's, she herself receives a gift for marrying "Old Fishy Face." Thanks to *Sea Monsters*, we can imagine what is missing from Austen's book—a satisfactory ending for *both* Brandon and Marianne that will include sexual stimulation.

RETHINKING *SENSE AND SENSIBILITY*

When Richard Jenkyns wrote in 2007, "Jane Austen and . . . books abound," he had no idea of the forthcoming Austen "and" monster mashups.[85] Yet the conjunction of the Regency and the monster worlds provides a valuable means for chuckling at Austen's novels and discerning more about her works, particularly in contemplating what each version of her characters reveals to us. In the case of Brandon, Winters draws on both his admirable qualities and his shortcomings to show readers why he is worthy of Elinor's veneration and parody. In both novels Brandon stands apart from the community, and, in turning him into a monster, Winters graphically reveals why this is the case. *Sea Monsters'* Brandon becomes the overt symbol of complex concepts that are covertly a part of Austen's novelistic landscape, but here are manifest. It is much easier to see what desire and oversensitivity look like when they are placed upon a monster. Essentially, Winters makes Brandon more awkward so that twenty-first-century readers can definitely see all that is wrong with him: he is physically off-putting, he wears his heart on his sleeve (or his tentacles), he feels too much for Marianne, and he has trouble connecting with people. Through humor, Winters caricatures Brandon's weaknesses—namely, desire and sensibility—and through the grotesque, Winters brings the horrors of the deep to the surface.

Neither a mere spin-off of *Zombies* nor a travesty of Austen's work, as Janine Barchas and Kristina Straub have labeled it,[86] *Sea Monsters'* alternate universe provides readers with an instructive place to rethink Austen's novel—and to have a good time doing it. Readers who are familiar with both Austen's novel and Winters's adaptation stand to gain much from seeing how in his exposed state the monster Brandon exposes people's inability to control their emotions and their bodies. In the carnival world of *Sea Monsters*, a lack of control appears to be funny; in *Sense and Sensibility*, it is forbidden. This is a part of the overarching goals of parody, which encourages readers to take a step away from a source text and laugh in order to reconsider what is worth evaluating in the first place; in this case, it is Brandon, desire, (non)sense, and sensibility. Although it might make us squirm a bit, *Sea Monsters* allows Austen fans a delightful, productive way of revisiting a beloved Austen novel through the absurd. While the monster mashup paints a darker picture of Austen's world than most adaptations do, it also makes light of this space and her characters, too. Ultimately, the monster mashup participates in a continually developing Austen mediascape by comically, yet grotesquely, reinventing Austen's work.

NOTES

1. Tiffany Potter, "Historicizing the Popular and the Feminine: *The Rape of the Lock* and *Pride and Prejudice and Zombies*," in *Women, Popular Culture, and the Eighteenth Century*, ed. Tiffany Potter (Toronto: University of Toronto Press, 2012), 16.
2. Jane Austen and Ben H. Winters, *Sense and Sensibility and Sea Monsters* (Philadelphia: Quirk, 2009), 7.

3. Linda Troost, "The Undead Eighteenth Century: 2010 EC-ASECS Presidential Address," *Eighteenth-Century Intelligencer* (March 2011): 7.

4. John Wiltshire, *Recreating Jane Austen* (Cambridge: Cambridge University Press, 2001), 2.

5. Ben H. Winters, "This Scene Could Really Use a Man-Eating Jellyfish: How I Wrote Sense and Sensibility and Sea Monsters," *Slate*, last modified September 15, 2009, http://www.slate.com/articles/arts/culturebox/2009/09/this_scene_could_really_use_a_maneating_jellyfish.html (accessed May 18, 2018).

6. Marie Mulvey-Roberts, "Mashing Up Jane Austen: *Pride and Prejudice and Zombies* and the Limits of Adaptation," *Irish Journal of Gothic and Horror Studies* 13 (2014): 17.

7. Jill Heydt-Stevenson, "'Slipping into the Ha-Ha': Bawdy Humor and Body Politics in Jane Austen's Novels," *Nineteenth-Century Literature* 55, no. 3 (December 2000): 312, 311.

8. Hanne Birke, "Gothic Fiction Bites Back—The Gothification of Jane Austen at the Beginning of the 21st Century," in *Pride and Prejudice 2.0: Interpretations, Adaptations, and Transformations of Jane Austen's Classic*, ed. Hanne Birk and Marion Gymnich (Gottingen, German: V&R University Press and Bonn University Press, Gottingen, Germany, 2015), 247.

9. For more on a "knowing audience," see Linda Hutcheon, *A Theory of Adaptation* (New York: Routledge, 2006).

10. Winters, "This Scene."

11. Winters, "This Scene."

12. Winters, "This Scene."

13. Linda Troost and Eckart Voights-Virchow call *Zombies* a pastiche. See Troost, "Undead," 4, and Eckart Voigts-Virchow, "Pride and Promiscuity and Zombies, or: Miss Austen Mashed Up in the Affinity Spaces of Participatory Cultures," in *Adaptation and Cultural Appropriation: Literature, Film, and the Arts*, ed. Pascal Nicklas and Oliver Lindner (Berlin/Boston: Walter de Gruyter, 2012), 48.

14. Ben H. Winters, "I Write With Dead People: How to Collaborate With a Corpse," *Huffington Post*, last modified March 18, 2010, http://www.huffingtonpost.com/ben-h-winters/i-write-with-dead-people_b_347365.html (accessed May 18, 2018).

15. Winters, "This Scene."

16. Winters, "I Write."

17. Winters, "I Write."

18. Juliette Wells, "New Approaches to Austen and the Popular Reader," in *Uses of Austen,* ed. Gillian Dow and Clare Hanson (New York: Palgrave, 2012), 78.

19. Mulvey-Roberts, "Mashing Up," 32.

20. Amy Leal, "See Jane Bite." *The Chronicle of Higher Education*, last modified March 14, 2010, http://chronicle.com/article/See-Jane-Bite/64585.

21. Troost, "Undead," 6.

22. Troost, "Undead," 3.

23. Wells, "New Approaches," 79.

24. Wells, "New Approaches," 79.

25. Mary Ann O'Farrell, "'Bin Laden a Huge Jane Austen Fan': Jane Austen in Contemporary Political Discourse," in *Uses of Austen: Jane's Afterlives*, ed. Gillian Dow and Clare Hanson (New York: Palgrave, 2012), 193.

26. The cover adapts W. & D. Downey's 1897 *Mr Forbes Robertson and Mrs Patrick Campbell in "Nelson's Enchantress."* This image is also an adaptation, for it is a lithograph version of a photograph taken of two actors in their performance of Risden Home's *Nelson's Enchantress.*

27. Austen and Winters, *Sea Monsters*, 55.

28. Austen and Winters, *Sea Monsters*, 37.

29. Austen and Winters, *Sea Monsters*, 203.

30. Sigmund Freud, *Jokes and Their Relation to the Unconscious*, trans. James Strachey (New York: Norton, 1960), 58.

31. Henri Bergson, *Laughter: An Essay on the Meaning of the Comic*, trans. Cloudesley Brereton and Fred Rothwell (New York: Macmillan, 1914), 22.

32. Bergson, *Laughter*, 23.

33. Austen and Winters, *Sea Monsters*, 39.

34. Austen and Winters, *Sea Monsters*, 60.

35. Austen and Winters, *Sea Monsters*, 188.

36. Austen and Winters, *Sea Monsters*, 334.

37. Mikhail Bakhtin, *Problems of Dostoevsky's* Poetics, ed. and trans. Caryl Emerson (Minneapolis: University of Minneapolis Press, 1984), 218.

38. Bakhtin, *Problems*, 123.

39. Bakhtin, *Problems*, 190.

40. Bakhtin, *Problems*, 173.

41. Freud, *Jokes*, 202.

42. Freud, *Jokes*, 202.

43. Freud, *Jokes*, 230.

44. Bakhtin, *Problems*, 166.

45. Bakhtin, *Problems*, 177.

46. Austen and Winters, *Sea Monsters*, 37.

47. Freud, *Jokes*, 201.

48. Austen and Winters, *Sea Monsters*, 56.

49. Austen and Winters, *Sea Monsters*, 71.

50. Austen and Winters, *Sea Monsters*, 57, 56.

51. Austen and Winters, *Sea Monsters*, 56.

52. Freud, *Jokes*, 105.

53. Troost, "Undead," 3.

54. Bakhtin, *Problems*, 127.

55. Austen and Winters, *Sea Monsters*, 56.

56. Austen and Winters, *Sea Monsters*, 71.

57. Austen and Winters, *Sea Monsters*, 153, 183.

58. Austen and Winters, *Sea Monsters*, 183.

59. Austen and Winters, *Sea Monsters*, 114.

60. Austen and Winters, *Sea Monsters*, 114.

61. Freud, *Jokes*, 125.

62. Bakhtin, *Problems*, 127.

63. Gabriela Castellanos, *Laughter, War and Feminism: Elements of Carnival in Three of Jane Austen's Novels* (New York: Peter Lang, 1994), 29.

64. Austen and Winters, *Sea Monsters*, 69, 191.

65. Austen and Winters, *Sea Monsters*, 188, 183, 273.

66. Austen and Winters, *Sea Monsters*, 62.

67. Austen and Winters, *Sea Monsters*, 275.

68. Ben Dew, "Rewriting Popular Classics as Popular Fiction: Jane Austen, Zombies, Sex and Vampires," in *The Bloomsbury Introduction to Popular Fiction*, ed. Christine Berberich (New York: Continuum International Publishing, 2015): 286.

69. Austen and Winters, *Sea Monsters*, 41.

70. Austen and Winters, *Sea Monsters*, 49.

71. Austen and Winters, *Sea Monsters*, 163.

72. Austen and Winters, *Sea Monsters*, 274.

73. Austen and Winters, *Sea Monsters*, 321, 275.
74. Austen and Winters, *Sea Monsters*, 299.
75. Austen and Winters, *Sea Monsters*, 303.
76. Austen and Winters, *Sea Monsters*, 302.
77. Austen and Winters, *Sea Monsters*, 210.
78. Austen and Winters, *Sea Monsters*, 60.
79. Austen and Winters, *Sea Monsters*, 185.
80. Austen and Winters, *Sea Monsters*, 158.
81. Austen and Winters, *Sea Monsters*, 158.
82. Mikhail Bakhtin, *Rabelais and His World*, trans. Helene Iswolsky (Bloomington: Indiana University Press, 1984), 49.
83. Austen and Winters, *Sea Monsters*, 338–39.
84. Troost, "Undead," 4.
85. Richard Jenkyns, *A Fine Brush on Ivory: An Appreciation of Jane Austen* (Oxford: Oxford University Press, 2007), viii.
86. Janine Barchas and Kristina Straub, "Curating *Will & Jane*," *Eighteenth-Century Life* 40, no. 2 (April 2016): 1–35.

As editor of this collection, my greatest expression of gratitude goes to the contributors, who have been willing to think seriously about laughing and have thus been willing to share with me in this combination of two of my most favorite things to do.

The idea for this volume came out of a class that I have been teaching for several years at Clemson, and thus another debt of gratitude goes to the students who over those years have played along, asked both the right and the, at first, apparently wrong questions, and who have allowed me to convince them that Jane Austen is downright hilarious. Personal debts of gratitude are also to be paid to Cameron Bushnell, Mike LeMahieu, Brian McGrath, and Elizabeth Rivlin, members of the merriest writing group in all the land. And finally, neither this book nor the course that inspired it would have come out of me were it not for the 2012 NEH Summer Seminar brilliantly run by Devoney Looser and co-conspired by a tremendously gifted and generous group of participants. It was there that I learned to work with Jane Austen, and also there that I committed to the value of her laughter.

Work for this book has received support from several sources, including a SEED Grant from the Clemson University Research Grants Committee, and an Insight Grant from the Social Sciences and Humanities Research Council of Canada. It has also been supported by the scholarly assistance and invaluable resources of the Chawton House Library and Jane Austen's House Library; the Huntington Library in San Marino, California; the Lewis Walpole Library in Farmington, Connecticut; and, to a tremendous extent, the Jane Austen Collection at Goucher College. The contributors thank the librarians and staff assistants at all of these institutions. We also thank Greg Clingham for shepherding this project with attention and acumen, Pam Dailey for keeping all the moving parts moving, and Sam Brawand for her invaluable assistance with copyediting and indexing.

Addison, Joseph [and Richard Steele]. *The Spectator*. Edited by Donald F. Bond. 5 vols. Oxford Clarendon Press, 1965.

Allison, Sarah, Marissa Gemma, Ryan Heuser, Franco Moretti, Amir Tevel, and Irena Yamboliev. "Style at the Scale of the Sentence." *Literary Lab 5* (June 2013). https://litlab.stanford.edu/LiteraryLabPamphlet5.pdf (accessed May 4, 2016).

Anderson, Misty G. *Female Playwrights and Eighteenth-Century Comedy: Negotiating Marriage on the London Stage*. Basingstoke: Palgrave Macmillan, 2002.

Aristotle. *Nicomachean Ethics*. Edited and translated by Roger Crisp. Cambridge Texts in the History of Philosophy. Cambridge: Cambridge University Press, 2014.

Atkinson, Ronald F. "Humour in Philosophy." In *Humour and History*, edited by Keith Cameron, 10–20. Oxford: Intellect, 1993.

Atwood, Margaret. *Second Words: Selected Critical Prose 1960–1982*. Toronto: Anansi, 1982.

Auerbach, Emily. *Searching for Jane Austen*. Madison: University of Wisconsin Press, 2004.

Auerbach, Nina. *Romantic Imprisonment: Women and Other Glorified Outcasts*. New York: Columbia University Press, 1986.

Austen, Henry Thomas. "Biographical Notice of the Author." In *Northanger Abbey*, edited by Susan Fraiman, 190–96. New York: Norton, 2004.

Austen, Jane. *Catharine and Other Writings*. Edited by Margaret Anne Doody and Douglas Murray. Oxford: Oxford University Press, 1993.

———. *Charades Etc. Written a Hundred Years Ago by Jane Austen and Her Family*. London: Spottiswoode, 1895.

———. *Emma*. Edited by Richard Cronin and Dorothy McMillan. In *The Cambridge Edition of the Works of Jane Austen*. Cambridge: Cambridge University Press, 2005.

———. *Jane Austen's Letters*. Edited by Deirdre Le Faye. 3rd ed. Oxford: Oxford University Press, 1995.

———. *Juvenilia*. Edited by Peter Sabor. In *The Cambridge Edition of the Works of Jane Austen*. Cambridge: Cambridge University Press, 2006.

———. *Later Manuscripts*. Edited by Janet Todd and Linda Bree. In *The Cambridge Edition of the Works of Jane Austen*. Cambridge: Cambridge University Press, 2008.

———. *Mansfield Park*. Edited by John Wiltshire. In *The Cambridge Edition of the Works of Jane Austen*. Cambridge: Cambridge University Press, 2005.

———. *Northanger Abbey*. Edited by Barbara M. Benedict and Deirdre Le Faye. In *The Cambridge Edition of the Works of Jane Austen*. Cambridge: Cambridge University Press, 2006.

———. *Persuasion*. Edited by Janet Todd and Antje Blank. In *The Cambridge Edition of the Works of Jane Austen*. Cambridge: Cambridge University Press, 2006.

———. *Pride and Prejudice*. Edited by Pat Rogers. In *The Cambridge Edition of the Works of Jane Austen*. Cambridge: Cambridge University Press, 2006.

———. *Selected Letters*. Edited by Vivien Jones. New York: Oxford University Press, 2004.

———. *Sense and Sensibility*. Edited by Edward Copeland. In *The Cambridge Edition of the Works of Jane Austen*. Cambridge: Cambridge University Press, 2006.

Austen, Jane, and Another Lady. *Sanditon: Jane Austen's Last Novel Completed*. New York: Touchstone, 1998.

Austen, Jane, and Ben H. Winters. *Sense and Sensibility and Sea Monsters*. Philadelphia: Quirk, 2009.

Austen-Leigh, James Edward. *A Memoir of Jane Austen: And Other Family Recollections*. Edited by Kathryn Sutherland. Oxford: Oxford University Press, 2008.

Austin, J. L. "Intelligent Behavior: A Critical Review of *The Concept of Mind*." In *Ryle*, edited by Oscar P. Wood and George Pitcher, 45–51. London: Macmillan, 1970. First published in the *Times Literary Supplement*, April 1950.

———. "Pretending." In *Philosophical Papers*, 2nd ed., edited by J. O. Urmson and G. J. Warnock, 253–71. London: Oxford University Press, 1970.

———. *Sense and Sensibilia*. London: Oxford University Press, 1962.

Austin-Bolt, Caroline. "Mediating Happiness: Performances of Jane Austen's Narrators." *Studies in Eighteenth Century Culture* 42 (2013): 271–89.

Ayres, Philip. *Cupid's Addresse to the Ladies*. London: R. Bentley, [1683].

———. *Emblems of Love, in Four Languages*. London: Henry Overton, 1701?

———. *Emblems of Love, in Four Languages*. London: John Wren, 1750?

Bakhtin, Mikhail. *Problems of Dostoevsky's Poetics*. Edited and translated by Caryl Emerson. Minneapolis: University of Minnesota Press, 1984.

———. *Rabelais and His World*. Translated by Helene Iswolsky. Bloomington: Indiana University Press, 1984.

Balfour, Ian. "Free Indirect Filmmaking: Jane Austen and the Renditions (On *Emma* among Its Others)." In *Constellations of a Contemporary Romanticism*, edited by Jacques Khalip and Forest Pyle, 248–66. New York: Fordham University Press, 2016.

Barchas, Janine, and Kristina Straub. "Curating *Will & Jane*." *Eighteenth-Century Life* 40, no. 2 (April 2016): 1–36.

Barreca, Regina. *Untamed and Unabashed: Essays on Women and Humor in British Literature*. Detroit: Wayne State University Press, 1994.

Barthes, Roland. *A Lover's Discourse: Fragments*. Translated by Richard Howard, with a foreword by Wayne Koestenbaum. New York: Farrar, Strauss, Giroux, 1978.

Beard, Mary. *Laughter in Ancient Rome: On Joking, Tickling, and Cracking Up*. Berkeley: University of California Press, 2014.

———. "What's So Funny?" *Chronicle of Higher Education*, July 14, 2014.

Bennett, Jane. *The Enchantment of Modern Life: Attachments, Crossings, and Ethics*. Princeton: Princeton University Press, 2001.

Bergson, Henri. *Laughter: An Essay on the Meaning of the Comic*. Translated by Cloudesley Brereton and Fred Rothwell. New York: Macmillan, 1914.

Berlant, Lauren, and Sianne Ngai. "Comedy Has Issues." Introduction to Special Issue. *Critical Inquiry* 43, no. 2 (2017): 233–49.

Bermel, Albert. *Farce: A History from Aristophanes to Woody Allen*. New York: Simon & Schuster, 1982.

Berry, Edward. *Shakespeare's Comic Rites*. Cambridge: Cambridge University Press, 1984.

Bilger, Audrey. *Laughing Feminism: Subversive Comedy in Frances Burney, Maria Edgeworth, and Jane Austen*. Detroit: Wayne State University Press, 1998.

Birke, Hanne. "Gothic Fiction Bites Back—The Gothification of Jane Austen at the Beginning of the 21st Century." In *Pride and Prejudice 2.0: Interpretations, Adaptations, and Transformations of Jane Austen's Classic*, edited by Hanne Birk and Marion Gymnich, 245–60. Gottingen, Germany: V&R University Press and Bonn University Press, 2015.

Blair, Hugh. *A Sermon on the Duties of the Young*. London and Edinburgh: T. Cadell, Jr., W. Davies, and W. Creech, 1799.

Blunt, Anthony. *Artistic Theory in Italy, 1450–1600*. Oxford: Clarendon Press, 1940.

Booth, Michael R. "Comedy and Farce." In *The Cambridge Companion to Victorian and Edwardian Theatre*, edited by Kerry Powell, 129–44. Cambridge: Cambridge University Press, 2004.

Booth, Wayne C. "Control of Distance in Jane Austen's *Emma*." In *Jane Austen's "Emma": A Casebook*, edited by Fiona Stafford, 101–21. New York: Oxford University Press, 2007.

Bourdieu, Pierre. *Outline of a Theory of Practice*. Translated by Richard Nice. Cambridge: Cambridge University Press, 1997.

Braverman, Amy. Interview with Robert J. Thompson. "Culture Jock." *University of Chicago Magazine* 98, no. 2 (2005). http://magazine.uchicago.edu/0512/features/thompson.shtml (accessed May 18, 2018).

Bree, Linda. "*Emma*: Word Games and Secret Histories." In *A Companion to Jane Austen*, edited by Claudia L. Johnson and Clara Tuite, 133–42. Oxford: Wiley-Blackwell, 2009.

Brontë, Charlotte. *Jane Eyre*. Edited by Richard Nemesvari. Peterborough, ON: Broadview Press, 1999.

Brown, Julia Prewitt. "The Feminist Depreciation of Austen: A Polemical Reading." *Novel: A Forum on Fiction* 23 (Spring 1990): 303–313.

———. *Jane Austen's Novels: Social Change and Literary Form*. Cambridge, MA: Harvard University Press, 1979.

Brown, Lloyd W. "The Comic Conclusion in Jane Austen's Novels." *PMLA* 84, no. 6 (1969): 582–87.

Brown, Marshall. "Emma's Depression," *Studies in Romanticism* 53, no. 1 (2014): 3–29.

Brownstein, Rachel. "Jane Austen: Irony and Authority." *Women's Studies* 15 (1988): 57–70.

Burgan, Mary. "Mr. Bennet and the Failures of Fatherhood in Jane Austen's Novels." *Journal of English and Germanic Philology* 74 (1975): 536–52.

Burns, Margie. "Comic Resolution, Humorous Loose Ends in Austen's Novels." *Persuasions* 33 (2011): 238–43.

Butler, Marilyn. *Jane Austen and the War of Ideas*. Oxford: Oxford University Press, 1975; 1987.

Byrne, Sandie. *Jane Austen's Possessions and Dispossessions: The Significance of Objects*. Basingstoke: Palgrave Macmillan, 2014.

Byron, George Gordon, Lord. *The Complete Poetical Works*. Edited by Jerome McGann. 7 vols. Oxford: Clarendon Press, 1980–93.

Canuel, Mark. "Jane Austen and the Importance of Being Wrong." *Studies in Romanticism* 44, no. 2 (Summer 2005): 123–50.

Castellanos, Gabriela. *Laughter, War and Feminism: Elements of Carnival in Three of Jane Austen's Novels*. Writing About Women. New York: Peter Lang, 1994.

Cavaliero, Glen. *The Alchemy of Laughter: Comedy in English Fiction*. Basingstoke: Macmillan, 2000.

Cavell, Stanley. "Must We Mean What We Say." In *Must We Mean What We Say? A Book of Essays*, 1–43. Cambridge: Cambridge University Press, 1976.

———. *Philosophy the Day After Tomorrow*. Cambridge, MA: Harvard University Press, 2005.

———. *Pursuits of Happiness: The Hollywood Comedy of Remarriage*. Cambridge, MA: Harvard University Press, 1981.

Chandler, James. *An Archaeology of Sympathy: The Sentimental Mode in Literature and Cinema*. Chicago: University of Chicago Press, 2013.

Cicero. *Letters to Quintus and Brutus*. Translated by D. R. Shackleton Bailey. Loeb Classical Library. Cambridge, MA: Harvard University Press, 1972.

Clune, Michael W. *Writing against Time*. Stanford: Stanford University Press, 2013.

Connell, R. W. *Masculinities*. 2nd ed. Berkeley: University of California Press, 2005.

Connolly, William E. *Why I Am Not a Secularist*. Minneapolis: University of Minnesota Press, 1999.

————. *A World of Becoming.* Durham, NC: Duke University Press, 2010.

"Conundrum, Christopher." *A Pretty Riddle Book.* London: R. Bassam, 1785?

Conybeare, John. *A Sermon Preach'd before the House of Lords.* Oxford: James Fletcher, 1751.

Crary, Alice. *Beyond Moral Judgment.* Cambridge, MA: Harvard University Press, 2007.

Dadlez, E. M. "Form Affects Content: Reading Jane Austen." *Philosophy and Literature* 32, no. 2 (2008): 315–29.

Daly, Peter M. *Literature in the Light of the Emblem: Structural Parallels between the Emblem and Literature in the Sixteenth and Seventeenth Centuries.* Toronto: University of Toronto Press, 1979.

Dames, Nicholas. "Jane Austen is Everything." *Atlantic* 320, no. 2 (September 2017): 92–103.

Darwin, Erasmus. *A Plan for the Conduct of Female Education in Boarding Schools.* London: J. Drewry for J. Johnson, 1797.

Davis, D. Diane. *Breaking Up (at) Totality: A Rhetoric of Laughter.* Carbondale: Southern Illinois University Press, 2000.

Dawson, William James. *The Makers of English Fiction.* New York: Fleming H. Revell, 1905.

De Quincey, Thomas. *The Collected Writings of Thomas De Quincey.* Edited by David Masson. 14 vols. London: A. & C. Black, 1896–1897.

Deresiewicz, William. *Jane Austen and the Romantic Poets.* New York: Columbia University Press, 2012.

Dew, Ben. "Rewriting Popular Classics as Popular Fiction: Jane Austen, Zombies, Sex and Vampires." In *The Bloomsbury Introduction to Popular Fiction,* edited by Christine Berberich, 285–95. New York: Continuum International Publishing, 2015.

Dickie, Simon. *Cruelty & Laughter: Forgotten Comic Literature and the Unsentimental Eighteenth Century.* Chicago: University of Chicago Press, 2011.

Doody, Margaret Anne, *Jane Austen's Names: Riddles, Persons, Places.* Chicago: University of Chicago Press, 2015.

Dow, Gillian, and Clare Hanson, eds. *Uses of Austen: Jane's Afterlives.* New York: Palgrave Macmillan, 2012.

Dryden, John. *The Works of John Dryden.* General editor Alan Roper. Berkeley and Los Angeles: University Press of California, 1987. Reprint, 1989. *Prose 1691–1698.* Vol. 20. In *The Works of John Dryden.* Edited by George R. Guffey, Alan Roper, and A. E. Wallace Maurer. Berkeley and Los Angeles: University of California Press, 1987.

Elias, Norbert. "Essay on Laughter." Edited by Anca Parvulescu. *Critical Inquiry* 43, no. 2 (2017): 281–304.

————. *The History of Manners.* Vol. 1 of *The Civilizing Process.* Translated by Edmund Jephcott. New York: Pantheon, 1978.

Ellis, Markman. *The Politics of Sensibility: Race, Gender and Commerce in the Sentimental Novel.* Cambridge: Cambridge University Press, 1999.

Emsley, Sarah. "Laughing at Our Neighbors: Jane Austen and the Problem of Charity." *Persuasions On-Line* 26, no. 1 (Winter 2005): n.p. http://jasna.org/persuasions/on-line/vol26no1/emsley.htm (accessed May 20, 2018).

Erwin, Timothy. *Textual Vision: Augustan Design and the Invention of Eighteenth-Century British Culture.* Lewisburg, PA: Bucknell University Press, 2015.

————. "*Ut Rhetorica Artes*: The Rhetorical Theory of the Sister Arts." In *Haydn and the Performance of Rhetoric,* edited by Tom Beghin and Sander M. Goldberg, 61–79. Chicago: University of Chicago Press, 2007.

Faflak, Joel. "Jane Austen and the Persuasion of Happiness." In *Romanticism and the Emotions,* edited by Joel Faflak and Richard C. Sha, 98–123. Cambridge: Cambridge University Press, 2014.

————. *Romantic Psychoanalysis: The Burden of the Mystery.* Albany: State University of New York Press, 2008.

Favret, Mary. "Free and Happy: Jane Austen in America." In *Janeites: Austen's Disciples and Devotees*, edited by Deidre Lynch, 166–87. Princeton: Princeton University Press, 2000.

Fergus, Jan. "The Power of Women's Language and Laughter." In *The Talk in Jane Austen*, edited by Bruce Stovel and Lynn Weinlos Gregg, 103–22. Edmonton, AB: University of Alberta Press, 2002.

Finch, Casey, and Peter Bowen. "'The Tittle-Tattle of Highbury': Gossip and the Free Indirect Style in *Emma*." *Representations* 31 (Summer 1990), 1–18.

Fisher, Carrie. *Wishful Drinking*. New York: Simon & Schuster, 2008.

Fisher, Philip. *Wonder, the Rainbow, and the Aesthetics of Rare Experiences*. Cambridge, MA: Harvard University Press, 1998.

Fletcher, Angus. *Comic Democracies*. Baltimore: Johns Hopkins University Press, 2016.

Ford, Susan Allen. "Reading *Elegant Extracts* in *Emma*: Very Entertaining!" *Persuasions Online* 28, no. 1 (winter 2007). http://www.jasna.org/persuasions/on-line/vol28no1/ford.htm (accessed May 18, 2018).

Fordyce, James. *Sermons to Young Women, in Two Volumes*. London: A. Millar and T. Cadell, 1766.

———. *Sermons to Young Women*. New York: M. Carey, 1809.

Fraiman, Susan. *Unbecoming Women: British Women Writers and the Novel of Development*. New York: Columbia University Press, 1993.

Freud, Sigmund. *Civilization and Its Discontents*. Edited by James Strachey. New York: W. W. Norton, 1989.

———. *Jokes and Their Relation to the Unconscious*. Translated by James Strachey. New York: Norton, 1960.

The Standard Edition of the Complete Psychological Works of Sigmund Freud. Translated by James Strachey. 24 vols. London: Hogarth Press, 1964.

Fritzer, Penelope Joan. *Jane Austen and Eighteenth-Century Courtesy Books*. Westport, CT: Greenwood Press, 1997.

Fry, Paul H. "Georgic Comedy: The Fictive Territory of Jane Austen's Emma." *Studies in the Novel* 11, no. 2 (1979): 129–46.

Frye, Northrop. *Anatomy of Criticism: Four Essays*. Princeton: Princeton University Press, 1957.

———. "The Argument of Comedy." In *Narrative Dynamics: Essays on Time, Plot, Closure, and Frames*, edited by Brian Richardson, 102–9. Columbus: Ohio State University Press, 2002.

Fulford, Tim. *Romanticism and Masculinity: Gender, Politics and Poetics in the Writings of Burke, Coleridge, Cobbett, Wordsworth, DeQuincey and Hazlitt*. New York: St. Martin's Press, 1999.

Fullbrook, Kate. "Jane Austen and the Comic Negative." In *Women Reading Women's Writing*, edited by Sue Roe, 35–57. New York: Harvester Publishing, 1987.

Galperin, William. "Adapting Jane Austen: The Surprising Fidelity of *Clueless*." *Wordsworth Circle* 42, no. 3 (Summer 2011): 187–93.

———. "Austen's Earliest Readers and the Rise of the Janeites." In *Janeites: Austen's Disciplines and Devotees*, edited by Deidre Lynch, 87–114. Princeton: Princeton University Press, 2000.

Galperin, William H. *The Historical Austen*. Philadelphia: University of Pennsylvania Press, 2003.

Gay, Penny. "*Emma* and *Persuasion*." In *The Cambridge Companion to Jane Austen*, 2nd ed., edited by Edward Copeland and Juliet McMaster, 55–71. Cambridge: Cambridge University Press, 2011.

———. *Jane Austen and the Theatre*. Cambridge: Cambridge University Press, 2002.

Gayford, Martin. *Man with a Blue Scarf: On Sitting for a Portrait by Lucian Freud*. London: Thames and Hudson, 2010.

Gentile, Kathy Justice. "'A forward, bragging, scheming race': Comic Masculinity in *Northanger Abbey*." *Persuasions* 32 (2010): 78–89.

Giffon, Michael. *Jane Austen and Religion: Salvation and Society in Georgian England*. Basingstoke: Palgrave Macmillan 2002.

Gillooly, Eileen. *Smile of Discontent: Humor, Gender, and Nineteenth-Century British Fiction*. Chicago: University of Chicago Press, 1999.

Gisborne, Thomas. *An Enquiry into the Duties of the Female Sex*. 3rd ed. London: T. Cadell, 1798.

Glick, Peter, and Susan T. Fiske. "An Ambivalent Alliance: Hostile and Benevolent Sexism as Complimentary Justifications for Gender Inequality." *American Psychologist* 56 (2001): 109–18.

———. "Hostile and Benevolent Sexism: Measuring Ambivalent Sexist Attitudes Toward Women." *Psychology of Women Quarterly* 21, no. 1 (1997): 119–35.

Goffman, Erving. "Felicity's Condition." In *The Goffman Reader*, edited by Charles Lemert and Ann Branaman, 167–72. Malden, MA: Blackwell, 1997.

Goss, Erin M. "Homespun Gossip: Jane West, Jane Austen, and the Task of Literary Criticism." *Eighteenth Century: Theory and Interpretation* 56, no. 2 (2015): 165–77.

Graham, Kenneth W. "The Case of the Petulant Patriarch." *Persuasions* 20 (1998): 119–34.

Graham, Peter. *Jane Austen & Charles Darwin: Naturalists and Novelists*. Aldershot, UK: Ashgate, 2008.

Gregory, John. *A Father's Legacy to His Daughters*. Edited by Gina Luria. New York: Garland, 1974.

Grossman, Jonathan H. "The Labor of the Leisured in *Emma*: Class, Manners, and Austen." *Nineteenth-Century Literature* 54, no. 2 (Fall 1999): 143–64.

Grossmith, George, and Weedon Grossmith. *The Diary of a Nobody*. London: J. W. Arrowsmith, 1892.

Hagstrum, Jean H. *The Sister Arts: The Tradition of Literary Pictorialism and English Poetry from Dryden to Gray*. Chicago: University of Chicago Press, 1958.

Halperin, John. *The Life of Jane Austen*. Baltimore: Johns Hopkins University Press, 1984.

Harding, D. W. "Regulated Hatred: An Aspect of the Work of Jane Austen." *Scrutiny* 8 (March 1940): 346–62.

———. *Regulated Hatred and Other Essays on Jane Austen* (1940). Edited by Monica Lawlor. London: Athlone Press, 1998. Reprint. London and Atlantic Highlands, NJ: Athlone Press, 1998.

———. *Words into Rhythm: English Speech Rhythm in Verse and Prose*. London: Cambridge University Press, 1976.

Harris, Jocelyn. *A Revolution Almost beyond Expression: Jane Austen's Persuasion*. Newark, DE: University of Delaware Press, 2007.

———. *Satire, Celebrity, and Politics in Jane Austen*. Lewisburg: Bucknell University Press, 2017.

Hazlitt, William. *Selected Writings*. Edited by Jon Cook. Oxford: Oxford University Press, 1991; 2003.

Heckerling, Amy. *Clueless*. Directed by Amy Heckerling. 1995. Hollywood, CA: Paramount Home Entertainment, 2005. DVD.

Hegel, Georg W. F. *Phenomenology of Spirit*. Edited by J. N. Findlay. Translated by A. V. Miller. Oxford: Oxford University Press, 1977.

Heydt-Stevenson, Jillian. *Austen's Unbecoming Conjunctions: Subversive Laughter, Embodied History*. New York: Palgrave Macmillan, 2005.

———. "Games, Riddles and Charades." In *The Cambridge Companion to* Emma, edited by Peter Sabor, 150–65. Cambridge: Cambridge University Press, 2015.

———. "'Slipping into the Ha-Ha': Bawdy Humor and Body Politics in Jane Austen's Novels." *Nineteenth-Century Literature* 55, no. 3 (December 2000): 309–39.

Hobbes, Thomas. *The Elements of Law, Natural or Politic.* Edited by J. C. A. Gaskin. Oxford: Oxford University Press, 1994.

Hofkosh, Sonia. "The Illusionist: *Northanger Abbey* and Austen's Uses Of Enchantment." In *A Companion to Jane Austen*, edited by Claudia L. Johnson, 101–11. Chichester, UK: Wiley-Blackwell, 2009.

Hopkins, Robert. "General Tilney and Affairs of State: The Political Gothic of *Northanger Abbey*." *Philological Quarterly* 57 (1978): 213–24.

Horace. *Satires, Epistles and Ars Poetica.* Translated by H. Rushton Fairclough. Loeb Classical Library. Cambridge, MA: Harvard University Press, 1966.

Hutcheon, Linda. *A Theory of Adaptation.* New York: Routledge, 2006.

Hutcheson, Francis. *Inquiry into the Original of our Ideas of Beauty and Virtue.* 3rd ed. London: J. and P. Knapton, 1729.

———. *Reflections upon Laughter, and Remarks upon the Fable of the Bees.* Glasgow: Urie, 1750.

Irwin, Michael. *Picturing: Description and Illusion in the Nineteenth-Century Novel.* London: Allen & Unwin, 1979.

Jarvis, Simon. "How to Do Things with Tunes." *ELH* 82, no. 2 (2015): 365–83.

Jay, Martin. "Scopic Regimes of Modernity." In *Vision and Visuality*, edited by Hal Foster, 3–23. Seattle: Bay Press, 1988.

———. "Scopic Regimes of Modernity Revisited." In *Essays from the Edge: Parerga and Paralipomena*, 51- 63. Charlottesville: University of Virginia Press, 2011.

Jenkyns, Richard. *A Fine Brush on Ivory: An Appreciation of Jane Austen.* Oxford: Oxford University Press, 2007.

Johnson, Barbara. "The Alchemy of Style and Law," In *The Feminist Difference: Literature, Psychoanalysis, Race, and* Gender, 165–82. Cambridge, MA: Harvard University Press, 1998.

Johnson, Claudia L. *Equivocal Beings: Politics, Gender, and Sentimentality in the 1790s: Wollstonecraft, Radcliffe, Burney, Austen.* Chicago: University of Chicago Press, 1995.

———. *Jane Austen: Women, Politics, and the Novel.* Chicago: University of Chicago Press, 1987; 1988.

———. "Persuasion: The Unfeudal Tone of the Present Day." In *Persuasion (Norton Critical Editions)*, edited by Patricia Meyer Spacks, 268–306. New York: W. W. Norton, 1994.

Jones, Vivien. "Introduction." In *Selected Letters*, by Jane Austen, edited by Vivien Jones, ix-xxxv. New York: Oxford University Press, 2004.

Kant, Immanuel. *Critique of Judgment.* Translated by Werner S. Pluhar. Indianapolis: Hackett, 1987.

———. *Critique of Judgement.* Translated by Nicholas Walker. Oxford: Oxford University Press, 2007.

Keller, Catherine, and Chris Boesel, *Apophatic Bodies: Negative Theology, Incarnation, and Relationality.* New York: Fordham University Press, 2009.

Kelly, Helena. *Jane Austen, The Secret Radical.* London: Icon Books, 2016.

———. "The Many Ways in Which We Are Wrong About Jane Austen: Lies, Damn Lies, and Literary Scholarship." *LitHub*, May 3, 2017. http://lithub.com/the-many-ways-in-which-we-are-wrong-about-jane-austen/ (accessed May 19, 2018).

Kipling, Rudyard. *Debits and Credits.* London: Macmillan, 1926.

Klein, Robert. *Form and Meaning: Writings on the Renaissance and Modern Art.* Translated by Madeline Jay and Leon Wieseltier, with a foreword by Henri Zerner. New York: Viking Press, 1979.

Knox, Vicesimus. *Elegant Extracts: or Useful and Entertaining Passages in Prose.* London: Charles Dilly, 1790?

Knox-Shaw, Peter. *Jane Austen and the Enlightenment.* Cambridge: Cambridge University Press, 2004.

————. "Philosophy." In *Jane Austen in Context*, edited by Janet Todd, 346–56. Cambridge: Cambridge University Press, 2005.

Kramp, Michael. *Disciplining Love: Austen and the Modern Man*. Columbus: Ohio State University Press, 2007.

Lacan, Jacques. *Écrits: The First Complete Edition in English*. Translated by Bruce Fink. New York: Norton, 2006.

The Lady's Preceptor: Or, a Letter to a Young Lady of Distinction upon Politeness Taken from the French of the Abbe D'Ancourt, and Adapted to the Religion, Customs, and Manners of the English Nation. By a Gentleman of Cambridge. London, 1745.

Lascelles, Mary. *Jane Austen and Her Art*. London: Oxford University Press, 1939.

Lauber, John. "Jane Austen's Fools." *SEL: Studies in English Literature, 1500–1900* 14, no. 4 (1974): 511–24.

Lawrence, D. H. *The Erotic Works of D. H. Lawrence*. New York: Avenel Books, 1989.

Leal, Amy. "See Jane Bite." *Chronicle of Higher Education*. Last modified March 14, 2010. http://chronicle.com/article/See-Jane-Bite/64585 (accessed May 18, 2018).

Lee, Rensselaer W. *Ut Pictura Poesis: The Humanistic Theory of Painting*. New York: W. W. Norton 1967.

Lee, Wendy Anne. "Resituating 'Regulated Hatred': D. W. Harding's Jane Austen." *ELH* 77, no. 4 (2010): 995–1014.

Leonard, Robert Z. *Pride and Prejudice*. Directed by Robert Z. Leonard. 1940. Burbank, CA: Warner Home Video, 2006. DVD.

Leslie, Robert Charles, and Tom Taylor. *Life and Times of Sir Joshua Reynolds*. 2 vols. London: John Murray, 1865.

A Letter from a Father to His Daughter at a Boarding-School. London: G. Robinson, 1774.

Levinson, Marjorie. *Keats's Life of Allegory*. Oxford: Blackwell, 1988.

Levy, Judith. "Austen's Persuasion and the Comedy of Remarriage." *Partial Answers: Journal of Literature and the History of Ideas* 12, no. 2 (2014): 255–65.

Lewis, C. S. "A Note on Jane Austen," In *Selected Literary Essays*, edited by Walter Hooper. 175–86. Cambridge: Cambridge University Press, 1969.

Litz, A. Walton. "Persuasion: Forms of Estrangement." In *Jane Austen: Bicentenary Essays*, edited by John Halperin, 221–34. Cambridge: Cambridge University Press, 1975.

Looser, Devoney, ed. "Introduction: Jane Austen and Her Contemporaries." Special Issue. *Eighteenth Century: Theory and Interpretation* 56, no. 2 (2015): 147–49.

————, ed. *Jane Austen and Discourses of Feminism*. New York: St. Martin's, 1995.

————. *The Making of Jane Austen*. Baltimore: Johns Hopkins University Press, 2017.

Loveridge, Mark. "Francis Hutcheson and Mr. Weston's Conundrum in *Emma*." *Notes & Queries* 30, no. 3 (1983): 214–15.

Lynch, Deirdre, ed. *Janeites: Austen's Disciples and Devotees*. Princeton: Princeton University Press, 2000.

MacDonald, Gina, and Andrew MacDonald, ed. *Jane Austen on Screen*. Cambridge: Cambridge University Press, 2003.

Magee, William H. "Instrument of Growth: The Courtship and Marriage Plot in Jane Austen's Novels." *Journal of Narrative Technique* 17, no. 2 (1987): 198–209.

Mandal, Anthony, and Brian Southam, eds. *The Reception of Jane Austen in Europe*. London: Continuum, 2007.

Manguel, Alberto. *A History of Reading*. New York: Penguin, 1996.

Markovits, Stefanie. "Jane Austen and the Happy Fall." *SEL: Studies in English Literature 1500–1900* 47, no. 4 (2007): 779–97.

Marno, David. *Death Be Not Proud: The Art of Holy Attention*. Chicago: University Of Chicago Press, 2016.

Martial. *Epigrams*. Translated by D. R. Shackleton Bailey. Vol. 2 of 3 vols. Loeb Classical Library. Cambridge, MA: Harvard University Press, 1993.

Marx, Karl. *Surveys from Exile*. Translated and edited by David Fernbach. Harmondsworth: Penguin Books, 1973.

Mattu, Ayesha, and Nura Maznavi. "Jane Austen and the Persistent Failure of the White Imagination." *Establishment*, May 15, 2017. https://theestablishment.co/jane-austen -and-the-persistent-failure-of-the-white-imagination-9a3c75c4bb5d (accessed May 18, 2018).

Mazzeno, Laurence W. *Jane Austen: Two Centuries of Criticism*. Rochester, NY: Camden House, 2011.

McGrath, Douglas. *Emma*, by Jane Austen. Directed by Douglas McGrath. 1996. Santa Monica, CA: Miramax Home Entertainment, 1999. DVD.

Michie, Elsie. "Austen's Powers: Engaging with Adam Smith in Debates about Wealth and Virtue." *Novel* 34, no. 1 (2000): 5–27.

Miller, D. A. *Jane Austen, or The Secret of Style*. Princeton: Princeton University Press, 2003.

Minma, Shinobu. "General Tilney and Tyranny: *Northanger Abbey*." *Eighteenth-Century Fiction* 8, no. 4 (1995): 503–18.

Mitchell, Robert. "Suspended Animation, Slow Time, and the Poetics of Trance." *PMLA* 126, no. 1 (January 2011): 107–22.

Mohsin, Moni. "Austenistan." *Economist 1843* (October-November 2017): 90–95.

Moler, Kenneth L. "Some Verbal Tactics of General Tilney." *Persuasions* 6 (1984): 10–12.

Momus. "Afterword." In *Žižek's Jokes*, by Slavoj Žižek, edited by Audun Mortensen, 141–48. Cambridge, MA: MIT Press, 2014.

Monteiro, Belisa. "Comic Fantasy in Jane Austen's Juvenilia: Female Roguery and the Charms of Narcissism." *Persuasions* 30 (2008): 129–34.

Moretti, Franco. *Atlas of the European Novel*. New York: Verso, 1999.

———. *The Bourgeois: Between History and Literature*. London: Verso, 2013.

Morreall, John, ed. *The Philosophy of Laughter and Humor*. Albany: SUNY Press, 1987.

Morse, Joann Ryan. "The Course of True Love Never Did Run Smooth: Shakespearian Comedy in *Emma*." *Persuasions On-Line* 26, no. 1 (2005): n.p.

Mudrick, Marvin. *Jane Austen: Irony as Defense and Discovery*. Princeton: Princeton University Press, 1952. Reprint. Berkeley: University of California Press, 1974.

Mullan, John. *What Matters in Jane Austen: Twenty Crucial Puzzles Solved*. New York: Bloomsbury Press, 2013.

Mulvey-Roberts, Marie. "Mashing Up Jane Austen: *Pride and Prejudice and Zombies* and the Limits of Adaptation." *Irish Journal of Gothic and Horror Studies* 13 (2014): 17–37.

Nersessian, Anahid. *Utopia, Limited: Romanticism and Adjustment*. Cambridge, MA: Harvard University Press, 2015.

A New Collection of Enigmas, Charades, Transpositions, Etc. London: Hurst, Rees et al., 1810.

Northcote, James. *The Life of Sir Joshua Reynolds*. 2 vols. London: Henry Colburn, 1818.

O'Farrell, Mary Ann. "'Bin Laden a Huge Jane Austen Fan': Jane Austen in Contemporary Political Discourse." In *Uses of Austen: Jane's Afterlives*, edited by Gillian Dow and Clare Hanson, 192–207. New York: Palgrave, 2012.

Panagia, Davide. *Impressions of Hume: Cinematic Thinking and the Politics of Discontinuity*. Lanham, MD: Rowman & Littlefield, 2013.

———. *The Political Life of Sensation*. Durham, NC: Duke University Press, 2009.

Paris, Bernard J. *Character and Conflict in Jane Austen's Novels*. Detroit: Wayne State University Press, 1978.

Park, You-Me, and Rajeswari Sunder Rajan, eds. *The Postcolonial Jane Austen*. London: Routledge, 2000.

Paster, Gail Kern. *Humoring the Body: Emotions and the Shakespearean Stage.* Chicago: University of Chicago Press, 2004.

Pater, Walter. *Appreciations, With an Essay on Style.* London: Macmillan, 1944.

Pennington, Lady Sarah. *An Unfortunate Mother's Advice to Her Absent Daughters; in a Letter to Miss Pennington.* London, 1761.

Perkins, Pam. "A Subdued Gaiety: The Comedy of *Mansfield Park.*" *Nineteenth-Century Literature* 48, no. 1 (1993): 1–25.

Pfau, Thomas. "The Art and Ethics of Attention." *Hedgehog Review* 16, no. 2 (2014): 34–42.

Philostratus. *Imagines.* Translated by Arthur Fairbanks. Loeb Classical Library. Cambridge, MA: Harvard University Press, 1936.

Pinch, Adela. "Lost in a Book: Jane Austen's *Persuasion.*" *Studies in Romanticism* 32, no. 1 (Spring 1993): 97–117.

———. *Thinking about Other People in Nineteenth-Century British Writing.* Cambridge: Cambridge University Press, 2010.

Plato. *Plato's Examination of Pleasure: A Translation of the Philebus.* Translated by R. Hackworth. Cambridge: Cambridge University Press, 1958.

———. *The Republic.* Cambridge Texts in the History of Political Thought. Translated by Tom Griffith. Cambridge: Cambridge University Press, 2000.

———. *Theaetetus.* Translated by Harold North Fowler. Cambridge, MA: Harvard University Press, 1996.

Polhemus, Robert. *Comic Faith: The Great Tradition from Austen to Joyce.* Chicago: University of Chicago Press, 1982.

Poovey, Mary. *The Proper Lady and the Woman Writer: Ideology as Style in the Works of Mary Wollstonecraft, Mary Shelley, and Jane Austen.* Chicago and London: University of Chicago Press, 1984; 1985.

Poplawski, Paul. *A Jane Austen Encyclopedia.* Westport, CT: Greenwood Press, 1998.

Potter, Tiffany. "Historicizing the Popular and the Feminine: *The Rape of the Lock* and *Pride and Prejudice and Zombies.*" In *Women, Popular Culture, and the Eighteenth Century,* edited by Tiffany Potter, 5–24. Toronto: University of Toronto Press, 2012.

Praz, Mario. *Mnemosyne: The Parallel Between Literature and the Visual Arts.* London: Oxford University Press, 1970.

———. *Studies in Seventeenth-Century Imagery.* 2nd ed. Rome: Edizioni di Storia e Letteratura, 1975; 2001.

"Quanti, Q." *The Game of Quadrille.* Cheltenham: G. A. Williams, 1822.

Raw, Laurence, and Robert Dryden, eds. *Global Jane Austen: Pleasure, Passion, and Possessiveness in the Jane Austen Community.* New York: Palgrave Macmillan, 2013.

Reay, Katherine. *The Austen Escape.* Nashville, TN: Thomas Nelson Press, 2017.

Reynolds, Sir Joshua. *Discourses on Art.* Edited by Robert R. Wark. New Haven, CT and London: Yale University Press, 1975.

Richardson, Alan. *British Romanticism and the Science of the Mind.* Cambridge: Cambridge University Press, 2001.

———. *The Neural Sublime: Cognitive Theories and Romantic Texts.* Baltimore: Johns Hopkins University Press, 2010.

Ricks, Christopher. *Essays in Appreciation.* Oxford: Oxford University Press, 1996.

Ricoeur, Paul. *Time and Narrative.* Translated by Kathleen McLaughlin and David Pellauer. Vol. 1 of 3 vols. Chicago: University of Chicago Press, 1984.

Roberts, Warren. *Jane Austen and the French Revolution.* London: Athlone, 1979.

Rogers, Susan. "Emma at Box Hill: A Very Questionable Day of Pleasure." *Persuasions Online* 25, no. 1 (2004). http://www.jasna.org/persuasions/on-line/vol25no1/rogers.html (accessed October 5, 2016).

Rohrbach, Emily. "Austen's Later Subjects." *Studies in English Literature 1500–1900* 44, no. 4 (2004): 737–52.

———. *Modernity's Mist: British Romanticism and the Poetics of Anticipation*. New York: Fordham University Press, 2016.

"Rondeaulet, Sieur." In *A Treatise on the Charade*. Translated by Tobias Rigmerole. London: T. Davies, 1777.

Rothenberg, Molly Anne. "Jane Austen's wit-craft." In *Lacan, Psychoanalysis and Comedy*, edited by Patricia Gherovici and Manya Steinkoler, 184–205. New York: Cambridge University Press, 2016.

Rozik, Eli. *Comedy: A Critical Introduction*. Brighton, UK: Sussex Academic Press, 2011.

Rubenstein, Mary-Jane. "A Certain Disavowal: The Pathos and Politics of Wonder." *Princeton Theological Review* 12, no. 2 (2006): 11–17.

Rumbold, Kate. "'So Common-Hackneyed in the Eyes of Men': Banal Shakespeare and the Eighteenth-Century Novel." *Literature Compass* 4, no. 3 (2007): 610–21.

Ryle, Gilbert. *The Concept of Mind*. London and New York: Hutchinson's University Library, 1949. Reprint. London: Penguin, 1990.

———. "Jane Austen and the Moralists." *Oxford Review* 1 (1966): 5–18.

Rzepka, Charles. "Re-collecting Spontaneous Overflows: Romantic Passions, the Sublime, and Mesmerism." *Romantic Circles Praxis* (Winter 1998). https://www.rc.umd.edu/praxis/passions /rzepka/rzp.html (accessed May 18, 2018).

Said, Edward. *Culture and Imperialism*. New York: Knopf, 1993.

Schopenhauer, Arthur. *The World as Will and Representation*. Translated by E. F. J. Payne. Vol. 1 of 2 vols. New York: Dover, 1966.

Sedgwick, Eve Kosofsky. *Between Men: English Literature and Male Homosocial Desire*. New York: Columbia University Press, 1985.

Seeber, Barbara K. *Jane Austen and Animals*. New York: Routledge, 2013.

Seneca. *Ad Lucilium Epistulae Morales*. Translated by Richard M. Gummere. Vol. 1 of 3 vols. Loeb Classical Library. Cambridge, MA: Harvard University Press, 1925.

Siddons, Sarah. *Reminiscences of Sarah Kemble Siddons*. Edited with a foreword by William Van Lennep. Cambridge, MA: Widener Library, 1942.

Sigler, David. *Sexual Enjoyment in British Romanticism: Gender and Psychoanalysis, 1753–1835*. Montreal: McGill-Queen's University Press, 2015.

Silverman, Kaja. *The Threshold of the Visible World*. New York and London: Routledge, 1996.

Smith, Adam. *A Theory of Moral Sentiments*. Edited by D. D. Raphael and A. L. MacFie. Vol. 1. *The Glasgow Edition of the Works and Correspondence of Adam Smith*. General editor A. S. Skinner. Oxford: Clarendon Press, 1976–1983.

Solinger, Jason D. *Becoming the Gentleman: British Literature and the Invention of Modern Masculinity, 1660–1815*. New York: Palgrave, 2012.

Solnit, Rebecca. *Hope in the Dark: Untold Histories, Wild Possibilities*. 3rd ed. Chicago: Haymarket Books, 2016.

Soni, Vivasvan. "Committing Freedom: The Cultivation of Judgment in Rousseau's *Emile* and Austen's *Pride and Prejudice*." *Eighteenth Century: Theory & Interpretation* 51, no. 3 (Fall 2010): 364–87.

Southam, B. C. "General Tilney's Hot-houses." *Ariel* 3, no. 1 (1971): 53–63.

———, ed. *Jane Austen the Critical Heritage*. 2 vols. London: Routledge & Kegan Paul, 1968.

Southam, Brian C. "Jane Austen's Englishness: *Emma* as National Tale." *Persuasions* 30 (2008): 187–201.

Southward, David. "Jane Austen and the Riches of Embarrassment." *Studies in English Literature, 1500–1900* 36, no. 4 (Autumn 1996): 763–84.

Spacks, Patricia Meyer. "Austen's Laughter." *Women's Studies: An Interdisciplinary Journal* 15, nos. 1–3 (1988): 71–85.

Spaulding, John Gordon. *Pulpit Publications 1660–1782: Being a New Edition of "The Preacher's Assistant."* 6 vols. New York: Norman Ross, 1996.

Stanley, Jason. *Know How.* Oxford: Oxford University Press, 2011.

Stevens, Wallace. *The Collected Poems of Wallace Stevens.* Edited by John N. Serio and Chris Beyers. New York: Alfred A Knopf, 1971.

Stewart, Garrett. *The Deed of Reading: Literature, Writing, Language, Philosophy.* Ithaca, NY: Cornell University Press, 2015.

Stout, Janis P. "Jane Austen's Proposal Scenes and the Limitations of Language." *Studies in the Novel* 14, no. 4 (1982): 316–26.

Stovel, Bruce, and Lynn Weinlos Gregg, eds. *The Talk in Jane Austen.* Edmonton, AB: University of Alberta Press, 2002.

Tanner, Tony. *Jane Austen.* Cambridge, MA: Harvard University Press, 1986.

Tave, Stuart M. *The Amiable Humorist: A Study in the Comic Theory and Criticism of the Eighteenth and Early Nineteenth Centuries.* Chicago: University of Chicago Press, 1960.

Taylor, Charles. *A Secular Age.* Cambridge, MA: Harvard University Press, 2007.

Taylor, Megan. "Jane Austen and 'Banal Shakespeare.'" *Eighteenth-Century Fiction* 27, no. 1 (2014): 105–25.

Telfer, Elisabeth. "Hutcheson's Reflections upon Laughter." *Journal of Aesthetics and Art Criticism* 53, no. 4 (1995): 359–69.

Thompson, James. *Models of Value: Eighteenth-Century Political Economy and the Novel.* Durham, NC and London: Duke University Press, 1996.

Thompson, Robert J. Interview with Amy M. Braverman. "Culture Jock." *University of Chicago Magazine* 98, no. 2 (2005). http://magazine.uchicago.edu/0512/features/thompson.shtml (accessed May 18, 2018).

Todd, Janet. *The Cambridge Introduction to Jane Austen.* 2nd ed. Cambridge: Cambridge University Press, 2015.

Troost, Linda. "The Undead Eighteenth Century: 2010 EC-ASECS Presidential Address." *Eighteenth-Century Intelligencer* (March 2011): 1–11.

Troost, Linda, and Sayre Greenfield, eds. *Jane Austen in Hollywood.* Lexington: University Press of Kentucky, 2001.

Veen, Otto van. *Amorum Emblemata.* Antwerp: H. Swingenij, 1608.

Voigts-Virchow, Eckart. "Pride and Promiscuity and Zombies, or: Miss Austen Mashed Up in the Affinity Spaces of Participatory Cultures." In *Adaptation and Cultural Appropriation: Literature, Film, and the Arts*, edited by Pascal Nicklas and Oliver Lindner, 34–56. Berlin and Boston: Walter de Gruyter, 2012.

Walker, Eric C. *Marriage, Writing, and Romanticism: Wordsworth and Austen after War.* Stanford: Stanford University Press, 2009.

Watt, Ian. "Jane Austen and the Traditions of Comic Aggression: Sense and Sensibility." *Persuasions* 3 (1981): 14–15, 24–28.

Wattles, Jeffrey. *The Golden Rule.* Oxford and New York: Oxford University Press, 1996.

Weil, Simone. "Reflections on the Right Use of School Studies." In *The Simone Weil Reader*, edited by George A. Panichas, 44–52. Wakefield, RI: Moyer Bell, 1999.

Wells, Juliette. "New Approaches to Austen and the Popular Reader." In *Uses of Austen,* edited by Gillian Dow and Clare Hanson, 77–91. New York: Palgrave, 2012.

Wendorf, Richard. *Sir Joshua Reynolds: The Painter in Society.* Cambridge, MA: Harvard University Press, 1996.

White, Laura Mooneyham. "Emma and New Comedy." *Persuasions* 21 (1999): 128–141.

———. "Jane Austen and the Marriage Plot: Questions of Persistence." In *Jane Austen and Discourses of Feminism*, edited by Devoney Looser, 71–86. New York: St. Martin's Press, 1995.

The Whole Duty of Woman. By a Lady. Written at the Desire of a Noble Lord. London, 1753.

Williams, Robert I. "Play and the Concept of Farce." *Philosophy and Literature* 12, no. 1 (1988): 55–69.

Wiltshire, John, ed. *The Cinematic Jane Austen: Essays on the Filmic Sensibility of the Novels.* Jefferson, NC: McFarland, 2009.

———. *Jane Austen and the Body: "The picture of health."* Cambridge: Cambridge University Press, 1992.

———. *Recreating Jane Austen.* Cambridge: Cambridge University Press, 2001.

Winters, Ben H. "I Write With Dead People: How to Collaborate With a Corpse." *Huffington Post.* Last modified March 18, 2010. http://www.huffingtonpost.com/ben-h-winters/i-write -with-dead-people_b_347365.html (accessed May 18, 2018).

———. "This Scene Could Really Use a Man-Eating Jellyfish: How I Wrote Sense and Sensibility and Sea Monsters," *Slate.* Last modified September 15, 2009. http://www.slate.com /articles/arts/culturebox/2009/09/this_scene_could_really_use_a_maneating_jellyfish .html (accessed May 18, 2018).

Wollstonecraft, Mary. *The Vindications: The Rights of Men and the Rights of Woman.* Edited by D. L. Macdonald and Kathleen Scherf. Petersborough, ON: Broadview Press, 1997.

Woolf, Virginia. *The Common Reader: First Series.* Edited by Andrew McNeillie. New York: Harcourt, 1925.

Wordsworth, William. *Selected Poems and Prefaces.* Edited by Jack Stillinger. Boston: Houghton Mifflin, 1965.

Wright, Nicole M. "Alt-Right Jane Austen." *Chronicle of Higher Education* 63, no. 28 (March 12, 2017).

Zizek, Slavoj. *First as Tragedy, Then as Farce.* London: Verso, 2009.

———. *The Sublime Object of Ideology.* London: Verso, 1989.

Zuccaro, Federico. *Idea de' Pittori, Scultori, e Architetti.* Turin, Italy: A. Disserolio, 1607.

Zupančič, Alenka. *The Odd One In: On Comedy.* Cambridge, MA: MIT Press, 2008.

SOHA CHUNG is a PhD candidate in the English Department at Texas A&M University, where she is completing her dissertation investigating the representations of female laughter in nineteenth-century British novels in order to examine the role of gender in women's experience and the expression of pleasure. Her research interests include nineteenth-century British literature, gender studies, and theories of emotions.

SEAN DEMPSEY is assistant professor of nineteenth-century British literature at the University of Arkansas. He has published on a range of Romantic and post-Romantic writers, including Wordsworth, Keats, Shelley, T. S. Eliot, and Robert Frost, and is currently completing a monograph titled *Postures of Attention: Formations of the Postsecular in British Romanticism*.

TIMOTHY ERWIN is professor of English at the University of Nevada, Las Vegas; the author of *Textual Vision: Augustan Design and the Invention of Eighteenth-Century British Culture* (Bucknell University Press, 2015); and Traveling Lecturer for the West for the Jane Austen Society of North America, 2016–2018.

ERIN M. GOSS is associate professor of English at Clemson University and the author of *Revealing Bodies: Anatomy, Allegory, and the Grounds of Knowledge in the Long Eighteenth Century* (Bucknell University Press, 2013). She is currently at work on a monograph exploring figures of repetition, automation, and complicity in eighteenth- and nineteenth-century British women's writing.

MICHAEL KRAMP is associate professor of English at Lehigh University. He is the author of *Disciplining Love: Austen and the Modern Man* (Ohio State University Press, 2007) and editor of *Jane Austen and Masculinity* (Bucknell University Press, 2018). He has edited and introduced special issues of *Rhizomes* focused on Deleuze and Photography and Austen and Deleuze, and has published articles on such figures as Deleuze, Foucault, Pater, Dickens, and Lawrence, as well as a series of articles on nineteenth-century visual culture.

MISTY KRUEGER is assistant professor of English at the University of Maine at Farmington. She has published on Austen, juvenilia, adaptation, and pedagogy. She was the 2017 Jane Austen Society of North America International Visitor and conducted research on Austen at Chawton House Library and the Jane Austen's House Museum.

ERIC LINDSTROM is associate professor in the Department of English at the University of Vermont. He is author of the book *Romantic Fiat: Demystification and Enchantment in Lyric Poetry* (Palgrave, 2011), and editor of the collection *Stanley Cavell and the Event of Romanticism*, Romantic Circles Praxis series (University of Maryland, 2014). His essays on Jane Austen, Romanticism, and modern poetry have appeared in such journals as *ELH, Studies in Romanticism, Essays in Romanticism, European Romantic Review, Criticism*, and *Modernism/ Modernity*. He is at work on a book manuscript on Jane Austen, Stanley Cavell, and ordinary language philosophy.

DAVID SIGLER is associate professor of English at the University of Calgary, with interests in Romanticism and literary theory. He is the author of *Sexual Enjoyment in British Romanticism: Gender and Psychoanalysis, 1757–1835* (McGill-Queen's University Press, 2015).

Civilization and Its Discontents, 71–72
civilizing process, 70–71
Clueless, 98, *103*, 107, 116, 121n26; directed
   by Amy Heckerling (1995), 98
comedy/comic: and the body, 11, 28, 40n46,
   45, 48, 70–71, 166, 171; as conservative, 9;
   as a form of thinking, 7, 128; and
   happiness, 7, 14, 63; and hope, 10, 14, 85,
   91, 109, 116, 130; and marriage, 6, 13, 63,
   101, 119n10, 128, 131–33, 135–36, 142, 149;
   as radical, 3, 9–10, 24, 32, 53, 59, 99, 167;
   relief, 170–72; and the split subject, 11;
   and style, 31, 33, 40n42; and wish
   fulfillment, 4, 7, 55, 57. *See also* affect
   (-ed, -ion); attention; community; design;
   discourse; farce; happiness; humor/
   humour; ideology; irony; jokes; laughter;
   love; marriage; persuasion; philosophy;
   politics (-al); reading; Shakespeare,
   William; social; tragedy; unconscious;
   wit (-ty); Zupančič, Alenka
community, 12, 43, 47, 53, 69, 84, 100–101,
   175–76; foundation of, 49; and happiness,
   58; and humor/comedy, 11, 50, 58–59, 162,
   171–73; idea of, 46–47; undermining of,
   42. *See also* Freud, Sigmund; Lacan,
   Jacques
Concept of Mind, The, 21, 23, 25–28, 36
conjugality, 5–6, 24, 54–55
Connell, R. W., 148
consciousness, 39n26, 45, 52–53, 70, 78n65;
   individual, 11; self-, 70; vehicular, 74
Crary, Alice, 27

Dadlez, E. M., 47, 142
Darwin, Charles, 6
Darwin, Erasmus, 8; *Plan for the Conduct of
   Female Education in Boarding Schools*
   (1797), 8
"Descartes' Myth," 23, 27
design, 108, 114–15, 155; of comedy, 59;
   definition of, 114; discourse of, 100, 116,
   118n4, 119n7; the formal metaphor of the
   sister arts in *Emma*, 118n4; syntax, 64
Dickens, Charles, 23–24, 34
Dickie, Simon, 9
discourse, 24, 42, 69, 117, 120n22, 155, 158;
   academic, 117; and comedy, 32, 58, 82,
   160; free indirect, 40n53, 53, 70, 95,
   121n25; meta-, 51; and philosophy, 11, 25;

symbolic, 100; visual, 114; and women, 82.
   See also design
disposition, 39n29, 47, 66, 73; as keyword in
   Emma, 82, 85, 107, 114, 122n40
dissensus, 68
Doody, Margaret Anne, 34–35

elasticity, 66, 73–74
Eliot, Anne, 46
Eliot, George, 4, 25
embodied mind, 64
Emma (Austen), vii, ix, 11–12, 129–33; and
   behavior and manners of the time, 27,
   70, 83, 90, 92, 95; comedy questioned,
   100–102, 119n9; and excuses, 37; and
   geography, 117; and Hegel, 22; and
   literature, 90, 95; monologues, 26; and
   politics, 26; theory of mind, 26, 36;
   visual field, 116; women, 82, 90, 115,
   119n15. *See also* happiness: perfect;
   laughter
Emma (characters): Bates, Miss, 26, 82,
   92–93, 101, 119n15; Bates, Mrs., 117;
   Churchill, Frank, 26–27, 36–37, 87, 90,
   113, 115–17; Coles, 87, 113; Dixon, Mr., 91,
   113; Elton, Mr. [Rev. Philip], 85–87,
   99–100, 102–4, 106–10: friend of Cher
   Horowitz, 103–4; Elton, Mr., and Psalms
   78:72, 114, 122n39; Elton, Mrs., 26;
   Fairfax, Jane, 26, 91, 113, 115; Goddard,
   Miss, 105; Goddard, Mrs., 101; Knightley,
   Mr. George, 26–27, 82, 101–2, 129, 133:
   rhetoric/judgment, 87–90, 94–95;
   Knightley, Mr. George, and social
   improvement, 93, 115–17; Knightley,
   Mr. George, and view of women's roles/
   behavior, 85, 87–88, 91–93, 95, 107;
   Martin, Robert, 86, 99–100, 102–3,
   105–8, 115, 117, 120n16, 121n26, 123n50;
   Perry, Mr., 101; Smith, Harriet, 27, 85, 99,
   104, 106–18, 122n39; Weston, Mr., 85, 93,
   109, 115; Weston, Mrs., 85, 87, 90, 93,
   107–8, 117–18; Woodhouse, Emma, vii,
   82, 85, 98, 131: as artist, 113, 115;
   Woodhouse, Emma, as comic butt, 98;
   Woodhouse, Emma, and visual comedy,
   99; Woodhouse, Mr. Henry, 70, 87, 93,
   101, 108, 115: as amiable humorist, 101
Emma (films), 12, 99–100, 103, 106–7,
   121n26; Box Hill picnic, 27, 36, 82–83,